THE TEACH YOURSELF BOOKS

ARCHÆOLOGY

Uniform with this volume and in the same series

Teach Yourself Anthropology

Teach Yourself Antique Collecting

Teach Yourself Archæology of the New Testament

Teach Yourself Archæology of the Old Testament

Teach Yourself Astronomy

The Teach Yourself Bible Atlas

The Teach Yourself Concise Encyclopædia of General Knowledge

The Teach Yourself Dictionary of Antiques

Teach Yourself Evolution

Teach Yourself Geology

The Teach Yourself Guide to Numismatics (A.B.C. of Coins and Coin Collecting)

Teach Yourself Heraldry and Genealogy

The Teach Yourself History of England

Teach Yourself Local History

Teach Yourself the Old Testament Story

TEACH YOURSELF
ARCHÆOLOGY

By

S. GRAHAM BRADE-BIRKS

M.Sc.(Manc.), D.Sc.(Lond.), A.L.S., F.Z.S., F.S.A.

Author of *Good Soil*

THE ENGLISH UNIVERSITIES PRESS LTD

ST. PAUL'S HOUSE   WARWICK LANE

LONDON EC4

TO
HILDA,
MARY,
ELIZABETH
AND
MARIANNE;

In spite of what they
may think
of
Archæology

First printed 1953
This impression 1967

ALL RIGHTS RESERVED

S.B.N. 340 05507 3

*Printed in Great Britain for the English Universities Press, Limited,
by Richard Clay (The Chaucer Press), Ltd., Bungay, Suffolk*

AUTHOR'S PREFACE

PLEASE remember you are going to *teach yourself* Archæology. This volume is really like a lot of small books rolled into one (their titles are in the list of *Contents*). If you do not find one little book (chapter) interesting, especially after you have read the two introductory ones, turn to another. Try number fifteen for instance, or numbers eighteen and twenty and come back, later on, to the earlier chapters.

The study of the Past

Archæology (Greek: αρχαιος *archaios*, "ancient"; λογος *logos* "study")—"The study of ancient things"—is a consideration of the things of the past. Sometimes the term is used in a limited sense to include only the study of things of extreme antiquity like prehistoric implements and earthworks in this country or the relics of ancient civilizations overseas such as those of Ur of the Chaldees and Ancient Egypt. In this book no such limitation is implied by the use of the word and although in these pages we shall seldom stray from our own country, everything that would interest the members of an archæological society today is comprised in our view of the subject. We are concerned with all that is past.

The continuous story of our nation we call its history: that, too, belongs to the past, but it is a narrative of events whereas archæology is mainly, though not entirely, the study of the things Man has employed to express himself; such things are the surviving evidences of Man's past activity. Thus in archæology we are concerned with tools and implements, with art and architecture; we investigate burial mounds, monuments and earthworks and are interested in all kinds of written records including, for example, ancient charters and parish registers. Coins, coats of arms and place names are among the things that may claim our attention and because all these are things invented and used by Man in the march of events which is chronicled as history, archæology is the handmaid of history. So historians draw upon archæology for some of the evidence which helps them to write the story of human progress down the centuries.

Acknowledgments

As every author should, I take full responsibility for statements of fact and opinion made in this book. Nevertheless I am greatly indebted to a large number of people for help in preparing it and it will be quite impossible to remember to mention them all by name. Among those I want to thank are: Miss M. Keer; Messrs. Frank Higenbottam, B.A., F.L.A.; Frank Jenkins; William Urry, B.A.; W. M. Thoseby, M.A.; M. R. Maitland-Muller, B.A.; Colin W. Walker, F.S.A. Scot.; Samuel Caldwell; George Easton; Robert H. Goodsall, F.R.I.B.A.; Ronald F. Jessup, F.S.A.; Charles C. Elam; G. P. Askew, B.Sc., B.Sc.(Agric.); Dr. Cornelius Davies, D.Sc.; Professor A. J. E. Cave, M.D., D.Sc.; Professor Michael J. O'Kelly, M.A., F.S.A.; and my younger daughter Elizabeth.

I acknowledge with thanks the kindness of authors, artists, publishers and other owners of interests and copyrights, for permission to reproduce material from published works, especially the following: Dr. H. C. Broholm and Miss Margrethe Hald of the National Museum, Copenhagen (Fig. 6 and Figs. 45–54 inclusive); the Controller of Her Majesty's Stationery Office (Figs. 1 and 33–35); the Trustees of the British Museum (Figs. 2–5, 9–17, 24–32, 37–41, 44, 55–67, 69–73, 77–86, 99, 104 and 105 taken from a number of their Guides); Professor Frederick E. Zeuner, D.Sc., F.G.S. (Fig. 7); Dr. H. Godwin, F.R.S. (Fig. 8); Messrs. William Heinemann, Ltd., the Rt. Hon. the Lord Moyne and Professor A. J. E. Cave, M.D. (Figs. 42 and 43); Messrs. B. T. Batsford, Ltd., and Dr. Joseph Raftery (Fig. 36); Kent Archæological Society (Figs. 101 and 113); *The Illustrated Carpenter and Builder* and Sydney E. Castle, Esq., F.R.I.B.A. (Fig. 100); L. F. Salzman, Esq., F.S.A. (Fig. 102) and the Society of Genealogists (Fig. 103).

I am grateful to Mr. Leonard Cutts, the Editor-in-Chief of this series, and to Mr. A. H. Dudley Tyas, both of the English Universities Press, for their kind help in steering this volume through the press. Their skill and experience have done wonders in squeezing in most of the things I wanted to say which would normally have been possible only in a much greater space than is available in a book so modestly priced.

S. GRAHAM BRADE-BIRKS

Godmersham
by Canterbury
Kent

CONTENTS

	PAGE
AUTHOR'S PREFACE	v

CHAPTER ONE
LOOKING AT THE PAST—Some general introductory remarks 13

CHAPTER TWO
HOW, WHEN AND WHERE?—Some further matters of general interest 21

CHAPTER THREE
MAN AND FLINT—The origin of the Human Race and a material much used for tools by Early Man . . 31

CHAPTER FOUR
THE DAWN OF INGENUITY—Man in the Old Stone Age . 37

CHAPTER FIVE
THE SOIL THAT MAN MOVES—The soil-mantle of the Earth as it appears to the Archæologist . . . 47

CHAPTER SIX
MAN, SOIL, ROCK AND THE EARTH—Geological matters of interest to the Archæologist 57

CHAPTER SEVEN
BETTER TOOLS—Man as implement-maker in the Mesolithic and Neolithic Ages 67

CHAPTER EIGHT
LEARNING TO USE METAL—Bronze first used for tools . 76

CHAPTER NINE
THEY BRING IRON—The Early Iron Age . . . 90

CHAPTER TEN
THE COMING OF THE ROMANS—Evidences of Roman rule in Britain 100

CHAPTER ELEVEN
ROMANS REALLY LIVED HERE—Getting a mental picture of the Roman centuries 109

CONTENTS

	PAGE
CHAPTER TWELVE	
BRITAIN BECOMES ENGLAND—The heathen English settle here	121
CHAPTER THIRTEEN	
THE ENGLISH CAME TO STAY—The period that lasted six hundred years	128
CHAPTER FOURTEEN	
THEY KNEW HOW TO BUILD—Architecture: Romanesque (Anglo-Saxon and Norman) and Gothic (Early English, Decorated and Perpendicular)	135
CHAPTER FIFTEEN	
GLORIOUS BUILDING—Ecclesiastical Architecture	140
CHAPTER SIXTEEN	
MAN MUST HAVE A HOME—Early Domestic Buildings (up to the fourteenth century)	151
CHAPTER SEVENTEEN	
CHANGES FOR THE BETTER—Houses attain greater comfort (from the fourteenth century onwards)	160
CHAPTER EIGHTEEN	
THE WRITTEN WORD—Learning to read ancient records	168
CHAPTER NINETEEN	
SOME QUEER CHARACTERS—Mainly about Runes and Ogham	174
CHAPTER TWENTY	
THE LANGUAGE OF SHIELD AND JUPON—Some principles of Heraldry	183
CHAPTER TWENTY-ONE	
WHAT'S IN A NAME?—Place-names and surnames tell their story	190
CHAPTER TWENTY-TWO	
THE PATCHWORK OF THE PAST—Archæology covers many subjects	194
CHAPTER TWENTY-THREE	
A COMPLEX PICTURE—Teach yourself by taking a wide view of the past	199
INDEX AND GLOSSARY	215

LIST OF ILLUSTRATIONS

Durovernum Cantiacorum . . . . *Frontispiece*

FIGURE		PAGE
1.	Stonehenge	14
2.	Neolithic polished axe	16
3.	Neolithic bowl	16
4.	Neolithic long barrow	17
5.	Bronze Age barrow	17
6.	Jacket of Bronze Age	22
7.	Wood sections	26
8.	Pollen of different trees	28
9.	Flaking stone	35
10.	Flake of flint	36
11.	Accident of Nature and "Eolith"	37
12.	Cave art	40
13.	Acheulian hand-axe	43
14.	Levallois and Mousterian cultures	44
15.	Aurignacian scraper	45
16.	Solutrean piercer	45
17.	Magdalenian grattoir	45
18.	Soil map	48
18a.	Key to map	49
19.	Horizons of a soil	50
20.	Riverside soils	53
21.	Testing soil for polish	55
22.	Soil being tested	56
23.	Three river-terraces	63
24.	Microlith of geometric type	67
25.	Rock paintings	68
26.	Mesolithic end-scraper	68
27.	Mesolithic end-scraper	68
28.	Microlith of geometric type	68

x   LIST OF ILLUSTRATIONS

FIGURE		PAGE
29.	Microlith of geometric type	68
30.	Microlith of geometric type	68
31.	Neolithic axe	69
32.	Neolithic arrow-heads	70
33.	Stonehenge	70
34.	Stonehenge	72
35.	Stonehenge	73
36.	Windmill Hill pottery	74
37.	Bronze Age spear-head	76
38.	Bronze Age halberd-blade	77
39.	Bronze Age incense-cup	78
40.	Bronze Age urn	78
41.	Neolithic canoe	79
42.	Long-headed race	80
43.	Short-headed race	81
44.	Evolution of the celt	82
45.	Bronze Age jacket	83
46.	Bronze Age stitching	83
47.	Bronze Age embroidery	84
48.	Bronze Age embroidery	84
49.	Bronze Age skirt	85
50.	Bronze Age jacket	85
51.	Bronze Age cord-sewing	85
52.	Bronze Age burial	86
53.	Bronze Age woman's grave	86
54.	Bronze Age shoe	86
55.	Bronze Age arrow-head	88
56.	Grave of first century B.C.	91
57.	Urn-field	91
58.	Loom-weight	92
59.	Weaving combs	93
60.	Mirror of Early Iron Age	93
61.	Early Iron Age swords	96
62.	Short sword from Halstatt	96
63.	A situla	97

LIST OF ILLUSTRATIONS

xi

FIGURE		PAGE
64.	Cistæ.	97
65.	Late Halstatt sword	97
66.	Early Iron Age pottery	97
67.	Pottery from Swarling	98
68.	Bronze figurine	103
69.	Roman tombstone	104
70.	Roman altar	104
71.	Roman amphora	105
72.	Lead pig	106
73.	Roman sarcophagus	107
74.	Roman written alphabet	111
75.	Roman pottery kiln	116
76.	The five orders	119
77.	Penny of Offa	121
78.	Anglo-Saxon glass	122
79.	A long brooch	125
80.	Gold ring with runes	127
81.	Saucer-brooch	128
82.	Applied brooch	128
83.	Keystone brooch	128
84.	Chip carving	129
85.	Teutonic art	129
86.	Scramasax.	133
87.	Anglo-Saxon belfry-window	140
88.	Masonry tooling.	141
89.	Norman window	142
90.	Single-lancet window	142
91.	Triple-lancet window	142
92.	Plate tracery	144
93.	Bar tracery	144
94.	Tracery with soffit cusps	144
95.	Decorated window	146
96.	Decorated window	146
97.	Perpendicular window	146
98.	Masons' marks	149

LIST OF ILLUSTRATIONS

FIGURE		PAGE
99.	Palæolithic dwellings.	151
100.	English barn	154
101.	A "hall" house	161
102.	Timber-framed house	164
103.	Seventeenth-century letters	170
104.	Coin of Philip II	171
105.	British coins	171
106.	Runic characters	174
107.	Mediæval inscriptions	181
108.	Arms of Knight	183
109.	Arms of Thomas Knight	183
110.	Arms of Lewkenor	184
111.	Arms of May	185
112.	Arms of Brodnax	185
113.	Stone with six brasses	187
114.	Arms of Austen	188
115.	Arms of Martin	188
116.	Military brass	200
117.	Incised marble slab	202
118.	A bas-relief	203
119.	Adam in stained glass	206
120.	Drawing in black pigment	207

A Romano-British town at the beginning of the third century of the Christian era. Our artist shows the walled capital of a Belgic tribe, the Cantii. This is Durovernum Cantiacorum, the modern Canterbury, as seen from the east. The place had only recently been walled, in obedience to an edict of the emperor Severus, to resist invasion. In the centre is the forum (the market-place) with the law court along its northern side. Nearby is the theatre, the largest of its kind in Britain. On Bab's Hill a group of citizens are interested in the work of an agrimensor (surveyor).

CHAPTER ONE

LOOKING AT THE PAST

SOME GENERAL INTRODUCTORY REMARKS

Archæology gives us an insight into the changing fashions of the past and shows us growth in human skill. The remembrance of the dead has given us much material for study. Archæology is a subject in which any intelligent person can attain sufficient proficiency to appreciate objects of the distant, and more recent, past and to make them tell their story.

What is Archæology?

An eminent archæological friend remarked to me one day of the remains of an iron bedstead serving as part of a fence in a cottage garden, "That is archæology." He meant, and explained that he meant, that that iron bed-head told its own story, the story of the change from the old-fashioned nineteenth-century iron-lath and straw-palliasse bed to the spring-mattress of later Victorian times. It was a guide-post to human progress. Similarly, in a suburban garden an unworn penny from the sixties of last century or fragments of pottery bearing the willow pattern turned up by the spade are evidences that the soil was cultivated in Victorian times. Just as anyone will recognize the approximate date of these familiar objects, the student of ancient pottery and money knows them just as well as we know our Victorian pottery and penny, and so is able to use occasional examples of coins or mere fragments of pottery of those earlier times to date any other work of Man with which they occur. The coin may be of negligible monetary value, the potsherds in themselves worthless, but the evidence they afford of date may be of great interest to archæologist and historian.

This is how the student of antiquities dates burial mounds, earthworks and ancient field cultivations. Among the remains of ancient cities, in the rubbish that obscures the foundations of its ruined buildings and in the debris filling its disused wells, ditches and rubbish pits, patient, careful, skilled excavation and sifting reveal similar evidence.

When trained archæologists undertake excavations, people often imagine that they are digging for hidden treasure, and though there may be great excitement among the archæologists themselves when a few recognizable fragments of pottery turn up, the casual visitor may be very disappointed if, after asking what has been found, he is shown such meagre fruits of much labour.

Growth in Skill

Speaking generally, the greater works of Man, the impressive ancient stone monuments, like Stonehenge, that everybody knows, or such spacious cathedrals as Lincoln or St. Paul's, are by no means Man's first attempts at that particular kind of work, but are the outcome of a long development of skill in

Stonehenge. Looking towards the South East.

FIG. 1.

From *Stonehenge Today and Yesterday*, by Frank Stevens. (London: H.M. Stationery Office, rev. ed., 1924.)

craftsmanship and construction, and though, to the general public, a great work may be most stirring and grand, making a special appeal to the imagination, the expert archæologist, anxious to trace the beginning of things, may find as much, or more, interest in some small cromlech (stone circle) or the ground plan of a ruined church of Anglo-Saxon times. So with earthworks, those that are spectacular are often well known, their details have been worked out by experts long ago and a great deal is known about them. As objects of study to help the learner to understand principles of construction they are of great importance. He can make reference to the works in which they have been so fully studied and described. Nevertheless, the smaller works of Man must also have their place in our study if we are to form a general impression of the way in which, down the ages, the soil has been used to provide bank and ditch as features of Man's defensive earthworks which the stresses of conflict and the anxieties of cold war have demanded.

Changing Fashions

A tendency of human beings everywhere, in all ages, which is of the greatest service to the archæologist when he is trying to unravel his problems, is changing fashions.

Take our own generation. In agriculture the horse plough has been displaced by the tractor-drawn implement. In coinage nickel has replaced silver; the small silver threepenny piece has been superseded by its bronze equivalent. In the house plain utility pottery, or at the least new design of ornament, has taken the place of the elaborately decorated tea services of Victorian times; stainless-steel knives are found where before there was labour-consuming cutlery of ordinary steel. We might run right through the range of human activity and find everywhere a replacement of old by new, so that an old object in use is a survival into the present, while the fashion of the new is more prized for its greater suitability. Side by side with this is a fuller appreciation of much in the art of past generations which is unequalled by modern achievement, not in all fields but in some. Thus " old masters " are sought for their timeless excellence, their combination of a high standard of artistic conception and skilful execution. The new takes its place here not necessarily because it excels what has gone before, but because the old ceases to be made when its executants die or stop production; after all, Man's need of works of art as well as of tools and other objects of everyday use can obviously only be met from available output, even when that output is inferior to the things that were formerly produced. So fashions change, either because new inventions supersede old styles or because a human factor (it may be death or economic pressure) brings production of some desirable object to an end.

The employment of materials also shows a sequence; we have it in Britain in the successive uses of stone, bronze and finally of iron for weapons of war and tools of peace. There is also a sequence in the style of workmanship which is an indication of progress in the skill with which Man handles the materials from which he makes his goods. In the case of flint implements we have it in the advances from the first tentative chippings by our remote ancestors through the well-planned but somewhat clumsy hand-axes of Chelles and Le Moustier to a better and more serviceable object. Then there are the advances of Neolithic times, which in the end produced beautifully ground and polished implements which must always remain fine examples of skill and patience. It is the end of one period of development, and is succeeded by the beginning of another, for here is a change in the material used for the best tools, and a new age of progress is brought in and bronze is used for the first time in this country. It is clear that such a change and development provided materials for assigning, by association, all kinds of human workmanship to their proper place in a time-sequence of Man's progress.

In architecture the invention of new methods of handling materials and new appreciation in design produced a sequence which " dated " the work.

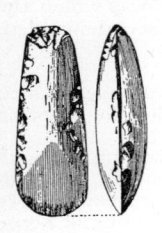

FIG. 2.—Neolithic polished axe, from the Thames at Teddington. Scale ⅛.

From *Flint Implements*, by William Watson.

The earliest pottery Man made must have perished because of its imperfect workmanship and treatment, but some of the earliest earthen vessels that have survived are of extremely rough construction, and from this beginning we can see a development of design as time went on and there is an obvious increase of skill in producing better ware. The different stages of improvement provide different types of pottery, and this enables experts to assign work in each category to its proper chronological place. Here again, then, every age has its own fashion or style. Greater efficiency in using materials or an alteration, sometimes a decline, in artistic ability brings about the change which an archæologist can turn to good account for purposes of "dating". This use of different types as a means of identifying periods of time is called *typology*.

Remembrance of the Dead

The earliest remaining memorials of the dead about which we can be certain are the barrows of Neolithic times (see Chapter Seven). These are followed in turn by burial mounds of the Bronze Age, of the Early Iron Age, of Romano-British days and of the Anglo-Saxon period.

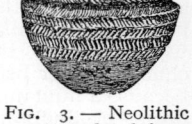

FIG. 3. — Neolithic pottery bowl, from the River Thames at Mortlake. Scale ⅛.

In spite of the racial differences which break the continuity of this series of superficially similar burials, there are certain features common not only to these but indeed to all monuments to the dead.

First, they are all dictated by the attitude of the living to the memory of the dead. For example, a great character beloved by those surviving him has universally demanded a worthy memorial.

LOOKING AT THE PAST

Second, they were all influenced by the religious beliefs of their time:

(*a*) Under certain circumstances the living might fear the spirit of the dead, and this might determine the site and nature of the burial and memorial.

(*b*) Sometimes belief in survival after death has led to material provision for the needs of the departed on a

FIG. 4.—Neolithic long barrow (restored), from the south, West Kennett, Wiltshire. The mound was 336 feet long when it was excavated in 1860. It was 40 feet wide at the west end and 75 feet wide at the east end; this was also the higher end, about 8 feet. There was originally a line of Sarsen stones all round the foot of the mound, and the spaces between the uprights were filled in with dry walling as shown in illustration.

journey to another world or in his life there. This may have included the building of a residence; the provision of means of transport, a ship, horses or a chariot, for example; the supply of tools and weapons and of money, food, domestic utensils and even personal attendants.

(*c*) Defence against evil spirits or their propitiation has been known to result in means for misleading them or denying them facilities for interference with the affairs of the dead or the living.

Third, materials of construction were governed by:

(*a*) *Custom.* Fashions change, but once a fashion is established there is a tendency for changes to come

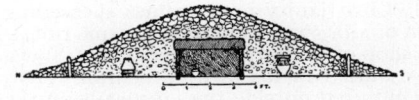

FIG. 5.—Section of a Bronze Age barrow, Ford, Northumberland. In the middle is a stone cist (chest) for the unburnt body. Enclosing-stones at or inside the margin of the mound recall the stone chamber and the ring-fence of the long barrows of Neolithic times (compare this with Fig. 4). The scale is in feet, four in all.

gradually, so that a general likeness in the form of burials or memorials may long continue. At the same time, it must be remembered that two or more methods of burial or of perpetuating the memory of the dead may be customary at the same time, as inhumation and cremation in England today and, strikingly enough, these two methods were also in use, side by side, in this country during part of the Bronze Age.

(b) *Availability of Desirable Materials.* A material that is suitable and has been used in one district may not have been available in another, and has therefore had to be replaced by something else or to have been brought from a distance. Because materials common and ready to hand in one area are unknown in another, there may be great differences between contemporaneous burials and memorials in two separated districts. This is particularly well seen in the contrast between a region where rocks are hard and plentiful and one in which no stone, or very little, occurs. Cairns can readily be erected where stone is ready to hand, while nothing of that exact kind can be made in the absence of stone.

(c) *Cost.* In all ages burials and memorials of the poor must of necessity be less elaborate than those of their wealthy neighbours.

(d) *Personal Choice.* Flexibility in this matter is strictly limited by the other factors involved, and is generally confined to details; for example, the variety of material and exact form of the burial or memorial.

Fourth, the site chosen depended upon the immediate circumstances. The avoidance of badly drained places to preclude flooding, and elevation for prominence, are factors to be considered in the siting of burial places. The necessity for hurried burial in time of plague or war or the desire to honour some prominent personage by interment in a local or national shrine may determine the place. In Roman law adults could not be buried in cities; and the English (A.D. 449–1066) at first—no doubt proud of their Roman tradition after their conversion to Christianity in the times succeeding St. Augustine's mission of A.D. 597—followed the same rule, so that Cuthbert (Archbishop of Canterbury, died A.D. 758) was the first of his line to be buried in his own cathedral. His predecessors had all been interred outside the city walls, in the neighbouring abbey of St. Peter and St. Paul (St. Augustine's).

Archæology for All

Let it never be thought for a moment that the clever people who know all the answers, or at least know all the long words, have a right to monopolize the study of antiquity. Archæology is for everybody. It enables the ordinary man to add interest to life in a rather drab modern world. It makes a

LOOKING AT THE PAST 19

walk to our work along a rather dilapidated old street in an industrial town a joyous and almost adventurous pilgrimage, for there the very beginner in archæology can look with appreciation at quaint features of a bygone fashion or the graceful ornament of wood or metalwork that has survived the successive stages by which a once fashionable street has been demoted to the level of the commonplace. These things can be observed and noted, and thus they will come to be part of the archæology we can teach ourselves.

"Let's Have a Dig!"

As you teach yourself archæology there will come a time when you want to dig. Perhaps there are ancient earthworks of unknown age in your neighbourhood, or the banks that mark outlines of prehistoric cultivation plots on a hillside near at hand; or you may notice strange lines and other markings on a grassy field, especially after a period of very dry weather, or there may be pits or mounds whose origin is unknown. What is to be done?

If you dig in a haphazard manner you will disturb evidence which might be a great help to an expert in deciding the purpose and date of the thing that puzzles you. In the eighteenth century one well-known excavator used to employ a gang of men to dig into ancient burial mounds. We are inclined to think of our ancestors as leisurely people; but, notwithstanding this impression of ours, whereas in this twentieth century an experienced archæologist might occupy many days in investigating a single barrow (burial-mound) this eighteenth-century gentleman makes us shudder at his bustling vandalism. Here is part of his record of one small investigation:

> "On the right hand side of the military Roman road . . . stand nine very fair, though small tumuli sepulchrales [i.e., burial mounds] of the ancients. . . . I had often cast a wishful look at them and from time to time had promised myself the future pleasure of examining their contents. But . . . I did not set about opening them till the 16th of July 1771; on the morning of which day, arriving at this spot in my way to Kingston Down [where later in the day he dug into no less than twenty-four burial-mounds, unearthing bones in every one and finding urns, beads, knife blades, nails, rings, buckles, studs and other objects] rather earlier than usual and being provided with plenty of labourers . . . I thought that a good opportunity to put my intention with regard to these so publicly situated tumuli into execution. So setting ourselves immediately to the business we finished our work in little more than two hours."

[This is an average of about fifteen minutes for each tumulus.]

The untold damage wrought by this eighteenth-century digger with his army of labourers is clear enough, of course, to you. The enormity of his proud catalogue of destruction startles you; but the unskilled excavator today, on a smaller scale, will do the same *kind* of damage. The *amount* of damage is merely determined by opportunity!

Then, you may well ask, ought the inexperienced but interested person to refrain entirely from digging in search of evidence of Man's past? Without skilled supervision, yes. But there are plenty of opportunities in these days for gaining experience, because those who are engaged in the excavation of ancient sites are only too glad to have the offer of volunteer labour, and your service in this kind of work will not only have helped the skilled archæologist but will give you some of the necessary experience which may *eventually* qualify you to undertake original excavation of your own. The secretary of any archæological society will be able to put you in touch with those who need help of the kind mentioned.

LITERATURE

On the subject of books and how to consult them, see the end of the next chapter.

CHAPTER TWO

HOW, WHEN AND WHERE?

SOME FURTHER MATTERS OF GENERAL INTEREST

A common-sense view of the past is important if we are to get the best from our study. The subjects of dates and dating are briefly reviewed, and a word is added about deciding where objects we find came from.

The Critical Faculty

An interested friend was pointing out to me the other day that the expert is not endowed with any senses ordinary mortals do not possess. He seldom smells or tastes any object he is investigating, nor does he often listen to any sound it may emit. He depends principally upon sight and touch, and these are two senses you and I possess as well; yet the expert sees things we may not notice, and he has experience which enables him to compare, mentally, an object under review with other objects he has previously seen and handled.

The archæologist has to learn to weigh evidence. Sometimes the solution of a problem is long delayed, and then suddenly it bursts upon the investigator or is revealed to him by the chance remark of someone in possession of further knowledge. I well remember the problem of some worn brick pillars in a college quadrangle; it was very puzzling. How had the bricks come to be worn like that? In places the wearing was high up, at shoulder level; in other instances it was low down, near the ground, as though a chained animal had worn the brickwork by the continual rubbing of the chain. Suggestion followed suggestion until at last someone who really knew came along. He was an old man, and he well remembered how, when he was a boy, knives had habitually been sharpened there upon the bricks, sometimes high up, sometimes low down. So the puzzle was solved; and, in the end, how simple the explanation was!

In attempting the solution of an archæological problem always take a common-sense view; remember that early Man made his tools for use; so we may be able to get some idea of their use by handling them. Ancient ornaments, clothes and weapons differ from those we use today only because of changed fashions and circumstances. Tracks and roads were used in olden days as we use ours, for getting about from place to place. The essential purposes of a modern house were likewise met by the earliest homes of men. So we can prosecute our enquiries in the knowledge that, fundamentally at least, human needs have remained much the same all down the centuries. So we are wise to proceed in our investigations from the known of this present day to the unknown of yesterday. We should not expect some fantastic and out-of-the-way use for an object that we are considering, but look rather for a somewhat commonplace answer to our questionings.

The value of an open mind can hardly be over-emphasized, for preconceived notions are liable to hinder discovery. I can

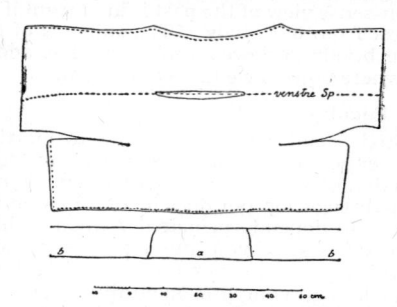

Fig. 6.—Pattern of a woman's brown woollen jacket of Bronze Age date found in a grave at Egtved, Jutland. The scale is in centimetres, 60 in all.

Drawn by Margrethe Hald. From *Bronze Age Fashion*.

illustrate this from a matter of personal experience. Some years ago I was anxious to discover the whereabouts of a place that figured in early records but the location of which was unknown to the present-day inhabitants of the district. The map was brought out and consulted. An air photograph was taken and examined, and by a study of roads and byways the site—an Early Iron Age one—was eventually identified, excavated and confirmed. But the point is this: the place is situated on heavy, clayey land, and had I used my knowledge as a geologist and taken into account the opinions of some authorities that no settlement of the Early Iron Age could occur upon clay, in the Chalk downland, I should never have found the site at all. Fortunately, incredible though it may seem, I was so preoccupied with the evidence of air photography and that of the ordinary maps, that I did not think about the geology, and so work went forward and, in an unusual situation, occupation from about 500 B.C. was verified.

I know of a massive earth bank about 12 feet high and perhaps 200 yards in length: it has long been an archæological puzzle and a subject of much discussion. "What was it for?"

From a knowledge of earthworks one would naturally reply, "It must have been for defence." But this bank is at the edge of an estate and runs directly uphill and downhill; moreover, it dies away both at the top of the hill and at the bottom, and there is no conceivable defensive purpose it could serve. Being at the edge of an estate, one natural suggestion made about it was that it might be a boundary mark. Here our answer must be, " Is it reasonable to suppose that a landowner would build an enormous earthwork to mark a boundary?" The answer must be in the negative. The puzzle has now been solved, and here is the explanation. The bank was built up, probably about 1730, to hide the boundary fence from anyone looking out from the mansion and to blend the grassland of the park around the great house into the landscape of the hillside (beyond the fence) which belonged to the neighbouring estate, so as to give a feeling of continuity and a vista of parkland melting into the distance.

Dates in Archæology

Historical dates are generally reckoned from the beginning of the Christian era; backwards as the years before Christ (B.C.) and forwards, as years of our Lord. For example, we speak of A.D. 1066 (Latin *anno Domini* 1066) or, in English, " in the year of our Lord 1066 ".

In comparatively recent times we can give accurate dates. The exact chronology of many Roman and Anglo-Saxon events in this country is known. Everybody knows A.D. 1066, the date of the Norman invasion, and at least from that time forward precise dating of events is possible. When we go back into pre-history, dates are less certain, and if we study extremely far-off ages, we have to be content with rough estimates of the lapse of years. Authorities differ considerably about very ancient chronology, and in two different books written by different experts you may find that dates of happenings a few thousand years ago are quite differently given. This does not mean that the experts in question are inaccurate people; it means that strict computation is not possible and that different ways of calculating the passage of time in those ancient ages have been adopted by archæologists today. It is safe to foretell that with new methods of enquiry into chronology which are now being tested and perfected much more satisfactory dating will be possible, and already some remarkable results have been obtained.

One of the most important tasks of the student of the past is this *dating* of the works he is investigating. By dating is not necessarily meant assigning an exact year to the object under consideration, whether it be a coin, a piece of pottery, an implement, an earthwork, a castle or a cottage, but its reference to the proper period of history or prehistory. Sometimes, of course, the actual year may be ascertained, as when a cottage or a coin bears a date; in other cases only the century can be determined, and sometimes, especially with extremely ancient objects, we have to be satisfied with a very wide approximation.

Although we cannot give exact dates for periods of prehistory, it is helpful to the mind in reading to know the succession of the different " ages " and to have some idea of their length expressed in years.

Geologists also use rough computations of time in studying the materials of which the earth's crust is composed and, of course, it is natural that their later dates should overlap those of the earlier archæological " ages ".

In the following table we begin with the most recent times, and as we proceed we go deeper and deeper into the past. This is the way in which geologists express the relative ages of the sedimentary rocks of the earth in their chronological tables:

The twentieth century	From 1st January 1901 to the present day.
Victorian times	A.D. 1837—1901
William the Fourth's reign	1830—1837
Georgian era	1714—1830
The Stuart period	1603—1714
Tudor period	1485—1603
The fifteenth century	1401—1500
The Middle Ages	900—1400
Middle Anglo-Saxon times	597—900
The Lost Century *	420—597
The Romano-British period	A.D. 43—420
Early Iron Age †	500 B.C.—A.D. 43
Bronze Age	1900 B.C.—500 B.C.
Neolithic times	2300 B.C.—1900 B.C.
Mesolithic times	12,000 B.C.—2300 B.C.
Palæolithic times	540,000 B.C.—12,000 B.C
The age of Eoliths	?—540,000 B.C.

Dating Objects that are Found

Dating is largely possible (a) by association (b) by typology—which means by changing fashions. By association is meant that objects found together are frequently of the same age, and if sufficient examples of the association are known it becomes

* The so-called Lost Century (A.D. 420—597) is often called, very appropriately, " The Dark Ages ", because it is a period about which we know very little; yet " The Dark Ages " is sometimes used as a synonym for " The Middle Ages " (the time from the death of Alfred the Great, A.D. 901, to the death of Geoffrey Chaucer, the poet, A.D. 1400), so if you meet with the term " The Dark Ages ", be sure you know what the user means by it. Similarly, the term " Middle Ages " is employed somewhat loosely.

† We are, of course, still in the Iron Age; but we may consider its first phase to have ended (as indicated in the above table) with the beginning of the conquest of Britain by the Romans (A.D. 43) in the reign of Claudius.

more and more certain, as the evidence accumulates, that they are in fact contemporary.

In relative dating, a principle long used by geologists in studying sedimentary rocks can usefully be employed. In stratified materials the lowest are normally the oldest (see Chapter Six, p. 59). In a cave formerly occupied by Man the normal arrangement is that the latest materials lie on the surface, older materials below, the oldest at the bottom.

Another principle that is very obvious, when it is once pointed out, is that when a number of objects made at different known dates have been deposited together, the date of the deposit must be as late as the date of the latest object. For example, a box of eighteenth-century coins is found in a wall; the date of the latest coin in the box is 1761, so the box must have been put in place in, or after, 1761.

The presence of such things as fragments of datable pottery and coins in association with objects of which it was wished to know the age has proved very useful to many generations of archæologists; but the new methods of studying varves, radioactive carbon and the rest are not only important in themselves for their practical results, but they also foreshadow the progress we may expect for the future, when still other methods of dating ancient objects have been devised by ingenious investigators. In this way, no doubt, accurate determinations of age will add very considerably to the sum of human knowledge about the past.

Dendrochronology

One of the best-known natural records of the passage of the years is provided by the annual growth rings seen in the secondary wood of forest trees, so that when a tree is cut down we can count these annual rings and determine the age of the tree. But we can now go farther than this and use the annual rings as a record of the actual years of the calendar. This is possible because the different annual rings of the same tree are not all alike. If the season is a wet one the cells are larger than usual, and the appearance of the annual ring growing at that time is different and more prominent. If the season is very dry there is less growth, and again the annual ring looks abnormal; this time it is thinner than usual. Now it will be clear that the pattern of the succession of these annual rings will be an exact match for the succession of annual weather conditions. Familiarity with the weather pattern exhibited by the annual rings over a series of years will enable an investigator to recognize the actual years exhibited by the section of wood, and of course the records of individual trees will overlap with others, enabling us to extend the record to cover more and more remote periods. This method of computation is called Dendrochronology (Greek δενδρον, "a tree"). In England we generally wish to use it on oak, because this wood has been so widely used for building.

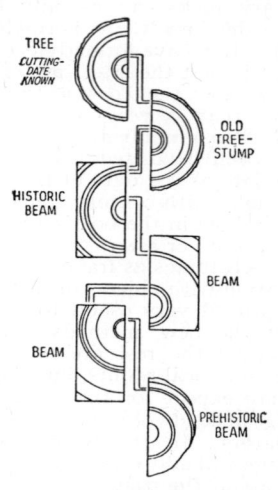

Fig. 7.—Schematic drawings of a series of wood-sections, illustrating cross-dating and how a chronological sequence is built up connecting prehistoric timber with modern trees.

From Professor Frederick E. Zeuner's *Dating the Past* (London : Methuen, 2nd ed., 1950). The drawings are based on work by W. S. Glock.

Radioactive Carbon

In the atmosphere there is a radioactive isotope of carbon with an atomic weight of 14, instead of 12. This isotope is produced in the upper atmosphere under the influence of cosmic rays. The proportion of C_{14} to C_{12} remains constant, because new atoms of the isotope are produced at the same rate as their disintegration takes place. Both C_{12} and the isotope are taken up as CO_2 into the substance of plants, so that both become part, for example, of the wood. In the wood C_{14} disintegrates normally, but naturally it is not replaced there as it is in the atmosphere, so the proportion of C_{14} to C_{12} goes on decreasing. This continues, of course, after the wood is cut. By the use of a special instrument which can detect extremely small amounts of radioactivity, the radioactive carbon present can be estimated, and hence the age of the wood can be calculated with a considerable degree of accuracy. Some accurate results have been obtained with wood of ancient date (of an age known from historical data). This proves that the method is a sound one.

Varves

One of the earliest methods of dating by a natural " clock " is that of studying the varves or annual deposits of fine-grained sediment during the Glacial period in Scandinavia. The turbulent waters after the spring melt were able to carry and deposit somewhat coarse sediment; later on when the rush of water subsided finer materials were laid down, and the finest sediment of all was laid down in the winter, so that there was a sharp contrast between this and the first grains laid down the following spring; in fact, a marked differentiation quite comparable with that of annual rings in wood. These varves a are measure of the passage of the years, but the chronology is only relative, and does not give us the actual date in years B.C. at which deposition occurred.

Pollen in Peat (See Fig. 8, p. 28)

Pollen grains of different plants are of different shapes and sizes, and the distinctions can readily be recognized under the microscope. The succession of different trees dominating the land surface after the Glacial period is known, and in peats accumulated in prehistoric times the pollen grains present are an index of the trees of neighbouring woodlands. By a count of the different pollen grains (of the different species of trees present) succession of the different layers in the peat can be correlated with the woodland flora of the neighbourhood. In this way the characteristics of the different layers can be defined, and a relative age scale can be established for application and use in other places.

Provenance in Archæology

More difficult perhaps than dating objects is the determination of their provenance, i.e., the locality of their origin and design. Most of us would recognize today a model of a chalet as a piece of work from Switzerland, and the same might be true of a paper-knife with a carved handle representing edelweiss, though both these objects might come from an adjoining part of the continent of Europe. Similarly, most of us would recognize a piece of cloth covered with hieroglyphics and representations of Amen-ra, Anubis and Thoth as being of Egyptian origin; yet, you know, we might be mistaken, for that sort of thing has been produced in England, taken out to Egypt and sold there as an ancient Egyptian product. Still with the idea of a model chalet from Switzerland or a representation of Amen-ra from Egypt, the principle of determining provenance

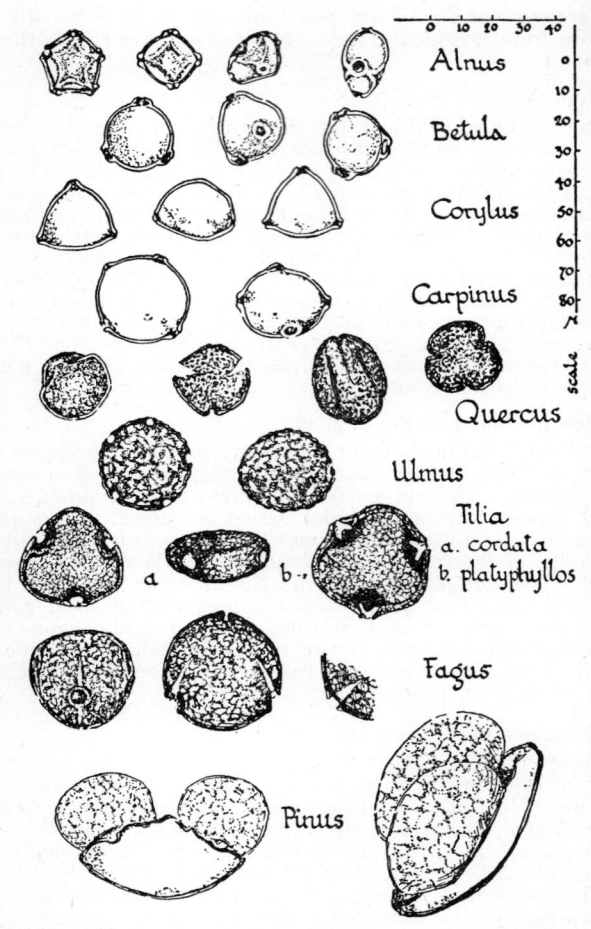

FIG. 8.—The pollen of different trees to indicate how easily botanists can distinguish the pollen grains in ancient peats. Here are represented pollen-grains of the more important trees found in Post-glacial deposits. Scale: one millimetre = 1000μ.

From the work of Dr. H. Godwin, F.R.S.

HOW, WHEN AND WHERE?

can be understood. Familiarity with the products of Swiss wood-carvers enabled us to recognize this isolated piece of work, and it is only when we have become familiar with the styles of a country (in the age under consideration) that we can speak with certainty.

LITERATURE

Books to guide you in your studies are most important.

You will learn to use the articles in various Encyclopædias upon archæological topics For your own particular area you will consult the *Victoria History* of your own county. You will also find that the various *British Museum Guides* are of great assistance, and you will learn to use them freely; sometimes local museums provide *Guides* to their own collections, and these, of course, should be used. Go also and look at the books in your own local library under the heading of Archæology and in the specialized branches of the subject, consulting the library staff, who will be only too willing to help you. Do not forget the Local History collection in the Reference Library. Even if the books you require are not in stock, the Librarian will try to borrow them from another library; there may be some charge for postage.

A most helpful book if you are asked to assist with digging is *Field Archæology*, by R. J. C. Atkinson (London: Methuen, first published 1946).

There is a general book of great use in deciding what books to read and, of course, gives far more information than can be offered in a volume the size of this present book. It is *British Archæology: A Book List for Teachers* (London: The Council for British Archæology, to be obtained from the Council, c/o Institute of Archæology, Inner Circle, Regent's Park, London, N.W.1). The 1949 issue of this useful work costs 1s. 6d.

The Historical Association, 21 Bedford Square, London, W.C.1, prepared a *Local History Handlist* published for the Association in 1947 by Staples Press, London. This available to the public at 1s. 1d., post free. It is a well-classified list covering: Topography; Village and Manorial History; County Administration and Justice; Town History; Trade, Commerce and Industry; Warfare on Land; Ports and Shipping; Education and Learning; Local Worthies—Biographies and Portraits; Societies and Institutions concerned with Local History and Antiquities, and their Publications; as well as most of the subjects with which the present volume deals (2nd ed. 1953).

Prehistoric Britain, by Christopher and Jacquetta Hawkes (Harmondsworth, Middlesex: Penguin Books, reprinted 1952). This contains a useful list of publications.

Prehistoric Ireland, by Joseph Raftery (London: Batsford, 1951). The above two books cover the prehistoric archæology of our islands. You may find the following works useful for consultation:

> (a) *Everyday Life Series*, by Marjorie and C. H. B. Quennell (London: Batsford) as follows: (i) *Everyday Life in the Old Stone Age*; (ii) *Everyday Life in the New Stone, Bronze and Early Iron Ages*; (iii) *Everyday Life in Prehistoric Times*; (iv) *Everyday Life in Saxon, Viking and Norman Times*.
>
> (b) *A History of Everyday Things in England*, by Marjorie and C. H. B. Quennell (London: Batsford) as follows: I. *1066–1499*; II. *1500–1799*; III. *1733–1851*; IV. *1851–1948*.
>
> (c) A series of books by C. W. Airne (Manchester: Thomas Hope and Sankey-Hudson) as follows: (i) *The Story of Prehistoric and Roman Britain Told in Pictures*; (ii) *The Story of Saxon and Norman Britain*

Told in Pictures; (iii) *The Story of Mediæval Britain Told in Pictures*; (iv) *The Story of Tudor and Stuart Britain Told in Pictures*; (v) *The Story of Hanoverian Britain Told in Pictures*.

Publications of your local and county archæological, historical and record societies (including parish register societies) will also be useful. Additional works that may be mentioned are:

Three books by V. G. Childe, *Man makes Himself* (Thinkers' Library) (London: Watts, 1948); *What Happened in History* (Harmondsworth: Penguin, 1950); *Prehistoric Communities of the British Isles* (London and Edinburgh: W. and R. Chambers, first published 1940).

Beginning in Archæology, by Kathleen Mary Kenyon (London: Phœnix House).

Field Archæology: Some notes for beginners, issued by The Ordnance Survey (London: H.M.S.O.).

Illustrated Regional Guides to Ancient Monuments Series. Vol. I. *Northern England.* Vol. II. *Southern England.* Vol. III. *East Anglia and the Midlands.* Vol. IV. *South Wales* (London: H.M.S.O.).

A Handbook of the Prehistoric Archæology of Britain (issued in connection with the 1st International Congress of Prehistoric and Protohistoric Sciences, London, 1932) (Oxford, 1932).

Periodicals. These should be noted:

Antiquity: A Quarterly Review of Archæology (Ashmore Green, Newbury, Berks: H. W. Edwards).

The Antiquaries Journal, which has a complete list of new publications on Archæology in each issue (London: Society of Antiquaries, & Geoffrey Cumberlege, Oxford University Press).

The Journal of Roman Studies (Society for the Promotion of Roman Studies: London).

CHAPTER THREE

MAN AND FLINT

THE ORIGIN OF THE HUMAN RACE AND A MATERIAL MUCH USED
FOR TOOLS BY EARLY MAN

The origin of Man is a topic of absorbing interest; its study depends upon a vast amount of evidence, much of which has been gathered during the last hundred years. Among the materials Man has used for making his implements, flint is of great importance.

The Origin of Man

A GOOD many years have now passed since scientists first seriously undertook enquiries about the origin of Man. It is, of course, a topic which interested Man himself before the dawn of history, for in the first two chapters of the Bible are written down two different accounts of Creation including the creation of Man (Genesis 1.^{27} and 2.^{7}), and these accounts have parallels in the folk-lore of many ancient peoples. All of them, including the two incorporated in the book of Genesis, must have been handed down by word of mouth for long centuries before they were ever committed to writing. As far as the accounts of Man's origin given in the Bible are concerned, no biblical scholar today would maintain that they are to be accepted as literally true and historically accurate. Their value as history is quite independent of the spiritual truths that are taught by these same chapters. The Bible tells us the truth about God and about spiritual things, but it is not meant to be a scientific or archæological text-book.

It is a comfort to many religious people to know that there are many men and women, first-class scientists and archæologists, who have no difficulty in reconciling the findings of biology and archæology with the teaching of the Church. Very often matters which present great spiritual difficulties to people who have a limited knowledge of archæology and biology, and perhaps of religion too, are not the slightest stumbling blocks to men and women who have made a deeper study of these matters.

Much is Still Unknown

In spite of all that has already been discovered about the beginning of the human race and about the life of Man in the far-distant past, there is still an unbounded field of work to be covered by those who investigate these things. Before the days when the burial of the dead was methodically carried out, the likelihood of a human skeleton being preserved was only a remote chance. Occasionally, in limestone caves, water containing lime in solution has provided the material for adding calcium carbonate to bone, hardening and preserving it, and this is one of the most satisfactory ways in which fossil Man has been preserved for us.

A Century of Discovery

Knowledge about the physical characteristics of early humans and pre-humans has been gradually built up during the past century or so by the discovery of a number of their skulls and other bones, and bit by bit these pieces of fossil evidence have been fitted together to give us, not a complete genealogical tree, but a series of likenesses which can be taken to show the state of development of the human race at different times and also to point out for us how modern Man arrived at his present stage of development from his remote and less remote relatives.

It is concluded on anatomical grounds that the nearest living relatives of Man are the anthropoid apes—the gorilla, chimpanzee, orang utan and gibbon. Certain South African fossils of Pliocene age (some time between fifteen million and one million years ago) or early Pleistocene age (say one million years ago) are still more human in form, and may, in fact, be ancestral to the human stock.

Fossils of true men (but not of our species, *Homo sapiens*) have been found at Choukoutien, near Peking (called Peking Man), 1927–29 and since; in Java late in the nineteenth century, and at Mauer * near Heidelberg in 1907. The Choukoutien and Java remains * are skulls perhaps dating back more than half a million years; they are like us, but have some ape-like characteristics too. The fossil from Mauer is a single lower jaw found in a sand-pit. The teeth are of the human type. This fossil probably dates from the beginning of the " first " (i.e., Ante-penultimate) Interglacial period about half a million years ago.

An ape-like jaw, a canine tooth and the skull of a man referable to the same species as Modern Man (*Homo sapiens*) found at Piltdown, Sussex, were, for a long time, problematical. It is now known that the jaw and tooth are those of a modern anthropoid ape. The skull is that of a woman of late Pleistocene age.

A gravel-pit at Swanscombe* in North Kent with middle Acheulean flint tools, which date from the " second " (i.e., Penultimate) Interglacial period of about 250,000 years ago, also

* See Table (in Chapter Six, page 64) of Glacial and Interglacial periods.

yielded some skull bones (occipital and left parietal) which agree with those of Modern Man (*Homo sapiens*).

Two crania of individuals belonging to a race very close to *Homo sapiens* if not actually members of our species were found in deposits not later than the " third " (i.e., Last)Interglacial period (Upper Pleistocene, about 120,000 years ago) at Fontéchevade * (Charente) south-west France.

There are other instances which help to support the view that *Homo sapiens* had already evolved before the beginning of the Upper Pleistocene about 175,000 years ago. This is very early when compared with the conceptions held by palæontologists fifty years ago, but when we examine the record of fossil mammals as a whole it is not a surprisingly early date for a living species, and one might well expect that future discoveries will throw back the origin of *Homo sapiens* quite a long way.

But there is another species of human being, now extinct, well represented by fossil forms, which is of great interest.

In 1857 Dr. Fuhlrott found part of an extraordinary human skull with some other bones of the skeleton in the now famous Neanderthal cave near Dusseldorf, Germany. A similar skull had actually been found in a cave at Gibraltar in 1848. In later years many other remains of the same type have been found in Belgium, Jersey, Italy, Yugoslavia, South Russia, Siberia, Palestine and North Africa. Such remains are termed Neanderthal.

Neanderthal Man cannot be regarded in any sense as intermediate between the apes and Modern Man (*Homo sapiens*) and, as he must be regarded as a separate species of human being, his biological designation must indicate this; scientifically he is called *Homo neanderthalensis*.

Neanderthal Man was not as upright as Modern Man. His head and his brain were large. The brow-ridges of his skull were larger than those of Modern Man; the forehead was noticeably retreating; the brain-case had thicker walls than that of *Homo sapiens* and was flattened; the lower jaw had a receding chin.

A step forward in correlation was taken when two skeletons of *Homo neanderthalensis* were found in a cave at Spy * in Belgium associated with typical Mousterian implements and with bones of animals known to be characteristic of the last Glacial period. In many other places the same kind of association has since been found. We have already seen that long before this *Homo sapiens* was also living.

Neanderthal Man evidently died out, for no living race of human beings exhibits the physical features he possessed. Also it may be noted that the earlier Neanderthal (Mousterian) men were more like Modern Man than later Neanderthal Man was.

* See Table (in Chapter Six, page 64) of Glacial and Interglacial periods.

Flint

Flint is hard concretionary chalcedonic silica in nodular or tabular form, occurring originally in, and therefore always ultimately derived from, the Chalk formation. Where accumulations of flints are found in gravels or elsewhere they have always been derived from chalk. Silica, chemically, is silicon dioxide, SiO_2, a substance of which most grains of sand are composed. The statement that flint is chalcedonic, meaning that it is in the form taken by the semi-precious stone chalcedony, indicates that it is a mixture of atoms of silicon and oxygen regularly arranged in a structural pattern, which we call crystalline, mixed with non-crystalline (amorphous) irregularly arranged molecules of silicon dioxide. Upon this internal arrangement of flint depends the characteristic way in which it breaks when struck. This manner of breaking produces a scar shaped like a mussel-shell, and so it is called a conchoidal (shell-like) fracture. The strength and direction of the blow determine the exact nature of the fracture, and this property of flint is therefore extremely important in the use of this stone for making tools. The silica in flint was derived from very small quantities of it occurring in the original limy mud which afterwards dried to form chalk. Much of this silica was no doubt present in the scattered skeletons of plants (especially diatoms) and animals (especially siliceous sponges) which originally lived in the sea in which chalk was formed. This silica by physical attraction moved in solution through the mud towards some centre, around which it accumulated to form what is known as a concretion. Isolated concretions are nodular (i.e., irregular, lumpy, round-edged masses), but if the concretions are numerous enough they may form a complete stratum or plate and, so, take on the tabular form. In the recognized Mohs's scale of hardness, flint has a hardness of 7, which means that it is about as hard as a steel penknife and a little harder than glass.

The Flaking of Flint

Flint can be worked in three ways : (i) It can be flaked by a blow; (ii) it can be flaked by pressure; (iii) it can be polished by grinding or rubbing.

In flaking by the first method, to be effective the blow must be delivered on a flat part of the flint. This flat area is called, by archæologists, the striking platform. The result of a blow (owing to the chalcedonic structure which has already been explained) is that fracture of the flint takes place in a characteristic and predictable manner. The fracture spreads outwards and downwards, beginning straight; but, as the force is expended, becoming first a smooth curve outwardly convex and eventually forming ripples at right angles to the general direction of the fracture. When circumstances allow and the blow is directed in the right place (for example, in the middle of the upper surface of a piece of tabular flint) a complete conical body of flint will fall out of the plate. But if the blow is directed where this is impossible at the *edge* of a striking platform, only that part of the cone which is represented by the

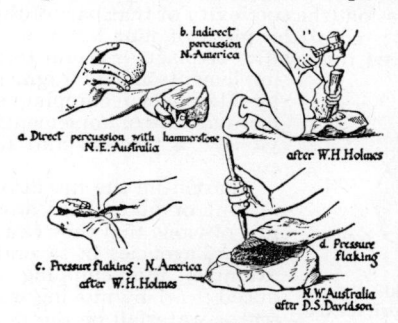

FIG. 9.—Methods of flaking stone.
From *Man the Toolmaker*, by Kenneth P. Oakley.

flint available can be developed. It will, of course, be roughly the shape of a cockle-shell (this is the conchoidal fracture already explained, Latin, *concha*, " a shell ").

The second kind of flaking is by pressure. If two flints are pressed together (for example, by the wheels of a vehicle passing along a flint road) tiny, and larger, flakes are *pressed* off their edges. The same result can be obtained by Man. Characteristically it can be done with a blunt pencil of flint called a *fabricator*. Upon the fabricator, held against the flint to be chipped, pressure is exerted so that a small flake is detached.

When a block of flint has been shaped by repeated blows and a primary form has been established, finer work, often called secondary chipping, can be carried out by pressure with a fabricator.

The third way in which flint can be worked is by polishing. This method was adopted in late Neolithic times, and some beautiful examples of polished implements have been found. Although it is easy to polish flint by using modern mechanical methods, it must have been a very laborious job in ancient times.

As far as flaking is concerned, I do not think it took Early Man long to make flint implements. I have made a tolerable flint arrow-head with a steel hammer in half an hour or so, and with practice that time might be much reduced.

In association with the main features of the fracture, which have already been mentioned, shallow fissures in the flint are produced in the general direction of the force of the blow, and a small fracture is often produced as a prominent feature near the top of the concavity. This is called the bulbar scar.

Terms used in connection with flint flaking also include the following : point of percussion (where the blow is delivered); bulb of percussion (the convexity of that part of the cone which is developed); core (the piece of flint left when flakes have repeatedly been removed); artefact (a useful term to include implements and *all* fragments produced by Man when chipping stone in his manufacture of implements); flake (obviously, a piece of flint flaked from a core).

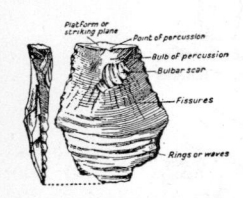

FIG. 10.—The ideal flake of flint, in which all the conchoidal features are clearly visible. Scale ⅕.

From *Flint Implements*, by William Watson.

Apart from the intentional chipping of flint or other hard stones by Man, it is obvious that they can be flaked by natural agencies in several ways. For example, this chipping can be produced : (*a*) by moving water, as when sea or waterfall or the flood waters of a river throw one freely-moving stone against another; (*b*) by the battering of a fixed stone by others carried in water; (*c*) by stones falling upon one another; (*d*) by movement or pressure of rock or soil.

In all these cases, and you may be able to think of others, the chipping might be expected to be either haphazard or produced by blows from a single direction. But when there are two or more regular directions in which the blows producing the chipping have been delivered and when there is also an absence of the haphazardly produced flaking, the accidental production of the final shape seems to be impossible. Then it is easier to believe that such a chipped stone is the work of Man than to think that it is the result of natural agencies, such as those we have mentioned.

LITERATURE

Books on this branch of the subject are briefly mentioned at the end of the next chapter.

CHAPTER FOUR

THE DAWN OF INGENUITY

MAN IN THE OLD STONE AGE

Here we go back a million years and speak briefly about Eoliths; then the long years and centuries of the Old Stone Age (the Palæolithic period) are considered, and we see a little of the great progress made by the human race during that great expanse of time.

Eoliths

A MILLION years ago the lands we call Britain and Ireland were still joined to the Continent. About that time something that puzzles us today was happening in the part of Europe we call southern England. Irregular pieces of flint were being chipped along their edges and were being given

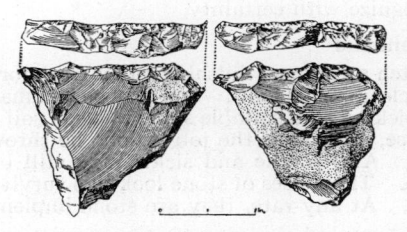

FIG. 11.—Accident of Nature and "Eolith". *On the left:* Flint with edges chipped by natural agency, below Eocene beds, Grays, Essex. *On the right:* Edge-chipped flint from Kent claimed by Benjamin Harrison as an "eolith". The scale is in inches, two in all.

From *Man the Toolmaker*, by Kenneth P. Oakley.

shapes that would make them useful to Man in a variety of ways. Some could be employed as scrapers or perhaps for breaking up the fibres on the back of the skins flayed from wild animals killed in hunting; such treatment would make the skins pliable. Other chipped flints were beak-shaped; they might be handy for skinning animals and preparing them for food.

How were these flints chipped?

Some people have argued that they were produced by natural

causes, one stone flaked against another without any hand to hold them. Other people are firmly convinced that these are implements purposely made for use by our remote ancestors in the dawn of human intelligence; and so they are called Eoliths (dawn-stones, from Greek ἠώς, *eos*, " dawn ", λίθος, *lithos*, " a stone ").

These chipped flints have been found in large numbers in the southern counties of England.

Whether the eoliths that have so far been discussed really were the work of Early Man or not, it is quite clear that flint implements cannot have originated except through stages which began with the use of the unchipped stone and went on to a form in which chipping was of the rudest description. Tools we can clearly recognize as Man's work were the final result of a long period of increasing skill.

It is obvious that this problem of the eoliths is one for people experienced in the study of stone tools, so we ought to pass on to learn something about the more readily identifiable types of later times, those of the Palæolithic, Mesolithic and Neolithic Ages. We can always come back to the eoliths when we have a better mastery of the problems of identification. Although eoliths must be the earliest in date of Man's stone artefacts, we have to admit that they are the most difficult of all early human tools to recognize with certainty.

Stone Implements

If you watch a gardener finishing off his work for the day you will see him cleaning his tools. You may be fortunate enough to notice him picking up a suitable stone to clean soil off his spade and, of course, as soon as the job is done he throws the stone down again. Also scythe and sickle may still be sharpened with a stone. These uses of stone look like survivals from the remote past. At any rate, they are stone implements still in use.

To some extent in some parts of the world, copper took the place of stone several thousand years before the beginning of the Christian era. In this country about 1900 years before Christ men began to use bronze (an alloy of copper and tin), while implements of iron (which is more difficult to obtain from its ores than copper and tin) came into use here about 500 B.C. But for long after metal was first made into tools, stone implements remained in use. Indeed, in the Bronze Age so highly was bronze prized that men made flint objects which imitated in shape the rarer, more desirable bronze tool or weapon, just as articles today made in plastics imitate the form and decoration of more expensive products normally made in metal or earthenware.

Flint was the usual kind of material from which early implements were made, but Man has always used any convenient material ready to his hand. In East Africa, for example, obsidian, a glassy rock, has been used for tool-making in comparatively recent times. A friend of mine was able to match an obsidian implement he brought back with him from East Africa with one in flint which he found on the North Downs of Kent.

Other hard rocks used by Early Man for making tools include quartzite and chert; such tools are not easily blunted by use.

Implements are made by Australian aborigines from bottles and telegraph insulators. They chip the glass or earthenware much as Early Man chipped flints, and produce very similar results.

Evidences of Palæolithic and Mesolithic Man

So remote are the Palæolithic (Old Stone) Age and the Mesolithic (Middle Stone *) Age, and so great is the period of time that they cover, that we cannot expect to have more than a very rough idea of all the changes that must have taken place in human activities and conditions of life over such a vast passage of time as five thousand *centuries*. Such a period baffles our imagination, but mentioning it in hundreds of years perhaps conveys more to the mind than speaking of half a million years.

We may assume that before the beginning of the Palæolithic era, Man and his ancestors had had very many centuries to learn to use wood and bone and shell and stone to aid them in their hunting, fishing and food gathering. It is not surprising when all the circumstances are taken into consideration that neither the bones nor the rude dwelling-places of these very first implement makers have been discovered.

Evidence for the existence and habits of Man in Palæolithic and Mesolithic times is, however, available. It is provided by stone tools, by rare and isolated examples of skulls, generally imperfect, and of other bones. As far as Mesolithic times are concerned, evidence is also provided by implements of bone, shell, antler, and by the finding of carved and engraved bones. In both Upper (late) Palæolithic times and the Mesolithic Age the drawings and paintings made by primitive artists on the walls of caves and rock shelters are found.

The Dawn of Human Ingenuity

When Man—or some man-like animal—first took stones into his hand and used them, he was probably unconcerned about exact shape and size. But with Early Man casual use would lead to selection, and selection would arouse a desire to chip the stone to a more convenient shape. Quite obviously the earliest

* Use the term " Middle Stone Age " with caution. In South Africa the phrase does not mean Mesolithic, but Upper Palæolithic.

of these shaped stones would be mere adaptations of the natural form.

Try to picture in your mind's eye an early ancestor of ours

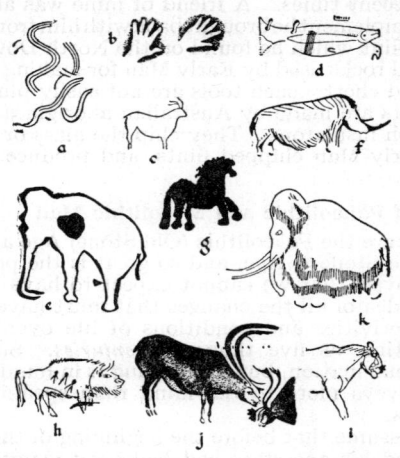

FIG. 12.—Upper Palæolithic cave art. *a–c, e,* "Early-Middle Aurignacian"; *d, f, g,* "Late Aurignacian" (Perigordian); *h–k,* Magdalenian.

a, Snake-like scribbles in yellow ochre, La Pileta (Malaga); scale $\frac{1}{50}$.
b, Hands stencilled in red ochre, Castillo (Santander); scale $\frac{1}{40}$. *c,* Engraving of ruminant, Pair-non-Pair (Gironde); scale $\frac{1}{60}$.

After Daleau.

d, Salmon engraved on roof of rock-shelter, Gorge d'Enfer, near Les Eyzies (Dordogne). Note associated bird's head, tally marks(?) and dumb-bell-shaped holes; scale $\frac{1}{60}$.

After Peyrony.

e, Elephant painted in red ochre, Pindal (Oviedo); note heart; scale $\frac{1}{36}$.
f, Woolly rhinoceros painted in red ochre, Font-de-Gaume, near Les Eyzies; scale $\frac{1}{40}$. *g,* Horse painted in black oxide of manganese, Lascaux, near Montignac (Dordogne); scale $\frac{1}{40}$. *h,* Wounded bison, engraved on floor of cave, Niaux (Ariège); scale $\frac{1}{4}$. *i,* Engraving of cave-lion, Combarelles (Dordogne); scale $\frac{1}{40}$. *j,* Reindeer painted in black (male) and in red (female), Font-de-Gaume, near Les Eyzies; scale $\frac{1}{80}$. *k,* Engraving of mammoth, Font-de-Gaume, near Les Eyzies; scale $\frac{1}{24}$.

Mainly after Breuil and associated authors.

From *Man the Toolmaker*, by Kenneth P. Oakley.

first using his new-found ingenuity. And never forget that, side by side with things that time has spared and preserved, there must have been many objects of a perishable nature made

THE DAWN OF INGENUITY 41

from wood and shells and the skins and bones of animals which were found useful in winning from Nature the essentials of life and in using them in the primitive activities of every day. Lumps of clay and dried mud, turves torn from the earth, the sinuous stems of climbing plants, great branches of trees and logs would often prove useful, while slate and slabs of stone must often have served for seats and tables.

If in studying flint implements and all the remains that archæology has discovered, we try to imagine in a common-sense way the mode of life of our remote ancestors, it will make our enquiries all the more enlightening. If we wish to avoid fantastic explanations we shall always remember that Early Man had the same fundamental needs we still experience. He needed food, warmth and shelter. Remember also that he had the same instincts as ourselves, many of the same fears and some of the same aspirations.

The Old Stone Era

Half a million years ago Man had then already attained very considerable skill in the shaping of various kinds of stone for a variety of uses. He was already very proficient in the manufacture of the so-called hand-axe.

It was in England towards the end of the seventeenth century that such an object as a hand-axe was first recognized with certainty as human workmanship. The individual implement in question is of flint, and was found in the Thames Valley gravels; it is still to be seen at the British Museum.

The Old Stone Age, or technically the Palæolithic (Greek παλαιὸς, *palaios*, " old "; λίθος, *lithos*, " a stone "), era covered an almost incredibly long period of time. Very careful consideration of a wealth of material gathered, especially from river gravels, rock shelters and caves has enabled the experts to work out a succession of types, each of which is characterized by a special kind of workmanship and by definite forms and shapes in the finished tools.

The frequency with which flint tools of the different subdivisions of the Palæolithic Age occur in the gravels of river terraces indicates that they must have been used in some way in association with the streams. Perhaps these implements were used in connection with fishing. The so-called " hand-axes " could have been used for skinning animals.

These works of Man are of such usual occurrence that where gravel used to be dug by hand labour, the workmen would pick out and sell them to any archæologist who wished to acquire them. They can readily be recognized with a little practice, and the best way to become acquainted with the typical forms is to study a good series of these implements in a museum or in a private collection.

From what has already been said, it will be realized that the "cultures" of the clearly defined groups of types of tools found in this country, belonging to different periods of the Palæolithic Age, are likely to represent the work of different races or peoples who came from the eastward in successive movements or waves, bringing their knowledge and skill with them. But the idea of "races" and "peoples" in relation to different styles or fashions or types of workmanship must not be too easily accepted. It does not necessarily follow that all communities using the same type of implement were in blood relationship. Thus a map to show the distribution of well-known types of implements may be no indication at all of racial boundaries.

Growth in Skill

During the Palæolithic age there was a great increase of skill in the manufacture of implements. Over the past hundred years investigation has shown that a Palæolithic site may have characteristic stone implements and that, having been studied there, those particular kinds may turn up again and again in other places, and so indicate a similar way of life or culture. Thus implements first studied from the Dordogne cavern called Le Moustier, near the right bank of the River Vézère, and from that fact called Mousterian, occur in many places in Europe and Asia. The implements in question form the Mousterian *culture*. The local examples of any culture regarded individually are called *industries*; thus we may speak of the Mousterian industry of Kent's Cavern, Torquay, meaning by that the implements of that culture occurring as the tools of the men living at Kent's Cavern.

Thus we have the following Palæolithic cultures as important examples:

Abbevillian—named from Abbeville on the Somme.
Acheulian—from St. Acheul in the Somme valley just above Amiens.
Levalloisian—after the Levallois–Perret quarter of Paris.
Mousterian—from the cavern called Le Moustier, in the Vézère valley.
Aurignacian—Aurignac is in Haute Garonne, 40 miles south-west of Toulouse.
Solutrean—called after Solutré, department Saône-et-Loire.
Magdalenian—from a place on the right bank of the Vézère, not far from the ancient castle of La Madeleine.

Implements of Abbevillian age are flattish lumps of flint coarsely flaked round the edge from both sides so as to produce a large irregularly oval or pear-shaped hand-axe which is the core of the original flint pebble. Such flaking as this can be

THE DAWN OF INGENUITY

produced either by hitting the flint with another flint or lump of rock used as a hammer or by striking it against the edge of a massive stone. It might take thousands of years for the new methods to become known over the breadth of a continent, but eventually the new style supplanted the old.

Contemporary with Abbevillian core-tools we find flakes fashioned as implements. This early flake industry is called Clactonian, from Clacton-on-Sea, Essex, where gravels provided the first-studied implements of this kind. The flakes themselves are coarse, and were probably made by striking the flint against a very large stone. The tools frequently show the

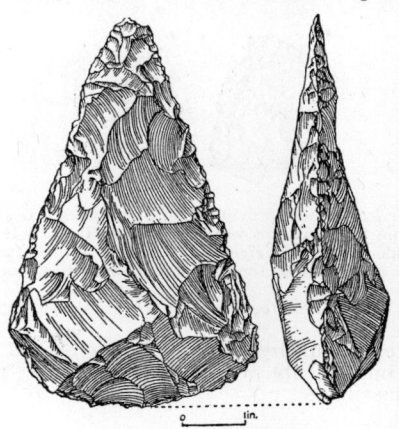

FIG. 13.—Acheulian hand-axe associated with the Swanscombe skull. See p. 32. The scale-line represents 1 inch.
From *Man the Toolmaker*, by Kenneth P. Oakley.

bulb of percussion. The edges of the flakes are trimmed. It may be mentioned that a wooden spear-head, of yew, of this age was found at Clacton. This is the only Palæolithic wooden implement so far discovered in Britain. Another spear, also of yew, was obtained from a Levalloisian site in Germany.

The next culture we must mention is the Acheulian. Its implements are principally core-tools, especially oval to pointed hand-axes for cutting and scraping. These tools are fairly smooth in outline, and have shallow flaking, probably produced by knapping with bone, hard wood or soft stone. They are of a more perfect form than Abbevillian hand-axes and have a more effective cutting edge.

Flake-tools of the Levalloisian culture were more elaborate

and more carefully executed than the implements of earlier cultures. They were typically produced from cores previously shaped by preliminary chipping to the form of a depressed cone. Skilful knapping from the prepared core provided either oval or long narrow flakes which were implements in themselves and needed no further treatment. Sometimes the butt of the flake bears traces of the preliminary chipping of the core. This kind of butt is termed *faceted*. In such implements the bulb of percussion is prominent if a hard hammer stone was used to strike the flake from the core, but it is flatter if a softer tool was employed for the purpose.

FIG. 14.—*On the left:* Cordiform (heart-shaped) hand-axe of the Levallois culture, from the Levallois working floor at Baker's Hole, Northfleet, Kent. Scale ⅓. *On the right:* Hand-axe of the type found in the Mousterian culture, from the type site, Le Moustier, Dordogne, France. Scale ⅙.

From *Flint Implements*, by William Watson.

The Mousterian culture is largely characterized by carefully made flake implements with edges trimmed, probably by pressure against bone.

TABLE OF PREHISTORIC AGES IN BRITAIN

Early Iron Age	500 B.C. to A.D. 43
Bronze Age	1900 B.C. to 500 B.C.
Neolithic Age (when farming began)	2300 B.C. to 1900 B.C.
Mesolithic Age	12,000 B.C. to 2300 B.C.
Palæolithic Age	540,000 B.C. to 12,000 B.C.

Peoples of Late Pleistocene Times

The closing phases of the Pleistocene period during the final glaciation of northern Europe brought with them a remarkable development of skill and the production of a wide variety of implements not only in stone but also in bone, antler and

THE DAWN OF INGENUITY 45

ivory, and many of the men of this period (approximately between 115,000 and 14,000 years ago) were also real artists, shaping and engraving bone, reindeer-antler and mammoth ivory, and painting, on the walls of rock-shelters and caves, realistic hunting scenes and other illustrations of their daily life (Fig. 12).

The peoples of this late Pleistocene epoch were:

Those of the Châtelperronian culture (the type site is at Châtelperron). Their typical tool was a flint blade fashioned as a knife, one edge very sharp and straight, the other curved up to the point and blunted by trimming.

The Cro-Magnon (= Aurignacian) people were workers in

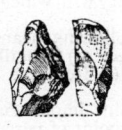

FIG. 15.—Nosed scraper, of the Aurignacian culture from Belcaire Bas, St. Léon-sur-Vézère, Dordogne, France. Scale slightly under ⅓.

From *Flint Implements*, by William Watson.

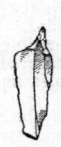

FIG. 16. — Upper Palæolithic flint tool. Solutrean piercer, or "hand-drill", Laugerie Haute (Dordogne). Scale ¼.

From *Man the Toolmaker*, by Kenneth P. Oakley.

FIG. 17.— Palæolithic flint tool. Double-ended grattoir (end-scraper) Magdalenian, Grotte des Eyzies (Dordogne). Scale ⅓.

From *Man the Toolmaker*, by Kenneth P. Oakley.

bone and antler; they were also artists using ochre. Cro-Magnon is a cave or rock shelter in a cliff overlooking the valley of the Vézère.

The Gravettian culture followed (named after La Gravette). The typical tool is a pointed blade curved on both edges, one blunted, one sharp. The men of this culture were hunters and artists, and made statuettes of women in bone, ivory, stone and pottery. They used red ochre and made personal ornaments by piercing shells, including fossils and animal teeth.

The Solutreans were very skilled in pressure flaking and made beautiful flint implements. They, too, were artists.

Lastly, mention must be made of the Magdalenian culture, which owed its characteristics to Gravettian and other influences. The implements produced were very varied, and exhibited great skill in working flint (especially blades), reindeer-antler, bone and ivory. The Magdalenians made barbed harpoons, needles with eyes and many other implements.

The well-known and often illustrated paintings of the Altamira cave in north-east Spain were executed by them, and they decorated their implements with engraved hunting scenes and with animal and human figures after the manner of present-day Eskimos. In England a culture akin to the Magdalenian occurs: it is called the Creswellian.

EXERCISE

Notice the fracture of different substances: coal, for example, when chipped with a hammer breaks irregularly with a jagged fracture. In other substances, such as glass, where an edge is chipped the fracture is shell-shaped (conchoidal).

In you live in a district where flint occurs naturally, note the conchoidal fracture resulting whenever flint is chipped. The result of a blow is predictable in a material like this; it does not split irregularly in all sorts of directions. Upon this predictable property depends the facility with which Early Man produced implements from flint.

Familiarize yourself as far as possible, by any of the following means open to you, with the appearance and form of flint implements: (*a*) from illustrations in books; (*b*) from examples in museums and (*c*) from the actual handling of specimens.

Make drawings for yourself of the way in which flint implements are made—to illustrate such matters as striking platform, point of percussion, cones and bulbs of percussion, bulbar scar, fissures and rings (ripples) produced in flaking. (NOTE: Do not be afraid of attempting drawings, even if you have never made them before; after all, they are for your own guidance. Teach yourself to record what you see.)

Become familiar with frost pitting of flint and its "starch" (columnar) fracture.

LITERATURE

There is a vast literature about flint implements and the men of the Old Stone Age. The general works listed at the end of Chapter Two contain a good deal of information on these topics. You will also find the first volumes in the series "Everyday Life" and "The Story of . . ." in the same list useful. You should see *Man the Tool-maker*, by K. P. Oakley (London: Trustees of the British Museum), and *Flint Implements: an account of Stone Age techniques and cultures*, by William Watson (London: Trustees of the British Museum); also *The Old Stone Age*, by M. C. Burkitt (Cambridge: University Press, 1933).

CHAPTER FIVE

THE SOIL THAT MAN MOVES

THE SOIL-MANTLE OF THE EARTH AS IT APPEARS TO THE
ARCHÆOLOGIST

To make earthworks for defence and burial mounds
to commemorate his dead, Man has moved the soil. He
has been doing this from very early times. If the archæologist is correctly to interpret his examination of Man's
disturbance of natural soil, he needs some at least of the
information that is given in this chapter.

The Soil that Man Moves

IN certain branches of his work the archæologist is very closely
concerned with the soil, and unless he understands how soil is
formed and is familiar with important changes which commonly take place in it subsequently, he is exposed to the
danger of drawing incorrect conclusions from the examination
of the surface layers in some of his excavations.

Almost everywhere the soil forms the natural outer covering
over the rocks of the earth's crust. But the soil is not everywhere the same. Its exact nature depends upon a number of
things, including the kind of rock material from which its
mineral part has been formed. It is better, therefore, when
speaking of "the soil" in this general way, when we mean the
whole outer covering of the land of the world, to call it the *soil-
mantle*. On limestones the soil-mantle may be quite thin
(frequently it is only about five inches below the surface that
we come to the hard rock); on soft sandstones in fairly flat
areas it may be very deep, and the roots of some plants may
go down into it forty feet or more. It is quite obvious that the
soil-mantle in these two places will give the archæologist very
different materials to deal with when he is excavating.

Soil consists of a number of constituents. Apart from
stones, its bulk is generally made up of mineral particles of
many different sizes, the largest plainly visible to the naked
eye, the smallest so minute as to be indistinguishable even
under the most powerful microscope. All these different
sized particles can be classified into three grades: (1) *sand*,
which is gritty and the particles of which are visible to the naked
eye; (2) *silt*, particles smaller than sand and not individually
distinguishable with the naked eye (silt when handled moist,

48   ARCHÆOLOGY

but not wet, is not sticky); and (3) *clay*, a material that is plastic and sticky when moist.

According to the proportions in which sand, silt, and clay occur in a soil it is called a light, medium or heavy soil.

FIG. 18.—Soil Map.

Soil also contains the decomposed and decomposing debris of plants: leaves, stems, stalks and roots, and we must not forget that two other important things, air and water, are present too.

Individual Soils

We may well speak of individual parts of the soil-mantle, one, for example, lying over a limestone and another developed from soft sandstone, as individual soils. Thus we can speak of the many soils of the world as comprising the soil-mantle much as the individual scraps of cloth contribute their substance to a patchwork quilt. Actually many thousands of different soils all over the world make up the soil-mantle, which, while it hides the rocks from view in most places, supports a variety of vegetation.

The Soil-profile

This is not the place to go into a long discussion of all the characteristics of individual soils. I shall be content to say

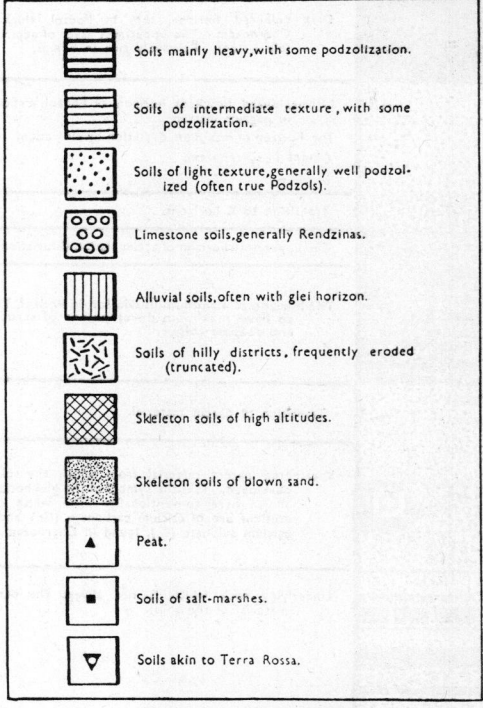

- Soils mainly heavy, with some podzolization.
- Soils of intermediate texture, with some podzolization.
- Soils of light texture, generally well podzolized (often true Podzols).
- Limestone soils, generally Rendzinas.
- Alluvial soils, often with glei horizon.
- Soils of hilly districts, frequently eroded (truncated).
- Skeleton soils of high altitudes.
- Skeleton soils of blown sand.
- Peat.
- Soils of salt-marshes.
- Soils akin to Terra Rossa.

Fig. 18a.—Key to Map.

that every soil has a number of natural properties, of which the following are important for purposes of recognition and characterization: (a) geological history of the mineral part of the soil; (b) topography of the soil. It is characteristic of it, individually, that either it lies on a steep hillside, or forms part of a level expanse or has some intermediate slope between the two extremes; (c) its own peculiarities of *natural* drainage; (d) its chemical characteristics from acid to alkaline; (e) its

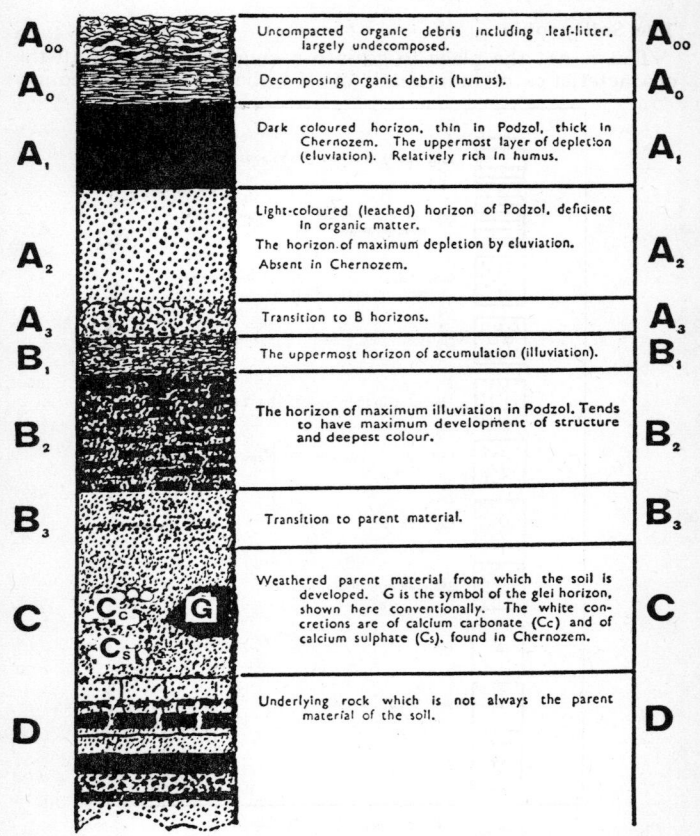

A_{oo}	Uncompacted organic debris including leaf-litter, largely undecomposed.
A_o	Decomposing organic debris (humus).
A_1	Dark coloured horizon, thin in Podzol, thick in Chernozem. The uppermost layer of depletion (eluviation). Relatively rich in humus.
A_2	Light-coloured (leached) horizon of Podzol, deficient in organic matter. The horizon of maximum depletion by eluviation. Absent in Chernozem.
A_3	Transition to B horizons.
B_1	The uppermost horizon of accumulation (illuviation).
B_2	The horizon of maximum illuviation in Podzol. Tends to have maximum development of structure and deepest colour.
B_3	Transition to parent material.
C	Weathered parent material from which the soil is developed. G is the symbol of the glei horizon, shown here conventionally. The white concretions are of calcium carbonate (Cc) and of calcium sulphate (Cs), found in Chernozem.
D	Underlying rock which is not always the parent material of the soil.

Fig. 19.—Diagram of the horizons of a soil. When seen in elevation, as here shown, the section is called a soil-profile, and such a view provides much useful information about a soil, enabling an expert to classify it and to recognize the mode of its formation.

soil-profile. The last-mentioned term is a technical one, and about it something more must now be said.

The soil-profile is the view of a soil which we obtain on the wall of a pit which we specially dig. We see the same thing when excavations are made for roads or buildings. Quite often (but not always) when we look at a soil in this way, we may find such a spectacular differentiation of the soil into layers (or, to be more accurate, horizons) that a child could see them at once. I shall speak of one such case. The succession is as follows : (i) On the surface there is a layer of pine needles mixed with the leaves and small twigs of a variety of trees; this litter is about two inches deep. (ii) Below this forest debris is a thickness of eight inches of well-decayed plant debris (humus) incorporated with loamy sand. Owing to the presence of the humus, the soil is very dark brown, almost black. (iii) The next ten inches is ashy grey loamy sand; this horizon is most spectacular, and looks as though somebody had deposited a layer of grey sand ten inches deep, but this is not so and, as we shall see later, its origin is entirely natural. (iv) Below the ashy grey soil is a horizon of four inches of compact dark chocolate-brown sandy loam succeeded by (v) five inches of sandy loam, mottled rusty-brown and pale brown. This horizon is succeeded by (vi) the rock, which is a pale yellow lightly consolidated sandstone.

To the experienced eye this soil-profile tells an unmistakable story and, since it is typical of the processes which characterize many soils in the British Isles, it will be no waste of time and space if we now consider its implications in a little detail. These implications are important for the archæologist.

(i) The surface layer is formed of the fallen leaves and other plant debris which gradually decay and become incorporated with the mineral matter to form the sort of material which characterizes (ii) the next horizon below. Here the sand grains which were originally, when part of the rock, yellowish brown have been bleached because humus is acid and has a solvent action upon the iron compounds which form the colouring matter and, often, also the cement of the sandstone rock. There is a great deal of decayed organic matter, and it gives this part of the soil a very dark tinge. Rain-water is constantly and, what is very important, *slowly* passing down through these horizons of the soil; the rain-water carries down with it acid and humus. For hundreds of years this process has been going on, and it has evidently removed all the colouring matter originally present in the upper part of the soil (the colouring matter in this case was the brown hydrated ferric oxide generally called Limonite; this is fairly easily removed downwards by acid soil-waters to be redeposited in a lower horizon).

The very ashy grey horizon (iii) has by this washing out (leaching) process lost all its colouring matter, but in the next two horizons, (iv) the chocolate brown and (v) the mottled brown and pale-brown horizons, that colouring matter has been reassembled to give, there, different intensities of colour reinforcing the iron compounds already present in the parent sandstone. Here the sand grains, instead of being bleached, are more thickly coated with limonite and similar materials than those of ordinary sandstone. These are horizons of accumulation.

It may now, I think, be readily appreciated that if we dig trenches into sandy soils in which the process of eluviation (depletion or impoverishment) and illuviation (accumulation or enrichment) has taken place we have to be very careful that we do not mistake the horizons produced by natural processes of soil-formation (pedogenesis) with layers of material deposited by our ancestors when they moved the soil in their constructional work.

Most soils in which a very marked profile has been developed as a result of the downward passage of acid-laden water through the uppermost layers are very ancient, and it has been suggested that their formation has taken thousands of years. The materials in which the most spectacular profiles are to be seen in Great Britain are the light sandstones and pebble-beds through which the water can pass rapidly after every rainstorm unless the land is very low-lying. These sandstones are also materials in which there is no lime to neutralize the effect of the acids which form in the surface layer of the soil from the decay of leaves and other plant debris. Sandstones are widespread in Britain. They are, of course, indicated in geological memoirs and bulletins and on geological maps, and these important publications of the Geological Survey should be consulted by every interested archæologist. It must, however, be emphasized that geological surveys are generally concerned with the rocks below the soil, and this, of course, is not the same thing as the soil itself.

In materials like clay (I mean real clay, not merely heavy soil) the soil-forming processes are naturally hindered, because there is no rapid downward movement of water in the soil and no passage *through* the clay itself at all. There is a soil-profile, but it might be passed unnoticed.

Between clay-rock and sandstone there are many intermediates. In some of these a very obvious soil-profile has been developed, in others it is not so noticeable.

In new sand-dunes, newly deposited river muds and on sea-shores there has not yet been time for soil-profiles to develop, and so little differentiation can be seen. Such materials are called *skeleton-soils*.

I have noticed some horizonation (produced *since* disturbance) in soil that had been moved a few years previously by excavators on a Roman site, and I see no reason to believe that a very great lapse of years is really necessary before horizonation may begin to show itself in skeleton-soils.

All excavators of chalky (and other limy) soils should know something about the special circumstances which have attended the formation of these soils. They are, generally speaking, thin soils, and all are formed from rock which consists very largely of calcium carbonate (chalk is an earthy limestone). Limestone soils in the British Isles nearly always contain enough fragments of rock, right up to the surface, to neutralize the acid produced by decaying vegetation immediately it is formed. There is, consequently, no acid available to bring about changes deeper down in the ground such as we have already seen producing very spectacular *soil-profiles* in sandy

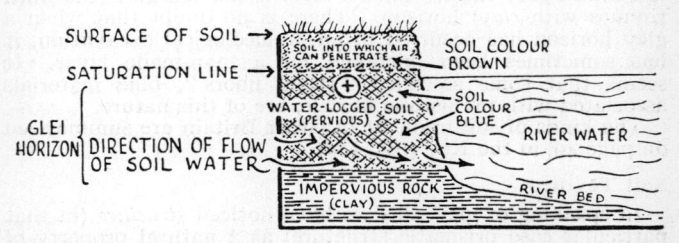

Fig. 20.—Diagram to illustrate the conditions of riverside soils.
Drawn by S. G. B.-B.

situations. The soil-profile over limestone (including chalk) frequently exhibits about five inches of soil containing fragments of the rock. The five inches rest immediately upon the limestone rock itself, which often has its upper layers fissured and fragmentary. Such soils are called *Rendzinas*.

It must, however, be remembered that chalk-rock and other limestones are quite frequently covered by deeper materials which have either been transported from far or near to their present situation by ice, water or wind or else have been derived from the insoluble residuum of the original rock, which generally consists of a reddish clayey deposit (sometimes called *Terra Rossa*). A well-known example of such a material is "Clay-with-Flints" a superficial geological deposit which has a fairly widespread occurrence over the Chalk formation in the part of England never covered by a moving ice-sheet during the Glacial period, that is to say south of a line from Bristol to London.

When soils are water-logged, as usually happens with riverside meadow soils, there is a shallow top horizon (say about eight inches deep) typically dark coloured and rich in organic debris; below this is a lighter-coloured horizon, often several feet deep and frequently showing a prismatic structure (i.e., this horizon then consists of lumps of similar shape which can be pulled out if there has been dry weather; these lumps are about four inches wide, two inches thick and about twelve inches high, but tapering away both at the top and bottom). In this horizon, especially towards its lower part, small black concretions, mainly of hydrated ferric oxide, occur, typically in sizes ranging from that of a wheat grain to that of a hazel-nut. Below the prismatic horizon is the permanently water-logged part of the soil. It contains a good deal of plant debris, and since air cannot penetrate from above, it is generally oxygen-hungry and contains blue iron compounds which give it a bluish-grey tinge. Such a layer is called a gley (the word rhymes with *clay*) horizon. There is no doubt that when a gley horizon has occurred in an archæological excavation, it has sometimes been mistaken for a man-made layer. It seems that some so-called " ritual floors ", blue materials associated with prehistoric burials, are of this nature.

The kinds of soil frequent in Great Britain are summarized on page 49, in the Key (Fig. 18a).

Soil Texture

In speaking of gley soils we have noticed *structure* (in that particular case prismatic structure) as a natural property of soils. Plates, prisms and crumbs in soils are structural units. But there is another characteristic of all soils which is of special interest to archæologists, the property known to soil scientists as *soil-texture*. It is a property which if carefully described by excavators in their reports would make these much more accurate, and would provide an item often valuable when comparing one report with another. Unfortunately texture is little understood by archæologists. The materials in excavations are frequently described as *clay*, for example, when they are nothing of the sort.

The texture of any soil is described by the farmer when he speaks of it as being heavy or light. By heavy he means difficult to work; a heavy soil needs more horse-power to plough it properly than a light soil. Incidentally, it is also true, as a rule, that light soils dry out more quickly after rain than heavy ones. Now a heavy soil turns out to be richer in clay than a lighter one, and that gives us a clue at once to what is meant by texture. As has already been briefly indicated soil-scientists (pedologists) recognize three grades of mineral matter in the soil-mantle. First, there is *sand*; this is gritty to the touch, and you can see the individual sand particles with the naked eye. *Silt* is the second grade, and its particles are finer than those of sand and cannot be seen individually without magnification with a lens. However, silt particles impart no plastic or sticky property to the soil when it is handled moist, the particles do not stick together, and when we handle silt or a soil rich in silt we find no grittiness (which is found with sand), but instead a textile-like quality which, for want of a better term, may be called smooth or silky. *Clay*, the third and last grade, is sticky when moist but not wet.

A soil in which there is such a good balance between sand, silt

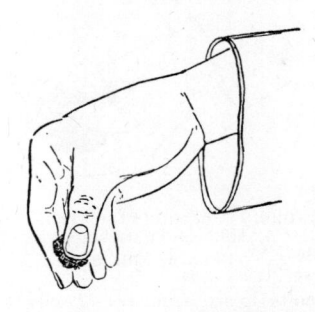

FIG. 21.—Soil texture. Testing soil for polish with thumb and two fingers.

Drawn by H. K. B.-B.

and clay that it is not gritty or silky or sticky when moist (not wet) is a *loam*. A soil heavier than a loam will be either silky or sticky to handle when moist. The heaviest textured soils of all (technically silty clay loam, clay loam, clay) will all take a polish *in the hand* when moist if pressed between finger and thumb. Those not quite so heavy but heavier than loam are silty loam and silt loam. Such soils will be silky to the touch when moist, but cannot be polished between finger and thumb.

Soils lighter than loams are all gritty to the touch; they are: (i) sandy loams, which, in the moist condition, will form a stable, cohesive ball; (ii) loamy sands, which will not form a stable cohesive ball, but will soil the fingers, and (iii) sands, which, when moist, will neither form a stable ball nor soil the fingers.

LITERATURE

For references to books on this topic. see note on Literature at the end of the next chapter.

EXERCISE

Look at the soil in your own garden. Note the colour of the surface soil. If you are not familiar with its lower horizons take the first opportunity to see its deeper parts. How does it fit the descriptions already given in this chapter? Is the colour lighter as you dig down?

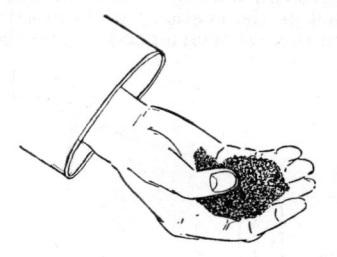

FIG. 22.—Soil texture. A handful of soil being tested for grittiness, silkiness or stickiness.

Drawn by K. H. B.-B.

Take an opportunity to see a number of soils in section (soil-profile) and note the horizons. Make drawings of what you see.

Handle several soils in a moist (but not wet) condition. Take up a handful of the first. Can you recognize, by touch, sand? or silt? or clay? If it is a gritty (i.e., sandy) soil, look at the individual particles of sand. Write a little report something like this: "SOIL A: *Test for Texture.* Moist soil handled. Did not feel gritty (therefore not a sandy soil) nor silky (therefore silt was not dominant), nor sticky (therefore not a clayey soil). Constituents therefore fairly well balanced; therefore a LOAM."

CHAPTER SIX

MAN, SOIL, ROCK AND THE EARTH

GEOLOGICAL MATTERS OF INTEREST TO THE ARCHÆOLOGIST

The geological matters that concern the archæologist dealt with in this chapter follow naturally upon what was written in Chapter Five.

Early Cultivations

As soon as soil on a slope is stirred it begins to move downhill under the force of gravity. This happens even when the slope is very slight. It should be remembered too, in this connection, that however slight the annual downward movement is, in the course of a century it will be multiplied a hundredfold and also that in dealing with this subject we are thinking of trends which have been operative for thousands of years.

Thus it was true that if a man cultivated *the same plot* on a slight slope, year after year, a considerable depth of the soil from the upper border of his plot was removed from the surface, so that the soil became shallower in that part, while there was an accumulation of soil along the lower boundary of the plot. If this process was continued for many years by the same man or by a succession of occupiers and if a similar process was going on all down the slope because the local community as a whole was at work cultivating the soil, eventually the whole group of cultivators produced what we may see today, a series of step-like strips on the hillside or any lesser slope. These strips are often called linches or lynchets, and it may even be that a parish has derived its name from their occurrence in the place. This is a possibility with Linch in Sussex and Sellindge in Kent.

The accumulation of soil at the bottom of the strip is sometimes called the positive lynchet, and the denuded line at the top the negative lynchet.

There is a great interest for the archæologist in these strip cultivations on slopes, because they may tell him a good deal about the farming activities of Early Man. The surface soil of land that is cultivated today, or has been cultivated in the past, contains small pieces of broken pottery left there because vessels containing food were sometimes taken out into the fields to the farm-workers and got broken. Sometimes too, no doubt fragments of crockery were carried out with manure to be spread on the fields. Pieces of farm implements and personal property, like pipes and coins, may also be left in the surface soil; iron will rust away in time, but implements of flint and coins remain practically for ever. From the nature of the pottery found on a lynchet we may infer something about the date of the cultivation; and the repeated association of fragments of a certain age with one kind of lynchet is good evidence that that type of cultivation was usual in the period in question. The nature of flint implements found may help in dating the site. Like so many things in archæology, the accumulation of many scraps of information, picked up over many years of study by many observers in different parts of the country, contribute to the full picture.

At first, and we know that cultivations go back to Neolithic times, Man no doubt did little more with his implements than scratch the surface soil before sowing his seed. It is presumed that these early implements were mainly made of perishable materials, especially wood. Later on, something like the *caschrom* or foot-plough still used in Skye was employed by Early Man, and only after a very long period of time did anything we can call a *plough* in the modern sense come into use. It would appear that when it was in common use in the Early Iron Age the plough was drawn under such conditions of soil-depth, implement-type and size of plough-team that the oxen doing the work required a "blow" (i.e., time to recover breath) after ploughing a length of about ninety yards. The width of the strip was determined by the amount it was possible to plough in one day: when the ninety-yard furrow was used the width was about seventy yards, so that a day's work under such conditions would produce almost a square plot. Plots representative of a *day's work* are convenient units, and they may actually be picked out by their outlines on ancient farm sites. Our *acre* has this long history behind it, but it dates from the first century before Christ, when the Belgæ brought their better ploughs to south-east Britain. The plough team was strong enough to make a furrow 220 yards long or thereabouts (and 220 yards is still our furlong = furrowlong); the width of a day's work of that length was approximately 22 yards so that a day's work was a plot ten times as long as wide containing approximately 4,840 square yards, which is the measurement of our acre. Further enquiry into this subject will help to paint a more complete picture, but it is already clear that in the earliest days of cultivation, in the Neolithic and Bronze Ages, the type of implement used, no doubt a hand-tool or "digging stick", imposed no special field-shape upon the man at work. Probably the plots were often abandoned after no more than a few crops had been taken off;

this is a primitive way of maintaining the fertility of the soil without manuring.

The earliest Iron Age cultivations appear to have been the squarish ones to which reference has already been made. Last of all came the long (10 × 1) strips. These were certainly in use after the English invasion of A.D. 449, but it was only in small areas where the invading Belgæ settled about 75 B.C. that the heavier, more efficient plough they introduced could make this kind of long strip before the Roman conquest. How widespread in this country the long strip was in the Romano-British period is not yet known. I often think there was less of a break in agricultural practice and systems of land-tenure between Romano-British and English times than has generally been supposed and, of course, the old idea that our English ancestors, on arriving in Britain, drove the wild Celtic inhabitants to the far west, where they became the modern Cornishmen, Welsh and Cumbrians is a figment of the imagination of our ancestors. In fact, the invaders were probably too few in numbers to do much driving out. They were strong enough to impose their wills upon the conquered Britons and to change many of the outward forms of government and to introduce their language, but some of the deep-rooted institutions were probably unchanged, particularly those governing the life of the countryside, where work on the land must, of necessity, have been largely done, if not completely organized, by the subjugated race.

Stratification

Archæologists and geologists are on common ground when discussing stratification. The principles are the same whether we are considering a geological stratification dating back a hundred million years or one that interests the archæologist because it began just before the Roman conquest of Britain in the first century of our era.

An easy simile is provided by a pile of old newspapers. I take a morning newspaper and wish to keep it for future reference. If on the evening of 1st January I begin a pile by laying down the paper for that day, and on each subsequent weekday add to the pile the issue for that day, it will be clear that the oldest journal will be at the bottom of the pile and the latest at the top. This is the principle of stratification in a nutshell. When applied to the sedimentary rocks of the earth's crust it means that the uppermost layers or *strata* (singular, *stratum*) are the newest. Older materials are lower down in the sequence; the oldest are at the bottom.

In the debris of an ancient town the lowest layer that provides us with evidence of human occupation may contain fragments of coarse ware recognized at once by the experts as evidence of the activities of Man in the Early Iron Age. The layers above this yield a Roman coin and a piece of "Samian" ware (see page 113). Next above this, the strata contain fragments of Anglo-Saxon glassware. Higher still, there is a layer that yields fragments of fifteenth-century pottery and a coin. The top layer close to the surface provides ample evidence of its late date, including a penny of Queen Victoria's reign and a piece of a willow-pattern plate.

Just occasionally owing to great earth movement, such as folded up the crust of the earth to form the Alps, the original order of the geological beds is found reversed. A similar complication for the archæologist occurs when he is investigating an early site that has been disturbed by later operations, as, for example, when a mediæval rubbish-pit has been dug down through an occupation level of Roman date. The disturbance of the original lines of stratification and differences of colour and texture help the observer to unravel the evidence of relationship between the two deposits, each of which is separately dated by the relics it contains.

Rocks and Soil

The study of the past brings us at a number of points to the consideration of rocks and soil. Many of the relics of the past are found in the soil. This is true whether those relics be the bones of men and animals or the pottery, ornaments, coins, weapons, tools and other possessions our ancestors lost, hid, rejected or buried with their dead. Moreover, soil is the stuff in which plants grow.

The word "rock" is used here in the geological sense: a rock is any mineral material that forms part of the crust of the earth. So that not only are granite, limestone, slate and marble rocks, but so are clay and the softest of soft sandstones. Rocks come within the purview of the archæologist wherever they have been used by Man for building dwellings, places of worship, fortresses, bridges and tombs, whenever they have been used for making bricks or stone implements or when their ores have been won from the earth to provide metal for tools, weapons and ornaments.

The soil often falls within the archæologist's province, because again and again it has been moved to provide defensive ramparts and ditches or to make a variety of burial mounds, and those great heaps of earth designed to be fortified, the mottes, as they are called, of castles. Again, the soil has been dug out to form graves, storage pits, wells, places of refuge, trenches, mines and quarries. It is the raw material of the farmer's craft which, from prehistoric times, he has used for growing crops. It follows that in many parts of the country the long history of the use of the soil for the production of food

MAN, SOIL, ROCK AND THE EARTH   61

can be illustrated by studying the banks (linches, lynchets) and other irregularities of the ground which may indicate the outlines of corn plots dating back to Neolithic, Bronze Age or Early Iron Age times (see page 57).

GEOLOGICAL PERIODS OF THE LAST MILLION YEARS (OR SO)

	HOLOCENE = Recent (post-Glacial period)	
		22 000 years ago
	Other Glacial and Interglacial periods	
		480,000 years ago
	Cromer Forest Bed	
	Antepenultimate Interglacial	
	Chillesford Beds	
PLEISTOCENE		540,000 years ago
	Weybourn Crag	
	Norwich Crag	Corresponding to Early Glaciation (= Gunz)
	Butley Crag	
	Newbourn Crag	
	Walton Crag	
		790,000 years ago
PLIOCENE	Coralline Crag	
		1,000,000 years ago

The dates are, of course, very rough and tentative.
See also Table of Glacial and Interglacial periods, page 64.

" Recently " is One Million Years Ago

Modern computations of the age of the earth indicate that it is at least 2,000 million years old and probably a great deal older. About 500 million years ago the rocks of the Cambrian period (so called because they were first studied in Wales, although they are widely distributed throughout the world) began to be laid down as marine deposits. These were such materials as pebbles, sands and muds which became consolidated to form, respectively, conglomerates, flaggy sandstones and shales. The shales, which we can find in quarries today, contain the fossil remains of highly organized animal life (Brachiopoda and Trilobita), and this, of course, presupposes a very long evolution of living creatures in the days before the Cambrian period began (that is to say in what is known as the Pre-Cambrian period) and indicates a very much earlier date for the origin of life upon the earth. The reason that fossils showing the evolution of Brachiopoda and Trilobita from much simpler forms of life are not known from the Pre-Cambrian rocks is that this early record has been destroyed by the great disruptive forces which were frequently at work on the rocks of Pre-Cambrian age before Cambrian sediments were converted into hard rock.

We pass over 1,999 million years from the first 2,000 million years conservatively estimated as the age of the earth, and so come down to a time just one million years ago. About that date a marine deposit found in East Anglia had long been in process of formation. This material is called the Coralline Crag. At the time, in the latitude of Britain, the mean annual temperature was decidedly higher than it is now. Subsequently, increasingly colder conditions prevailed, and eventually the northern ice-cap became so extensive that at its greatest development it covered this country as far south as a line we might draw roughly from Bristol to London. Before the ice finally disappeared from the surface of our islands at the end of the Glacial Period it alternately advanced and receded, so that four glaciations are now generally recognized. The period of cold conditions prevailing in northern Europe from the end of Coralline Crag times until the ice sheet finally receded fell within the geological epoch called the Pleistocene, if we use this term to include the Red Crag (Walton Crag, Newbourn Crag, Butley Crag), Norwich Crag, Weybourn Crag, Chillesford Beds and Cromer Forest Bed, as well as both glacial and interglacial deposits with all contemporaneous materials. In the interglacial times the land surface was, of course, free for the activities of hunters and fishermen.

In the absence of vegetation immediately after glaciation, finely ground mineral particles left behind by the ice were very readily carried by wind, and this dust, coming to rest in the sheltered, less elevated areas of the land surface, filled in the hollows, such as river valleys, to a greater or lesser extent. This deposit is called loess, and it is found right across the Eurasian continent from China to the British Isles. Subsequently this wind-borne material was sometimes re-sorted by rivers and mixed with other sediments carried by the water.

The Work of Rivers

As soon as the ice had melted, rivers again became important in modifying the land-surface, and in areas never covered by ice their work had gone on, of course, throughout the glacial period.

As long as there is sufficient fall towards the sea, a river will scour its floor and deepen its bed, working deeper and deeper down into the rocks over which it flows, but as time goes on this work is reduced, because the fall of the land towards the ocean gets less and less. At long last there comes a time when the power of the water is insufficient to cut any deeper at all. The river is then said to have reached its base level of erosion.

Thereafter the erosive action of the river is entirely limited to the other kind of erosion it had always been carrying out, namely, the cutting away of its banks and the sides of the valley. If this kind of action continues long enough a wide plain is produced, and gravel, sand and mud deposited by the river cover very wide stretches of country. There is a common but erroneous belief that where a wide, flat valley floor exists, it means that that was at one time the width of the river. The fact is that an extensive valley floor is produced by the ever-changing course of the stream. The river swings from side to side of the valley, and is said to meander. The water is continually eating away one bank and depositing gravel, sand and mud on the opposite side. Where the water is running swiftly it removes material, where the current is slowed down by the curves it drops its load of mineral matter.

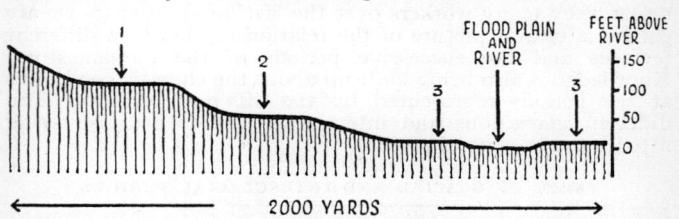

FIG. 23.—Diagram of river, flood-plain, and three river-terraces. The uppermost river-terrace is the oldest, and so is numbered one.
Drawn by S. G. B.-B.

In the course of this action the stream constantly changes its bed, and over the centuries removes and redeposits all the materials of the valley floor. The course of the stream itself moves down the valley, so that although at any given moment the river is comparatively narrow, in the elapse of centuries it has by its plough-like action worked upon the whole valley floor, bit by bit.

But sea and land do not remain indefinitely at the same levels. The sea may rise or fall, so may the land. If there is a relative uplift of the land, either by the fall of sea-level or by actual elevation of the land, the power of the river will be restored, and it will again begin to eat away the rocks of its bed. When the power of a river is restored in this way rejuvenation is said to take place. The former plain (base level of erosion), now elevated above the river, becomes a river terrace. On the other hand relative depression of the land surface tends to the deposition of materials carried in suspension by the river; this process, the reverse of rejuvenation, is called aggradation.

C

When river deposits are made under cold conditions, evidence of frost action is provided by characteristic frost-fracture of stones in the valley gravel.

In cases of extremely cold winters there was accumulation of ice and snow on the higher ground, and then each spring the melting of the frozen materials brought streams of mud and stones down the valley slopes, and the debris was deposited on the lower ground. The downflow of the loose surface materials, soil and subsoil alike, as a semi-liquid mass is called solifluction.

With all these features and deposits, the archæologist investigating human activities in river valleys must make himself as familiar as possible.

There is considerable interest for the archæologist in the study of river terraces, because Early Man's implements are found in the gravels of river valleys. As the result of much research by many workers over the last hundred years we are getting a clearer picture of the relationship between different terraces and the successive periods of the human story. Knowledge is also being built up about the climatic conditions at the periods represented by the different terraces. The different glaciations and interglacial periods are also being fitted into the general picture.

TABLE OF GLACIAL AND INTERGLACIAL PERIODS

Duration of period in thousands of years	
22	Post-glacial period = HOLOCENE
	———————————— 22,000 years ago
90	Last glaciation (= Würm) *Homo neanderthalensis* at Spy
	———————————— 115,000 years ago
60	Last interglacial period Man at Fontéchevade
	———————————— 175,000 years ago
65	Penultimate glaciation (= Riss)
	———————————— 240,000 years ago
190	Penultimate interglacial period (= Great Interglacial period) Swanscombe Man (*Homo sapiens*)
	———————————— 430,000 years ago
50	Antepenultimate glaciation (= Mindel)
	———————————— 480,000 years ago
60	Antepenultimate interglacial period Jaw at Mauer
	———————————— 540,000 years ago
250	Early glaciation (= Günz) Java Man; Man at Choukoutien
	———————————— 790,000 years ago

The Different Glaciations

On four occasions during the last 800,000 years the climate in the northern hemisphere has become so cold that for tens of thousands of years at a time the north polar ice-cap has occupied the land masses and seas of our part of Europe to produce a glacial period. At its maximum extent the moving ice sheet came as far south as London.

The last glaciation (called the Würm glaciation) lasted some 90,000 years, ending about 22,000 years ago. Before that the last interglacial period, still a cold time, lasted about 60,000 years. A glacial period (called the Riss glaciation) of some 65,000 years preceded this, and before that the penultimate, warm, interglacial period occupied about 190,000 years. Before that the Mindel glaciation of approximately 50,000 years succeeded the antepenultimate interglacial, probably cold, period of about 60,000 years. This, in turn, succeeded the Günz glaciation of perhaps 250,000 years.

Each glaciation withdrew water from the ocean to form ice and snow. These were piled up on the land and over the ice-sheet. Outside the areas of glaciation the river floors were therefore *relatively* elevated above the sea-level, and by rejuvenation were able to cut deeper into the rocks to form new base levels of erosion. During interglacial periods the water was restored to the sea, and the land level fell in relation to the ocean, so that aggradation took place.

But apart from rise and fall due to climate, there has been a progressive fall in the level of the ocean due to some unknown cause, probably a deepening of the ocean bed.

These changes and others of a minor nature are reflected by the base levels of erosion and by raised beaches to be found in river valleys and around coasts respectively.

Problems of absorbing interest and no little difficulty confront any archæologist who undertakes the study of this branch of the subject. Dating cannot yet be accurate and revision must constantly be in progress as research proceeds.

EXERCISE

Cultivations. Note the shapes of fields in your area. Squarish fields may indicate Celtic influence and small plough teams. (In Ireland, modern (nineteenth-century) redistribution of land has sometimes modified the layout.) The "Saxon" shape is 10 × 1. Can you identify this? How many fields have a furlong (220 yards) as one dimension? (This can conveniently be determined from a map.) Can you identify ancient fields in open country in your region? Draw sketch maps.

Stratification. Devise an exercise for yourself on this point. You can do it with a pile of books; arrange them in order of publication the earliest at the bottom.

Look at road excavations, note the stratification and evidence, if any, of earlier disturbances of the soil. In an ancient city you may recognize the stratification as follows (from below, upwards): undisturbed geological material, pre-Roman, Roman, Saxon (English), Mediæval, Modern. How far is this true of your own town? Make sketches of what you see.

Geological Materials and Processes. These you can study in quarries and natural exposures. In glaciated districts take note of the results of ice action. Also use museum collections. Make drawings.

The Work of Rivers. Observe for yourself the work of a local river, taking into account the points mentioned in this chapter. Can you recognize, locally, river terraces? Make your own diagrams.

LITERATURE

Geology is a subject with a vast literature. A general knowledge of this branch of science is very useful in many ways to the archæologist. A general view is taken in *Teach Yourself Geology*, by A. Raistrick (London: English Universities Press, first published in 1943). As far as the soil is concerned, the subject is covered in *Good Soil*, by S. Graham Brade-Birks (London: English Universities Press, first published in 1944). The relationships between archæology and geology and soil science (pedology) are mainly dealt with in isolated papers.

CHAPTER SEVEN

BETTER TOOLS

MAN AS IMPLEMENT-MAKER IN THE MESOLITHIC AND NEOLITHIC AGES

Man's skill increased with the centuries. An indication of some of the progress that marked the Mesolithic and Neolithic periods is given in this Chapter. Metal had not as yet been used in the making of tools.

The Mesolithic Age

THE Mesolithic period in Britain extended approximately from 12,000 B.C. to 2300 B.C. It began immediately after the last glaciation and before the age of polished tools. It is characterized especially by the occurrence of very small flint implements (sometimes called "pigmy flints") or *microliths*. Remarkable paintings in caves and on open-air rock faces in south-east Spain showing men hunting with bows and arrows belong to the Mesolithic period. To the same era belong the shell mounds or "kitchen middens" of Denmark. The men of Mesolithic times were evidently hunters, fowlers and fishermen, but in Palestine bone sickle-shafts fitted with flint teeth have been found on a Mesolithic site which goes back to about 6000 B.C. These teeth have an added layer of silica, showing that they were used for reaping cereals and took up from the stems of those plants the mineral matter which gives stiffness to the stalks of corn and other grasses.

FIG. 24.—Microlith of geometric type from Lakenheath, Suffolk. Scale ⅔.

From *Flint Implements*, by William Watson.

During this period several cultures are recognized, especially the following :

Azilian (named from Le Mas d'Azil (Ariège) in southern France). This has a characteristic type of harpoon which has been found in Yorkshire and in Scotland. Microliths of typical shape have been found in England.

Tardenoisian (from Tardenois (Aisne), North France). To this belong many microliths. A burin or graver of characteristic form is typical. These tools frequently occur on what were sandy, elevated sites. They have been found near Huddersfield and in Lincolnshire and in the south of England. Belonging to the Tardenoisian culture in England is a type of implement, called the

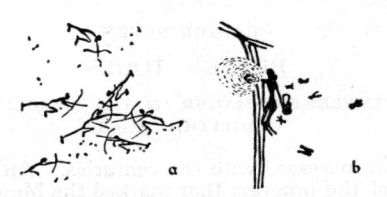

FIG. 25.—Stone Age rock paintings in eastern Spain.

a, Fighting with bows and arrows; red ochre, in rock shelter at Castellón. Scale $\frac{1}{16}$.

After Hernández-Pacheco.

b, Collecting honey on cliff with aid of grass-ropes or lianas; red ochre in cave, N.W. of Bicorp (Valencia). Scale $\frac{1}{4}$.

After Obermaier.

From *Man the Toolmaker*, by Kenneth P. Oakley.

Thames Pick, sometimes dredged from that river. It is a long bar of flint nearly triangular in section with a chisel-edged, rounded working end produced by blows delivered

FIG. 26. 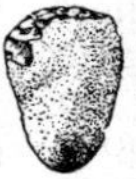   FIG. 27.    FIG. 28. 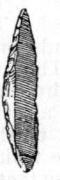   FIG. 29.    FIG. 30.

FIGS. 26–30. FIG. 26.—End-scraper of the Mesolithic Forest culture, from Lower Halstow, Kent. Scale slightly under $\frac{1}{2}$. FIG. 27.—Mesolithic end-scraper, from Kelling Heath, Norfolk. Scale slightly under $\frac{1}{2}$. FIG. 28.—Microlith of geometric type, from Lakenheath, Suffolk. Scale $\frac{2}{3}$. FIG. 29.—Microlith of geometric type, from Warcote Hill, Yorkshire. Scale $\frac{2}{3}$. FIG. 30.—Microlith of Geometric Type, from Lakenheath, Suffolk. Scale $\frac{2}{3}$.

From *Flint Implements*, by William Watson.

from the sides of the implement and not along its length. In Denmark, with similar tools is found the so-called Shell-mound Axe (*grand tranchet*). It has its cutting edge produced by a single blow, delivered from the side of the implement, called the *tranchet* blow.

BETTER TOOLS

Maglemosian (called after Maglemose—i.e., The Great Bog—Zealand, Denmark). This culture was well developed in the Baltic area, and is represented in England by microliths and by harpoons found in Yorkshire and Hertfordshire, in the North Sea off the Norfolk coast and in the Thames at London.

The Neolithic Age

The Neolithic period, the age of polished implements, may be dated tentatively in England as occupying the period from around 2300 B.C. to about 1900 B.C. The probable time of the final separation of this country from the Continent by the submergence of the land which formerly united them was about 6500 B.C. This relative depression of the land and encroachment of the sea thus began in Mesolithic times, and it went on right through the Neolithic period.

If we regard the Palæolithic period as having extended from about 540,000 B.C. to 12,000 B.C. and the Mesolithic period from 12,000 B.C. to 2300 B.C. we get the lengths of the Palæolithic, Mesolithic and Neolithic periods as covering 528,000, 9,700 and 400 years respectively.

In point of fact, it is difficult to decide what we really mean by the Neolithic period, because so many implements which are highly finished stone tools and weapons survived into the Bronze Age or did not come into use until bronze had been introduced into Britain; this is particularly noticeable with flint arrow-heads, which imitate, in shape, the bronze article which, at the time, would be rarer and more precious.

Fig. 31.—Neolithic axe, of flint, unpolished, from Great Bealing, Suffolk. Scale ⅕.

From *Flint Implements*, by William Watson.

The implements called Neolithic, in the wide sense, include polished stone axes, some of them perforated, leaf-shaped arrow-heads, polished flint knives, flint daggers and flint sickles. In addition to flint, hard stones in wide variety were used in the manufacture of the implements.

No earlier period provides anything so elaborate as characteristic Neolithic implements. The highly finished ground and polished tool or weapon is extremely easily recognized. One well-known type of implement is called a *celt* (from a supposed Low Latin word *celtis*, " an axe "). This has nothing to do with the Keltic or Celtic race. The celt is an axe-head with a cutting edge at the broader end, the narrower end having been thrust into a split stick used as a haft.

Some of the finest flint implements of the period have been

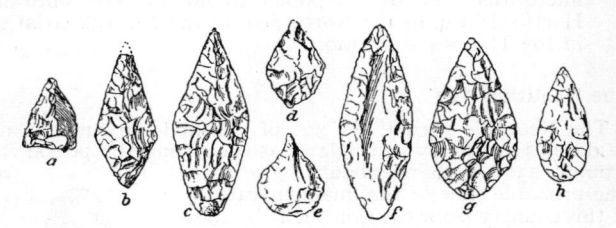

FIG. 32.—Varieties of Neolithic arrow-heads. Scale ¼.

Stonehenge
as it probably was. Plan & Bird's eye View.

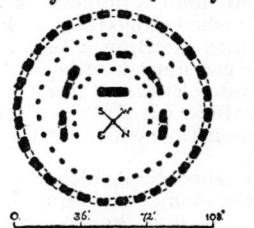

FIG. 33.—Stonehenge.

From *Stonehenge Today and Yesterday*, by Frank Stevens.
(London: H.M. Stationery Office, rev. ed., 1924).

found in Denmark: this part of Europe was geographically suited for long-undisturbed occupation, and therefore excellently adapted for the full development of any industry.

In addition to the highly polished implements of Neolithic

BETTER TOOLS

times, the folk of this period produced beautifully shaped, finely flaked tools. Once again, then, typology is important, for the shapes of such implements are characteristic. The best way to become familiar with them is to see a good series in one of the museums. They are in marked contrast with the heavy, bulky hand-axes of Palæolithic times (e.g. Fig. 13, p. 43).

The Neolithic period provides us with surprising art in the portrait busts, built in plaster upon human skulls, found at Jericho in Israel in 1953. These perhaps date back to 5000 B.C., long before the Neolithic period began in this country.

The Neolithic period included the time when Man began to build the great stone monuments, the best known of which is Stonehenge; but the latest of them (and this actually includes Stonehenge) belong to the transition in time between the Neolithic period and the Bronze Age. To this transitional time the names of the Chalcolithic period and the Æneolithic period have been given. The first syllables of these words mean " copper " from the Greek χαλκός, *chalcos*, and " brassy " from the Latin *æneus*. The second syllable is, of course, our old friend λίθος, " stone ".

The Great Stone Monuments

The Megalithic (large stone) structures are of three kinds—Menhir, Dolmen and Cromlech.

The Menhir, a single upright stone, may have been a memorial of an event or in honour of a hero. The word, in Celtic, means " tall stone ".

The Dolmen (meaning " table stone ") is a stone chamber consisting of several, generally three or four, stones set up on edge and covered by a horizontal slab or cap stone. This structure is probably all that is left of an elongate grave mound called a " long barrow ", the form of which has often been preserved in Britain. Typically it is found to consist of a burial chamber covered by a long earth mound (it may be more than 100 yards long, but smaller examples may be as short as 30 yards). Sometimes there is no stone chamber, sometimes there is one of wood, sometimes the chamber opens from a passage. Frequently there are many burials in one barrow.

The Cromlech (" stone circle ") is a ring of standing stones, generally surrounding a menhir or dolmen. The best-known example in Britain is Stonehenge in Wiltshire, erected about 1700 B.C. This is a late example, now in ruins. The monoliths have been trimmed with stone tools but at a time when bronze was just coming into use. The monument, which was built within an earthwork 300 feet in diameter, is made of three kinds of stones : (i) local Tertiary sandstone of a sort which, in southern England, occurs widely as massive slabs called grey wethers or sarsen stones (i.e. Saracen, meaning foreign stones). This material occurs naturally over the Chalk. (ii) One large slab of micaceous sandstone (i.e., a sandstone in which mica, a flaky light-reflecting mineral, is a prominent constituent). This came from the neighbourhood of Milford Haven, Pembrokeshire. (iii) Sixteen stones (originally more than thirty), monoliths of hewn igneous rock (diabase and

The Lithology of Stonehenge.

■ = Syenite and other foreign stone.
▨ = Sarsen—local Wiltshire stone.
□ = Fine grained micaceous sandstone.

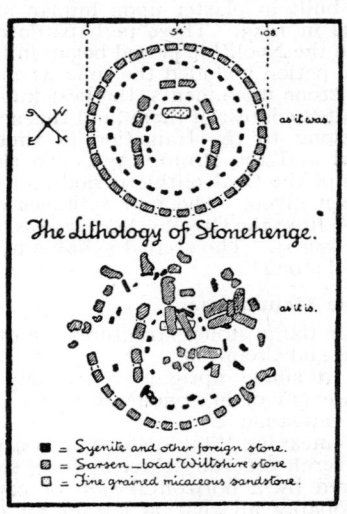

FIG. 34.—Stonehenge.
From *Stonehenge Today and Yesterday*, by Frank Stevens.
(London: H.M. Stationery Office, rev. ed., 1924).

rhyolite) which have been identified by mineralogical peculiarities as having come from the Preselau Hills of Pembrokeshire. In the Preselau area there are eight cromlechs of the same rocks, and it is presumed that a cromlech formerly standing in that area was carried by migrating people in Neolithic times and re-erected in Wiltshire, the slab of micaceous sandstone being brought at the same time.

The whole elaborate system of upright stones, including the local incorporated materials, was built in one period of continuous work.

Many fantastic ideas have been current from time to time about the origin and purpose of Stonehenge. Although the great stones were erected in connection with ancient religious rites, there is no evidence that they have anything to do with human sacrifices or with Druids. Druids were Celtic priests known in Gaul (ancient France) in the first century before

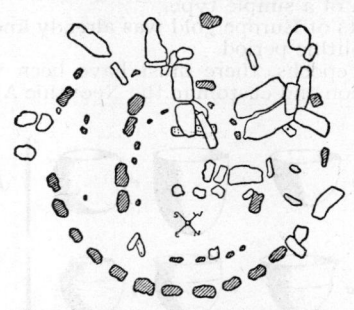

Upright stones shaded — Prostrate stones in outline.

FIG. 35.—Stonehenge.

From *Stonehenge Today and Yesterday*, by Frank Stevens
(London : H.M. Stationery Office, rev. ed., 1924).

Christ, and they were active and powerful in Anglesey in the first Christian century.

The alignment of stones at Stonehenge points to some relationship between the sun and the monument, perhaps as an indication of the seasons.

There are more than 200 sepulchral mounds or barrows near this cromlech.

The Possessions and Activities of Neolithic Man

From Neolithic times pottery survives. It is moulded by hand, no wheel being used. Shape and design give the appearance of an imitation of skin or leathern vessels. This bag-like earthenware includes the so-called Windmill Hill ware (named from a Wiltshire locality); it has a dark surface and is provided with slight decoration in the form of incised lines, grooves, flutings and punctures. Another English site for Neolithic pottery is at Fengate, Peterborough, hence the name Peterborough ware for pottery with more elaborate ornamentation, consisting of considerable decoration with pitting and cord and comb impressions. Rough clay spoons, like some from Neolithic graves in France, have been found in Sussex.

The flint sickle-blade and the saddle quern proclaim Neolithic man as an arable farmer (that is a cultivator of earable land, land that could be *eared*, an old word for ploughed (see

Genesis 45.⁶)). From the fact that his corn plots in Britain were small and irregular—when we are able to trace them out, today, by their surviving outlines—we may infer that he had no plough in the ordinary sense, but he may have employed a digging plough of a simple type.

In some parts of Europe gold was already known before the end of the Neolithic period.

As in other epochs, there must have been wide ranges of belief, occupation and custom in the Neolithic Age over Europe

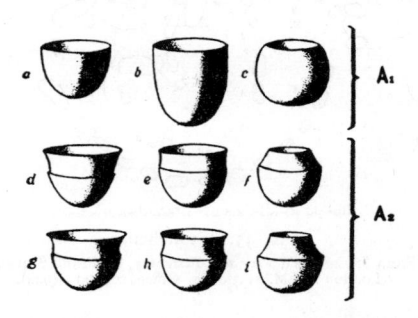

FIG. 36.—Diagram of the main types of Windmill Hill or Neolithic A pottery. A1 is the earliest simple bowl form; A2 is the developed group with neck and shoulder added to the bowl.

and Asia as a whole. The skill exhibited by Neolithic Man when he first appeared in this country must already have had a long history further east. The period began much earlier in the Danubian basin and the Middle East, so we must not generalize too much upon our knowledge of Neolithic people in Britain. Thus, true though it may be for our own area, we are perhaps making rather a sweeping statement when we say that Neolithic man was a farmer who kept cows, sheep, pigs and goats or that he fortified irregular areas on hilltops by a system of concentric, low ramparts protected externally by flat-bottomed ditches crossed by causeways or again, and specially, that he made flint-mines in the chalk.

It is recognized that some Neolithic flint-mines about 12 feet deep are simple pits and seem to have been dug with limb-bones of cattle and rough flint tools, not the finished kind of implements which we often picture Neolithic Man using.

Other pits, three times the depth, lead to underground workings and contain lamps made by hollowing out lumps of chalk, antler picks, flint tools and Neolithic pottery.

EXERCISE

Visit and examine any collections of Mesolithic and Neolithic implements available. Make drawings.

At the same time examine Neolithic pottery and any other relics of the New Stone Age available.

When opportunity arises visit Megalithic monuments, not only the well-known examples like Stonehenge, but any less-famous menhirs. dolmens and cromlechs within reach of your home or your holiday resort.

Long barrows, flint-mines and irregular cultivation areas of Neolithic Age should be examined as opportunity offers.

Trace, by means of maps, known sites of Mesolithic and Neolithic Age. Note possible lines of communication for trade. What conditions, in relation to water, woodland and defence, are likely to have prevailed in those ancient days? What arable land would be available in Neolithic times?

LITERATURE

A work of great general interest which will tell you about the way Early Man went about his work is *Prehistoric Europe*, by J. G. D. Clark (London: Methuen). This period is covered by some of the literature mentioned at the end of Chapter Two. For Stonehenge you will find a first-class account given in *Stonehenge Today and Yesterday*, by F. Stevens London: H.M.S.O. revised 1924).

CHAPTER EIGHT

LEARNING TO USE METAL

BRONZE FIRST USED FOR TOOLS

The story of Bronze Age people is briefly told. The wonders of craftmanship attained in Denmark by those who used bronze are mentioned.

Metal at Long Last

Man used implements made from flint and other hard stones for hundreds of thousands of years before he hit, at long last, upon metals as still more suitable materials from which to make tools and weapons.

The Raw Materials for Making Metallic Tools

In the days of stone implements not many places in these islands were far from a natural source of some suitable natural raw material for their manufacture—flint and other hard substances, such as indurated sediments and harder kinds of both metamorphic and igneous rocks. On the other hand, sources of copper and of tin to use with copper for the production of bronze occurred only in certain districts, and for most of the people a new need for trade arose either to bring in the metal that the craftsman needed for his work or to supply finished tools and weapons. Traders needed routes by which to travel, and when men travel they bring their own and other people's ideas with them. They tell travellers' tales and stir interest about distant places among the stay-at-homes. Thus tales of mystery and legends grow from fact and exaggeration. While any migration of communities or individuals to make permanent settlements must produce a flow of ornaments, tools and ideas—all these things may move effectively along trade routes with little or no change of population.

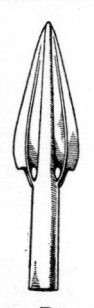

FIG. 37.—Bronze Age bronze spear-head, from Elford, Northumberland. Scale ⅙.

The metals available to Early Man were gold, copper, tin, bronze (copper with an admixture of about 10 per cent of tin)

LEARNING TO USE METAL

and iron. Gold had been known in some places in Europe at the end of the Neolithic era, but it was only rarely employed in implement making. However, it came early into use for the adornment of horses and men. In some parts of the world, for example in the valley of the Nile and in Mesopotamia, copper was the first metal to be made into implements, but it could not be cast satisfactorily in closed moulds, a fact which placed a limitation upon its utility. In any area in which copper was in extensive use, it would be possible to speak of a Copper Age in that region, but there was no such period in our country. Here, bronze implements can be dated back to about 1900 B.C., and iron was first used about 500 B.C.

The Bronze Age Begins

At the end of the Neolithic period in this country, great proficiency had been attained in the manufacture of stone implements. The great stone (Megalithic) monuments had succeeded the simpler and less-impressive erections of earlier days, and we can picture in our mind's eye a settled agriculture with well-established practices as well as a degree of organized society in which tradition and religion had developed over many centuries. In the south-west there had been an easterly extension of influence from what we call Wales. This is well illustrated by the transport of the Preselau stones by the builders of Stonehenge to the Wiltshire downland from South Wales, see page 72.

To get a working idea of conditions at the beginning of the Bronze Age in Britain we should perhaps remind ourselves

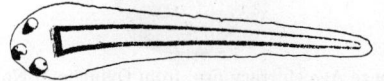

FIG. 38.—Bronze Age bronze halberd-blade, from Slieve Kileta Hill, co. Wexford. Scale ⅛.

that in Spain and southern France the use of bronze had already begun, and that among weapons made there were flat daggers, and also that right from the beginning of the Neolithic period of this country bronze was already employed in Mesopotamia and Egypt. When our Bronze Age began copper and bronze implements already in use in Ireland included the flat halberd. From all three of the sources just mentioned traders brought their wares to the southern and western ports of our island in the first days of the Bronze Age here, about 1900 B.C. About the same time from North-west Europe came the so-called Beaker Folk. Their name is indicative of the use in burial that they made of tall, cylindrical

78   ARCHÆOLOGY

pottery vessels often termed beakers; these were evidently to hold food and drink intended for the use of the departed. These beakers, occasionally provided with a handle, are of good thin ware, made without the use of a potter's wheel. They are generally found in round barrows with unburnt interments. Typical beakers are covered with ornament, and consist of a globular body and a neck. The neck is either cylindrical or an inverted cone. The pattern is usually arranged horizontally, but sometimes vertical ornament on the neck helps to distinguish that part of the vessel from the body. The ornament was, of course, impressed before baking the pottery; it consists of small rings

FIG. 39.— Bronze Age "incense-cup", from Beedon, Berks. Diameter 3¾ inches.

FIG. 40.—Bronze Age cinerary urn, from Ovingham, Northumberland. Scale ¼.

and of herring-bone and other linear designs, including cross-hatching, produced with wood or bone styles and dies and of cord-patterns applied by twisted thongs.

On the continent of Europe similar vessels are typical of the late Neolithic period or of the age which immediately succeeded it, called the Copper period, which is not recognizable in this country.

Chronology of the Bronze Age

Our picture for the beginning of our Bronze Age about 1900 B.C. must, then, be of the coming of distinct and sharply contrasted cultures : the Western Megalith builders with their Neolithic culture tending to move eastwards, i.e., from Wales towards the Midlands and South-east; traders in bronze from Ireland, Spain and southern France coming to the western and southern ports; the Beaker Folk with little or no knowledge of metal arriving from Europe on our eastern coast.

But the whole Bronze Age extended over many centuries in this country—actually it comprised almost as long a time as separates us today from the end of the Roman period—and

FIG. 41.—Dug-out canoe, from South Stoke, Sussex, as used by inhabitants of crannogs (artificial islands). From Neolithic times onwards crannogs were constructed.

that was naturally quite long enough for many of Man's ideas, customs, beliefs, industries and habits of life to change very considerably.

The first phase of the Bronze Age has been subdivided into:

(i) Early Bronze Age .. .. .. 200 years
(ii) Middle Bronze Period A .. .. 300 years
(iii) Middle Bronze Period B .. .. 400 years

(i) The Early Bronze Period (1900–1700 B.C.) was the time of the Beaker Folk when few metal implements, flat axes and daggers were being imported. The flat axe was used with a split stick as a handle. At this time short-headed and long-headed people were living here side by side. Burial was without cremation in round barrows.

(ii) In the Middle Bronze Period A (1700–1400 B.C.) flat and flanged axes were in use as well as daggers. The axe-head was more efficiently held in the cleft stick by hammering up the edges into flanges and by providing a cross rib on each face of the axe-head to prevent the stick from being split too far.

(iii) In the Middle Bronze Period B (1400–1000 B.C.) were developed the thrusting sword (rapier) and the form of bronze axe known as a palstave. The palstave is a development of the flanged celt. In it the metal covered by the split stick is thinned out and a side loop is provided for a securing cord. With the end of the Middle Bronze Period B, the first phase of the Bronze Age came to a close about 1000 B.C.

Then came, suddenly in East Anglia, a time in the Bronze Age (about 1000 B.C. in Lowland Britain) when striking improvements in metallurgy took place. It is most noticeable to us today; the rapier, or thrusting sword, gave place to the more formidable and efficient striking sword; the round shield came into use about the same time, and associated with these introductions there was greater efficiency in the manufacture of other bronze objects in large numbers. The spear-

MEDITERRANEAN

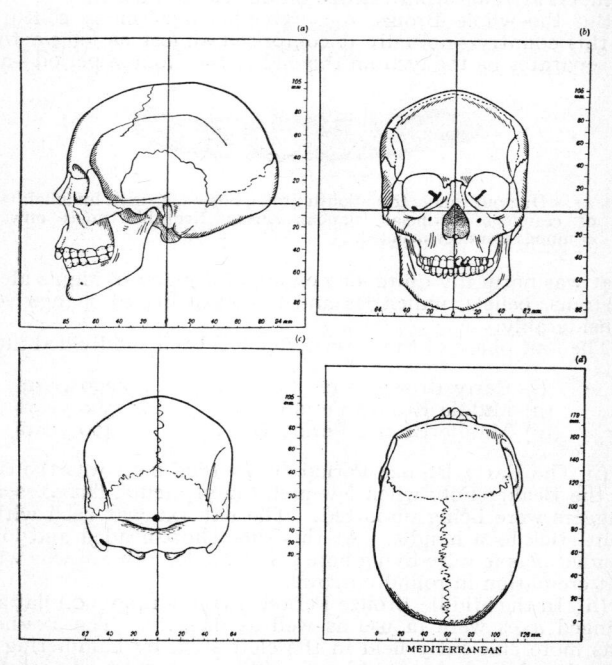

FIG. 42.—Long-headed race. This series of drawings shows clearly what is meant by a long-headed (dolichocephalic) race. This skull is that of an ancient Egyptian (Middle Kingdom, Abydos) belonging to the Mediterranean or Brown Race. Compare this with the illustration of the skull of a short-headed race (Fig. 43). (*a*) norma lateralis (profile); (*b*) norma frontalis (face view); (*c*) norma occipitalis (back view); (*d*) norma verticalis (top view).

Drawings made by Mr. E. J. Noon under the supervision of Professor A. J. E. Cave.

heads first developed wings, and finally they were made hollow, and so less metal was required for their manufacture. This phase (1000–500 B.C.) is the Late Bronze Period. It was the time of bronze founding when the socketed axe and the leaf-shaped sword were made and used.

In Bronze Age times, as in other ages, ideas from the east

could easily sweep in over the comparatively flat land of the country that lies south-east of a line drawn from modern Dorset to the north-east coast of England. The more mountainous

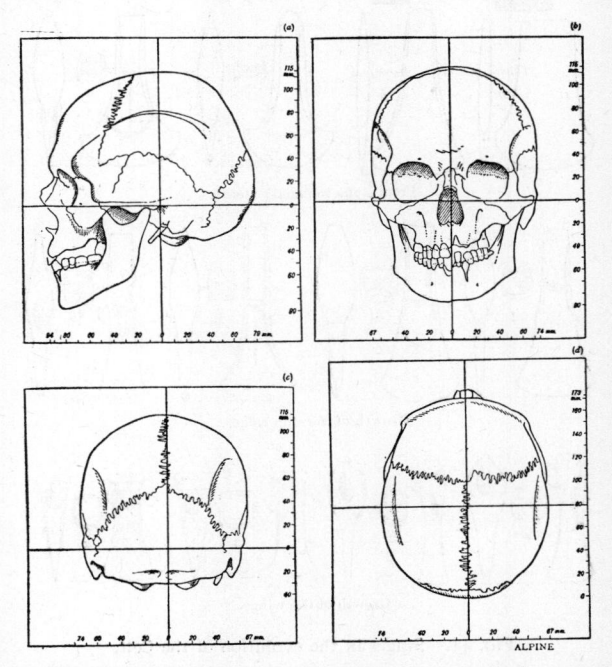

FIG. 43.—Short-headed race. Four aspects of the skull of a short-headed (brachycephalic) race. This skull is of the Alpine type, that of a male Slovene, aged thirty, from Perloka, Carniola. Aspects as in Fig. 42, with which this should be compared. The cephalic index is expressed by regarding the breadth of the skull as a percentage of the length. Skulls with a cephalic index between 70 and 75 are long-headed (dolichocephalic); between 75 and 80 are medium-headed (mesaticephalic) and those between 80 and 85 are short-headed (brachycephalic).

Drawings made by Mr. E. J. Noon under the supervision of Professor A. J. E. Cave.

country to the west of this line is less easily penetrable, and any chronology drawn up for one of these two regions is not likely to be strictly applicable to the other.

Chronologies of the Bronze Age have been attempted for

82   ARCHÆOLOGY

different countries. They are based, of course, upon typology,
i.e., upon the types of implements and ornaments which are

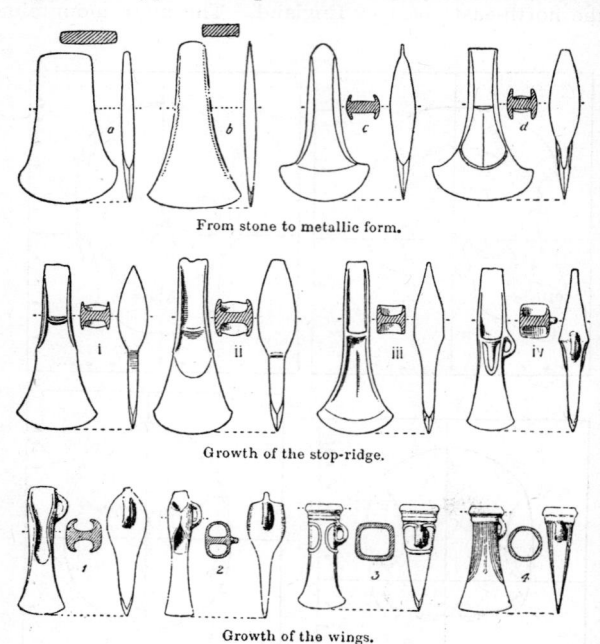

From stone to metallic form.

Growth of the stop-ridge.

Growth of the wings.

Fig. 44.—Stages in the evolution of the Celt.

characteristic of different portions of time. A chronology
that is well known is that for France devised by Professor
Montelius of Stockholm.

The Bronze Age in Denmark

Denmark was in a somewhat isolated position in Neolithic
and subsequent ages, and new cultures reached it late and often
had longer to grow and develop there before being superseded
by newer fashions. Certainly this was the case with the
Bronze Age, which is generally reckoned as beginning in
Denmark about 1500 B.C. and extending till about 400 B.C.
Two main chronological divisions have been recognized: the
former from 1500 B.C. to 800 B.C., and the latter from 800 B.C.

LEARNING TO USE METAL 83

to 400 B.C. Early Bronze Age objects from Denmark exhibited in London in 1948–49 included two solid bronze religious processional axes, more than a foot in length, and a ceremonial bronze sword which has, on the hilt, gold inlay consisting of gold-plated bronze discs alternating with horn, or some other impermanent material which has now disappeared, and amber. Amber was gathered on the North Sea coast of Jutland, and no doubt was traded for materials such as bronze and gold,

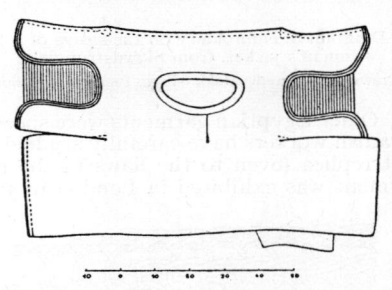

FIG. 45.—Pattern of a Bronze Age woman's jacket, from Skrydstrup field, west of Haderslev, Jutland. Scale in centimetres, sixty in all.

Drawn by Margrethe Hald. From *Bronze Age Fashion*.

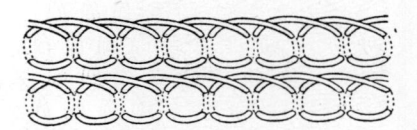

FIG. 46.—Diagram of the stitching by which ribs were made on the sleeve of a Bronze Age woman's jacket, from Skrydstrup field.

Drawn by Margrethe Hald. From *Bronze Age Fashion*.

which had to be imported. These objects alone are sufficient to convince anybody seeing them that Man in the Bronze Age had reached a high degree of artistic perception and had combined it with great skill in craftsmanship. It is difficult to believe that in these particular materials a modern worker in metals could excel his Bronze Age forerunner, even if he might equal in beauty and finish the work that he turned out.

Another set of interesting relics of the Bronze Age which has been provided by Denmark is everyday clothing. Owing to the peculiar conditions of the oxygen-hungry, wet burial-places the garments of sheep's wool in which both men and women were buried have been preserved in at least seven cases—those of four men and three women. This clothing is wool twill, and is the oldest everyday clothing of Man that has come

FIG. 47.—Diagram of embroidery on the sleeve of a Bronze Age woman's jacket, from Skrydstrup field.

Drawn by Margrethe Hald. From *Bronze Age Fashion*.

down to us. Older Egyptian garments were specially made for funerals. Danish workers have carefully studied this clothing, and an exact replica (even to the flaws in the material) of a woman's garment was exhibited in London in 1948–49. The

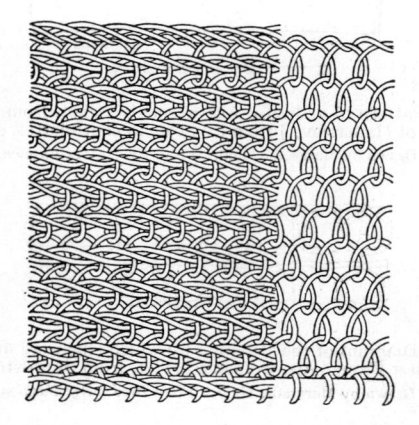

FIG. 48.—Diagram of embroidery at the neck of a Bronze Age woman's jacket, from Skrydstrup field.

Drawn by Margrethe Hald. From *Bronze Age Fashion*.

men's clothes consisted of a tight loin cloth, a cloak hanging loosely from the shoulders and a round cap.

In one case the woman's dress consisted of a smock with sleeves to the elbow and a corded skirt. The costume was held round the waist by a belt, and on this was fastened a bronze belt disc. In the two other cases the skirt was longer and came to the ankles. Sandals or shoes of cloth or leather

LEARNING TO USE METAL 85

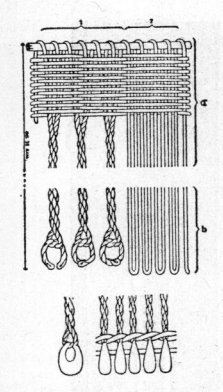

FIG. 49.—Diagram showing how a woman's corded skirt of Bronze Age date was made. The grave from which the skirt came was at Egtved in Jutland, Denmark.

Drawn by Margrethe Hald. From *Bronze Age Fashion*.

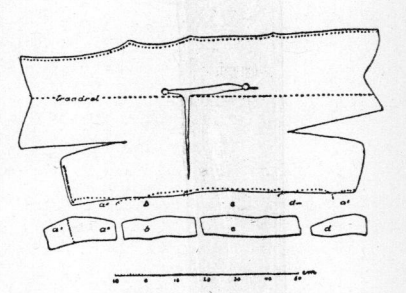

FIG. 50.—Pattern of a dark wool jacket (Bronze Age), found in a woman's grave at Borum, Jutland. Scale in centimetres, 60 in all.

Drawn by Margrethe Hald. From *Bronze Age Fashion*.

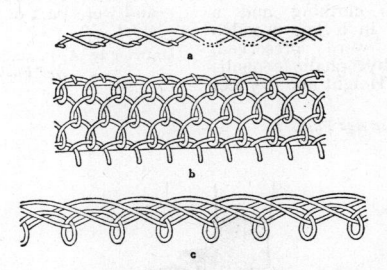

FIG. 51.—Diagrams showing the cord-sewing inside a man's cap of Bronze Age, from a grave west of Kolding near Vester Vamdrup, Jutland, Denmark.

Drawn by Margrethe Hald. From *Bronze Age Fashion*.

Fig. 52.—Bronze Age burial in an oak coffin, from a large barrow called "Borum Æshøj" west of Aarhus, Denmark. The body was that of a young man of about twenty. His clothing and a short dagger in a fine wooden *sword*-sheath were preserved. Cranium brachycephalic (cephalic index 80.3). Height about 5 feet 5 inches.

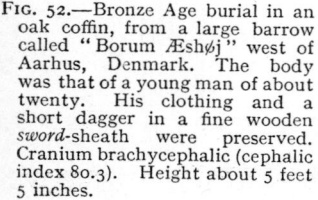

From *Bronze Age Fashion*.

Fig. 53.—Bronze Age woman's grave, from Ølby, Denmark. Round the neck is a bronze collar; the peculiar tubes below the belt-disc are made of thin bronze, and were part of the cords of the skirt.

Drawing by A. P. Madsen. From *Bronze Age Fashion*.

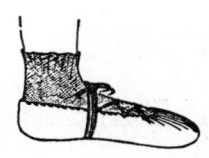

Fig. 54.—Reconstruction of a Bronze Age shoe, from Skrydstrup field, Jutland.

From *Bronze Age Fashion*.

were worn by both men and women. All seven burials just mentioned are dated by Danish experts as belonging to the second period of the Early Bronze Age (about 1400–1150 B.C.).

From the Late Bronze Age of Denmark come the earliest wind musical instruments in the world so far discovered. They are of bronze, the tubes conical and made in several pieces. Such instruments are called "lurs". They were made in pairs, and can be played well today by expert musicians. When one looks upon such objects as these, it is with some amazement that we realize that these great horns were really made more than 2,350 years ago (before 400 B.C.).

There is a modernity about many of these objects from the Bronze Age of Denmark which startles some people into the realization that these ancient craftsmen were not inferior to their present-day successors in the production of fine workmanship.

BRONZE AGE IN ENGLAND AND DENMARK

ENGLAND		DENMARK
	400 B.C.	
	500 B.C.	Late Bronze Age
Late Bronze Age	800 B.C.	
	1000 B.C.	
Middle Bronze Age, Period B		Early Bronze Age
	1400 B.C.	
Middle Bronze Age, Period A	1500 B.C.	
Early Bronze Age	1700 B.C.	
	1900 B.C.	

Daily Life in the Bronze Age

There is a fear that typology and chronology may so fully occupy our minds that we may forget to picture to ourselves the daily life of the peoples of the Bronze Age. To try to visualize the folk who occupied Britain for nearly fifteen hundred years as though they were all alike from the beginning to the end is, of course, incorrect, as incorrect as it is impossible, and we must think rather of an evolution of the ways of life from the day when the Beaker Folk, the Megalithic builders and the traders from southern Europe and Ireland met here at the beginning of the Bronze Age to the days at its close when the peoples of this land, already Celtic in race, were shallowly cultivating the land with their simple ploughs drawn by a pair of oxen and producing squarish fields which can still be traced by their outlines breaking the smooth surface of hillsides, especially in southern and south-eastern England. It is better to have a slightly incorrect mental picture of this succession of inhabitants than to have no picture in our mind at all.

How Changes Occurred

From what has already been said about immigration and trade routes it will be clear that new fashions and new materials were not necessarily introduced by new invading races nor that the use of a certain technique by a region must imply that the people inhabiting it were all of one and the same racial group with a common ancestry. Nor must we imagine that because men knew and possessed a certain metal they had entirely discarded the materials of an earlier period; for example, in the Bronze Age, and long after, men still used flint for implement making; partly, of course, because it was more readily available to most people, and therefore cheaper. Similarly, in the Early Iron Age (and in the Later Iron Age, too, in which we ourselves live) bronze, still very attractive for some purposes, continued in use.

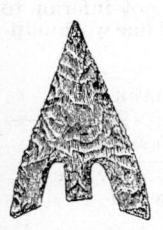

FIG. 55.—Bronze Age flint arrowhead, from Lambourn Downs, Wilts.

Remember that a long expanse of time gave ample opportunity for much development of form in implements and much change in daily life. So we are right to think of those relics that have survived as being mere representatives of the great range of objects in daily use, many of them, unlike those that have frequently come down to us, executed in perishable materials, including wood, skins and textiles. Again, we must remember that while the sequence Stone, Bronze, Iron is to be found in all parts of the world, the chronology is different in different places: especially are the corresponding periods of greatly different lengths in different countries, and this has given greater opportunity for the elaboration of technique in regions having a long history of the use of one material.

It is interesting that when men change from the use of one material to another for the manufacture of an object in common use the form established in the older material may be imitated in the new, as for example when early pottery of Neolithic date reproduced some of the features of the skin receptacles formerly used for the same purpose. Conversely, when bronze was still a rare metal and men still used flint for implement-making they sometimes imitated, in this very abundant medium, the form that bronze objects naturally took when they were cast in moulds.

EXERCISE

Pay attention to the changing fashions (typology) of the various subdivisions of the Bronze Age. Having become familiar from reading and from the examination of illustrations with the various relics of the period, pay a visit to the nearest museum with a collection illustrative of the Bronze Age. Note the advances in skill that occurred during the period. Make drawings, however rough, for your note-book to illustrate: (*a*) typology (changing fashions); (*b*) implements; (*c*) pottery; (*d*) burials.

Visit any Bronze Age sites within reach.

If opportunity occurs, help experienced excavators with their work. (This applies to other periods as well; excavators are generally glad of any help they can get. It is often best to communicate with the Director of Excavations, on the site, by letter.)

LITERATURE

Good information occurs in the general works mentioned at the end of Chapter Two, and for particulars of life and work see *Prehistoric Europe*, by J. G. D. Clark (London: Methuen). Some valuable information about agriculture will be found in *Prehistoric Sussex*, by E. C. Curwen (London: Homeland Association, first published in 1929, at 10s. 6d.).

For particulars about current excavations you should look in the *Archæological News Letter* (see note on Literature at the end of Chapter Two).

CHAPTER NINE

THEY BRING IRON

THE EARLY IRON AGE

A new metal, IRON, is introduced, and this has a profound influence upon Man's work in the world. With it he can do things that were never before possible. We are still in the Iron Age; the *Early* Iron Age began in Britain about 500 B.C. and extended into the first Christian century.

Dates Help us to Grasp the Subject

I THINK that it is generally a good thing to have a date and a mental picture upon which to build our growing knowledge in any period, even if that date must be altered and that mental picture modified later on by more accurate information and by new discoveries. If we think of outstanding inventions as having been introduced at certain times, and if we employ dates for important happenings in the past, we are helped to fit in particulars of other isolated facts as they come to our notice, and we are able to get a working impression about the epoch in which we are, at the moment, especially interested. For the beginner clear-cut impressions help to establish principles and foundations. The expert who knows the exceptions and uncertainties softens down the hard-and-fast lines in the picture without blurring the whole, because he knows enough details to make every part intelligible.

So, before we talk about the first use of iron in Britain, let us be bold in our consideration of the different races of men who lived here from about 2000 B.C. and get some impression, however imperfect, of the people who first handled metals in this country.

About 2000 B.C. there was an immigration of people related to the modern Irish. In other words they were Celts (or Kelts if we prefer to use this spelling to avoid confusion with the word *celt*, a kind of stone-axe which is not in any way connected with the race of men of whom we are now speaking). These first Celtic immigrants to Britain were the so-called Q-Celts. This is a designation based upon their language, but there is no reason to doubt that, in this particular case, there is a real racial distinction between these Q-Celts and the folk that followed them, the P-Celts, and the third and last wave of all, the Belgæ. The three great waves can reasonably be identified with peoples of these islands today: the Q-Celts with the Gaelic inhabitants, the Highlanders of Scotland and the Irish and the Manx; the P-Celts with the Welsh and the

FIG. 56.—Vertical section of a grave in the Belgic cemetery (first century B.C.) at Aylesford, Kent.

Cornish and the Cumbrians; and the Belgæ with those who were absorbed into the English population of South-eastern England after the invasion of A.D. 449. The distinction of

FIG. 57.—Circle of interments in the Belgic cemetery (first century B.C.) at Aylesford, Kent. Such a cemetery is often called an urn-field, from the occurrence of the burial urns.

language between Q-Celts and P-Celts is seen in the equivalence of Q and P sounds in some words used by these two races. Everyone knows the *Mac* (meaning "son of") of many Gaelic family names, *MacMichael*, for example. At the end of *Mac* is the *q* sound. In Welsh the corresponding element, for son, is *Ap*. In a number of surnames the *a* is lost, and we have such examples as Prichard (i.e., Ap-Richard), Pritchard, Prichett, in which the meaning *son* is represented by the *p* element. The P sound is represented by the first letter in *Britain* and *Briton*. If we accept the dates that have been assigned to the three invasions we shall perhaps be satisfied with 1800 B.C., 600 B.C. and 75 B.C. respectively. We can call them invasions of Goidels, Brythons and Belgæ. In this case we shall say that the Q-Celts brought bronze and the P-Celts iron with them from the Continent, and both brought also skill to produce and work the metal that came in with them. It need hardly be added that it cannot have been quite so simple as that, because individuals with knowledge of new materials and methods and small groups of immigrants at frequent intervals may have arrived before and after any large-scale influx of population; nor must we place too much emphasis upon exact dates or upon certainties of racial relationship and language. Nevertheless, the things that have been mentioned are useful pointers to begin with.

Different Kinds of Immigration

In considering the influx of men, ideas, materials and objects of daily use we must remember that there are several kinds of immigrations. (i) There may be violent invasions of a military or piratical nature, whereby earlier populations are subjugated and many of their customs and habits of life modified or swept away. Contrary to popular belief, such conquests seldom, if ever, result in a whole population being massacred or driven away to another area, though some family-groups or larger communities may migrate before the advancing flood of powerful invaders. To realize the import of the armed intrusions of prehistoric times we may recall the historic instance of the Norman Conquest. (ii) But there is the possibility of peaceful intrusion. Groups of craftsmen may come into a country to ply their trade in a more profitable area. They may be driven out of their original home by political, economic or religious pressure. They carry new ideas with them. The friendly textile-workers of the Low Countries and France that came to England in the sixteenth and seventeenth centuries provide a comparatively recent example, which must often have been paralleled in prehistoric days, and may in early ages have extended over long periods of time, a flourishing industry

FIG. 58.—Clay loom-weight, for hanging on the ends of the warp threads, four-sided, tapering towards the top, from Lakenheath, Suffolk. Early Iron Age. Scale $\frac{1}{12}$.

attracting from overseas other workers with new ideas. (iii) Again, traders, as transient visitors, are capable of influencing the life of the community.

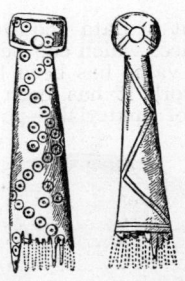

FIG. 59.—Bone weaving combs of Early Iron Age date. *On the left*, from Nether Wallop, Hants; *on the right*, from Haslingfield, Cambs. Scale ¼.

Halstatt and La Tène

Anyone coming to this country about the year 900 B.C. (and for four hundred years or so longer, till about 500 B.C.) would have found no iron implements in use yet. Flint was still largely used in everyday life, while the best kinds of tools and some ceremonial objects were made of bronze. Britain was still in the Bronze Age.

Yet, at that same time and, indeed, already for about a century before (since 1000 B.C. or thereabouts) wrought iron was in use at Halstatt some thirty-five miles south-east of present-day Salzburg in Austria. We know about this very early employment of iron in Europe from the excavation of burials at Halstatt, associated with which is a rich variety of grave-goods: pottery, weapons and ornaments. So considerable is the material at Halstatt and at other places which can be correlated with it, that it has been possible to work out a chronological classification, a kind of time-scale from discoveries made by archæologists. This time-scale is applicable to isolated finds in other places. The Halstatt period as a whole covers the time from 1000 B.C. to 500 B.C., and we shall speak further about it a little later on in the present book, see page 95.

Later in date is another important Early Iron Age site, which has also been used for drawing up some guide-posts in time for the use of students. It is La Tène, meaning *the shallow place* (in the lake, close to the shore), the relics of a fortified military post at the northern end of Lake Neuchâtel,

94 ARCHÆOLOGY

in Switzerland; its date is from about 250 B.C. to 100 B.C. However, the term *La Tène* is used to cover a longer period than this (as much as from 500 B.C. to the first century of the Christian era), and is subdivided in various ways by different workers.

By the employment of data acquired at Halstatt and La Tène and at other places which can be fitted into the scheme, a time-scale of great value has been built up. With such a chronological framework it has been possible to set out a detailed succession of materials—pottery, tools, weapons,

FIG. 60.—Back of a bronze mirror of Early Iron Age date, from Desborough, Northants. Scale ⅛.

articles of personal adornment—so that new finds continually fit into the classification and give us more and more information about Man's pursuits over the period as a whole, correcting an earlier misconception here and there and providing us with fuller pictures of the various phases of human activity.

Very full information is again obtained for this period by studying *typology*, that is to say, by becoming familiar with a wide range of objects in the different categories and knowing by their *type* (recognized by their shape, material, texture, mode of manufacture and ornament) into which place they fall in the general classification.

It is, once again, obvious that the best way to obtain this information is by familiarity with the objects themselves, to see and to handle as many examples as possible or, failing that, to study representations and detailed descriptions of the things in question.

In the compass of such a small work as this it is only possible to indicate the lines of progress you should follow in teaching yourself this part of the subject. The details must be left to you.

Perhaps it is now best to take a general view of the Early Iron Age classifications, and then we shall be in a better position to understand its implications for Britain.

Halstatt and La Tène

THE EARLY IRON AGE

La Tène IV	First century of the Christian era
La Tène III	First century B.C.
La Tène II	300–100 B.C.
La Tène I	500–300 B.C.
Late Halstatt	650–500 B.C.
Middle Halstatt	850–650 B.C.
Early Halstatt	1000–850 B.C.

Sword and Bucket at Halstatt

At Halstatt itself and in places where the culture can be closely related to it, one of the most satisfactory objects for study, to illustrate succession of types in the Halstatt period, is the sword (Figs. 61, 62 and 65).

The earliest of these swords were of bronze while iron was still scarce. One of the earliest is called the *antennæ* type, because its pommel was provided with curled projections. Another type, of the same time, was the leaf-shaped sword. These weapons belong to the years 1000–800 B.C.

The next stage is a large iron blade, 800–650 B.C.

The third and last phase is marked by a short iron sword with horseshoe-shaped pommel, 650–500 B.C.

Different authorities split the Halstatt period up differently, and what has just been said is sufficient to indicate the principles upon which classification can be carried out.

Bronze buckets of the Halstatt period are of two types. There is the *situla*, a vessel with a narrow base. It tapers upwards to a shallow shoulder with a vertical rim about the same height as the shoulder below it. The rim is normally

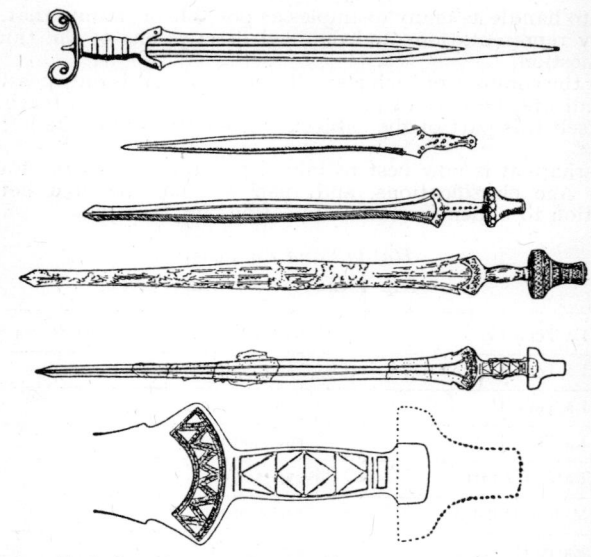

FIG. 61.—Early Iron Age swords. The top example is of bronze and has "antennæ"; next below this is a "leaf-shaped" bronze sword. Both these indicate transition from the Bronze Age. Next the blade is sometimes of iron while a tang of bronze is retained, showing that iron was still rare. (This phase is illustrated by the third example.) As the blade increases in length (which was possible and desirable when iron was available) the pommel increases in size to balance it: this is seen in the examples given. The period of the large iron sword, eighth and seventh centuries B.C. (4th and 5th examples), was the culmination of the process of development. The huge sword was replaced in the seventh century B.C. by a short sword with horse-shoe pommel (see Fig. 62). The fifth example (with part enlarged below) is a large iron sword with gold-foil (in part restored) from Halstatt. The top sword is shown reduced to $\frac{1}{12}$, the next three to $\frac{1}{8}$ and the last to $\frac{1}{20}$ and $\frac{1}{8}$.

FIG. 62.—Short sword with horse-shoe pommel which superseded the large sword about 650 B.C., from Halstatt. Scale $\frac{1}{10}$.

provided with two handles and a lid. The other bucket is the *cista*; it is parallel-sided with diameter and height not far from

Fig. 63.—Early Iron Age bronze pail (technically situla) with lid, from Halstatt, Upper Austria. Scale $\frac{1}{12}$.

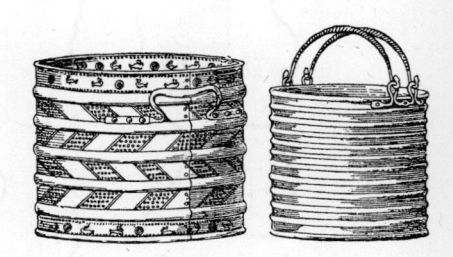

Fig. 64.—Early Iron Age. *On the left*, Bucket (cista) with broad hoops; scale $\frac{1}{10}$. *On the right*, cordoned bucket (cista); scale $\frac{1}{8}$. Both from Halstatt and both of bronze.

equal. Its rim may be provided with two loop handles, or fixed handles may be riveted below the rim.

Early Iron Age in Britain

In Britain the date generally given for the beginning of the Early Iron Age is 500 B.C., so that the greater part of the

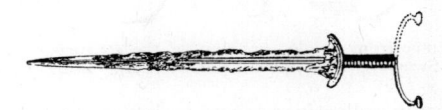

Fig. 65.—Short iron sword of late Halstatt appearance with horse-shoe pommel (antennæ type), from the River Thames. Scale $\frac{1}{12}$.

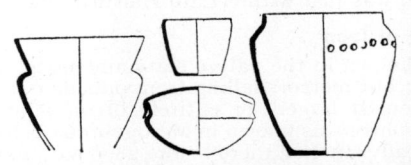

Fig. 66.—Early Iron Age pottery, from Park Brow, Cissbury, Sussex. Scale $\frac{1}{18}$.

centuries covered, in Austria, by the Halstatt period falls into the Bronze Age of Britain. However, a short iron sword from the Thames with horseshoe pommel which is preserved in the

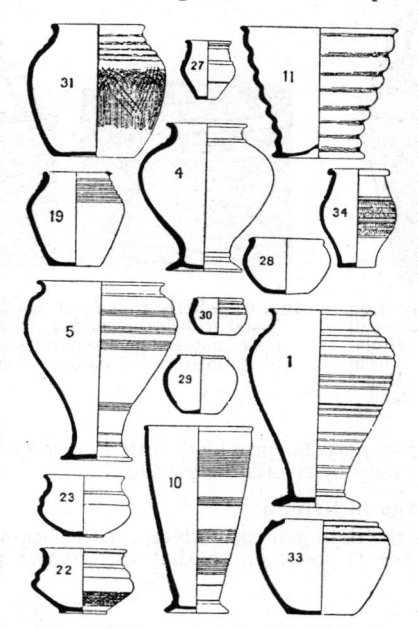

Fig. 67.—Pottery from Belgic cemetery (of the century 50 B.C.–A.D. 50), Swarling, Kent (profile and section). Scale $\frac{1}{12}$.

British Museum collections seems to belong to Late Halstatt, and pottery found near Cissbury in Sussex is of Late Halstatt type, so that it is almost certain that the earliest use of iron in Great Britain was just within Late Halstatt times.

The Coming of Iron

Iron is unknown in the native state among the rocks of the earth's crust, but meteors falling from outside our atmosphere sometimes consist largely or entirely of metallic iron. Iron from such a source was known in Mesopotamia before 3000 B.C. Iron was already smelted there before 2800 B.C., but it was rare until 1100 B.C.

From before 1900 B.C. iron was in use regularly in Asia

Minor. From about 1400 B.C. onwards, iron objects, largely daggers and dagger-blades, were exported from Asia Minor, North Syria and North-west Mesopotamia. Before 1300 B.C. smelted iron was being imported into Egypt. By 1100 B.C. Cyprus and Greece were in the Iron Age; by 1000 B.C. iron was in use at Halstatt, and before 500 B.C. it had reached France and Germany with the La Tène period of the Iron Age. An interesting article entitled " The Coming of Iron " was contributed to *Antiquity*, March 1936, by G. A. Wainwright. The above dates are those he gives.

EXERCISE

Follow the procedure suggested for the Bronze Age (see end of Chapter Eight) as far as visits to sites and excavations are concerned.

What trace of Early Iron Age cultivation can you find in your own neighbourhood? Compare rectangular plots, if they are still visible on hillsides, with the field-systems in Wales and Ireland. (Large-scale maps may be a help.)

As before, pay close attention to museum collections. Examine any models illustrative of the daily life of Early Iron Age peoples.

LITERATURE

The subject of the Early Iron Age is covered to some extent by several of the works mentioned in the list of books at the end of Chapter Two. For Early Iron Age cultivations consult E. C. Curwen, *Prehistoric Sussex* (London : Homeland Association, 1929).

CHAPTER TEN

THE COMING OF THE ROMAN

EVIDENCES OF ROMAN RULE IN BRITAIN

Roman influence was first felt through trade and travel. In the Early Iron Age, Julius Cæsar unsuccessfully invaded Britain, and then, in the first century of the Christian era, Britain was conquered by the Romans.

The Roman Period is Rich in Material for the Archæologist

It will be realized that much expert knowledge is necessary for the complete study of the antiquities of Roman Britain. This is clear when we remember that there are the ground-plans and buildings of Roman towns and country houses to be examined; roads, forts and other military works like Hadrian's Wall to be considered, and that the student has before him a great wealth of objects: altars and tombstones, both pottery and coins in bewildering variety, household utensils and personal ornaments, as well as objects belonging to such activities as agriculture, metal-working and weaving. Works of art, not often of a very high order, are also well represented. In spite of all the complexity presented by the antiquities which have just been mentioned, we can at least gain a general idea of life here between the first invasion of Julius Cæsar in 55 B.C. and the waning of Roman power during the first half of the fifth century of the Christian era. So in this chapter a broad view is taken of the antiquities of Roman Britain.

The Background of the Roman Period (say 55 B.C. to A.D. 410)

Before the military conquest, a religion common to inhabitants of Gaul (the modern France) and Britain, as well as relationships of blood, naturally resulted in a good deal of movement by individuals to and from this country. Continental traders also came here. All this made the political and cultural influence of Rome felt in Britain. In the absence of any written account by the inhabitants of Britain at this epoch, we rely upon the comments of foreigners and the results of archæological research to throw some light upon the life and ideas of those times.

So, then, here is a word-map of Roman Britain:

THE COMING OF THE ROMAN

55 and 54 B.C.	Julius Cæsar unsuccessfully invaded Britain in 55 B.C. and again in 54 B.C. Britain remained under its quarrelling tribal leaders for nearly a century. One, Cunobelin (about A.D. 5–40), who was the Cymbeline of Shakespeare, had coins inscribed (in Latin) " King of the Britons ".
A.D. 43.	In the reign of the Emperor Claudius, Aulus Plautius conquered all Britain south-east of a line from the Severn to the Wash.
A.D. 47–60.	Ostorius Scapula (Governor of Britain, A.D. 47–52) crushed a revolt in eastern Britain and established the frontier from Lindum (Lincoln) to the Dee and thence to Isca Silurem (Caerleon); it remained so until A.D. 60.
A.D. 61.	Suetonius Paulinus attacked North Wales and subjugated the religious (Druids') centre of Mona (Anglesey). Boudicca (incorrectly called Boadicea) Queen of the Iceni (in modern Norfolk) with a force of about 80,000 men seized the opportunity for revolt and massacred many Romans and rendered the Roman position in Britain very precarious. Suetonius crushed the rebellion with great slaughter and restored the frontier.
A.D. 61–71.	Peaceful consolidation followed (A.D. 61–71).
A.D. 71–85.	Expansion to the north and west next took place, and some control was exercised as far north as the Forth.
A.D. 85–119.	The barbarians of the north were turbulent.
A.D. 119.	The Emperor Hadrian came to Britain and built a wall from the Tyne (Wallsend) to the Solway (Bowness); this made consolidation and control possible. Local government and continuity with the past were maintained through a system of cantons based upon the pre-Roman tribal territories.
A.D. 122 onwards.	From A.D. 122 we must picture Britain as part of the Empire with many of its inhabitants, but especially those of the south-east, coming more and more to regard themselves as Romans.
A.D. 140–141.	In A.D. 140–141 Lollius Urbicus, Governor of Britain, built a solid wall of earth (with a ditch to its north) from the Clyde to the Forth, supported by ten strong forts, but the native tribes north of Hadrian's Wall were never subjugated.
A.D. 181–209.	From A.D. 181 to 209 there were mutinies in the army as well as external attacks in the north by Picts and Caledonians.
A.D. 209 and 210.	The Emperor Severus prosecuted two vigorous campaigns in A.D. 209 and 210 against the barbarians of the north, and then until the end of the third century the line of Hadrian's Wall held firm.
A.D. 286–293.	Carausius, who had been appointed Admiral to fight Frankish and Saxon pirates, made himself Emperor of Britain (A.D. 286–293).
A.D. 293–296.	He was murdered by Allectus, who died in defeat by Constantine's invasion of Britain (A.D. 296).
A.D. 296–350.	A peaceful period of half a century followed.
From A.D. 350.	From A.D. 350, Picts, Scots, Saxons and Attacotti invaded Britain. In A.D. 369 Theodosius was sent to the rescue, and he defeated these enemies.

	ARCHÆOLOGY
A.D. 383.	In A.D. 383 a revolt in the army made Magnus Maximus emperor in Britain. He invaded the Continent with the best troops; few of them ever returned. There followed a period of civil war and intrigue. Britain was cut off from Rome by the southern advance in Europe of Vandals and other barbarians.
A.D. 407.	In Britain, Constantine, native "emperor" (A.D. 407–411), took all the troops he could and invaded the Continent; he was defeated and executed. Depleted of trained defenders, the Britons were bidden by the
A.D. 410.	Emperor Honorius to defend themselves (A.D. 410). They still regarded themselves as Romans, and kept up an unequal fight until they were overwhelmed by
A.D. 449.	the English about forty years later.

The Pen and the Spade

The Roman period is exceptionally interesting from an archæological point of view. Roman writers have left accounts which have come down to us giving an outline picture of the Roman world as a whole in the years that intervened between the first invasion of Britain by Julius Cæsar (55 B.C.) and the beginning of the English settlement in the middle of the fifth century (say A.D. 449). There is, however, great uncertainty about detail, and especially about the course of events in Britain, so the spade has been very useful, here, in increasing our knowledge. Since the Second World War a great deal has been found out by the scientific examination of bombed sites, especially in ancient cities and towns. The last few years have thus been fruitful and have focused interest, especially locally, upon British antiquities of the first four and a half centuries of the Christian era.

Roman Antiquities

Roman antiquities, small and great, are very numerous in this country. The following are some important kinds which are worthy of careful study :

Roads: The main Roman roads make an impressive network by which the great military and civil centres could readily keep in touch with one another. Lesser roads linked less-important places. **Frontier Walls:** The more northern of these, of earth, runs from Clyde to Forth. Hadrian's Wall runs from Bowness-on-Solway to Wallsend-on-Tyne. **Camps, forts and fortresses:** The camp was temporary, the others permanent. The fortress was the station of a legion. The fort was a smaller place. All three were rectangular with rounded corners, in fact shaped in plan like a playing-card. **Civilian towns; ports and quays:** These either developed from military origins or grew up as settled conditions became established. **The detached house** and other buildings : These are often found on an estate (farm). The term villa means the estate, but it is often used for the country mansion or farm-house which stands upon it. Mosaic pavements sometimes occur. The farm-buildings are a necessary adjunct. In Britain we also find houses which were occupied by civil and military officials. **Fields** are indicated by outlines which were produced by cultivation. These outlines are generally ridges or banks.

THE COMING OF THE ROMAN

Coins are of such importance in all kinds of transactions, military and civil, that they occur in large numbers over the whole range of Roman occupation, both in time and space. Of course, they are very useful for helping to date objects found with them and to establish the age of levels at which they are found in stratified deposits. **Pottery:** In the home and as grave furniture a great variety of pottery was used. Styles and potters' marks make pottery an important factor in dating associated finds and the different levels reached in excavations. **Glassware** is found

FIG. 68.—A bronze figurine of Roman date (probably second century) depicting a devotee offering a libation to a deity from a small patera (plate) in the right hand. The attitude is typical of contemporary stone reliefs depicting sacrificial scenes at altars. Found at Barham, Kent. Original in Canterbury Museum. Height 3⅞ inches.

Drawn by S. G. B.-B.

both from homes and from burials. **Military objects** include arms and armour. **Personal possessions**, including shoes and ornaments, are an important and varied part of the spoil from excavations. Artistic works in bronze and stone occur. Models, perhaps children's toys, have been found. Pens, styles (for use in writing) and writing-tablets have been discovered. **Manufactures and Industry:** Pottery kilns are numerous. Agriculture is known not only from farm-buildings and field-patterns but also from implements. Metal-working and weaving have left relics. **Religion** is known from inscriptions on tombstones and from actual burials. Many heathen altars have survived. Some Christian remains are known.

We must, of course, remember that Roman antiquities in this country do not stand alone. On the Continent, apart

FIG. 69.—Roman tombstone from Caerleon. To Gaius Valerius Victor, standard-bearer of the 2nd Legion "Augusta". Length, 3 feet 11 inches.

From Antiquities of Roman Britain.

FIG. 70.—Roman altar to Mars, King's Stanley, Gloucestershire. Height, 1 foot 11½ inches.

From Antiquities of Roman Britain.

from Rome itself, great centres of Roman life are known and minor sites are innumerable. As a result, the material for study is immense, and we must not forget that it is largely elucidated by contemporary Roman literature.

Relics Widespread and Varied

The relics of four and a half centuries of Roman influence are not only spread widely over the English countryside but are to be found in Wales and southern Scotland as well. Indeed, they are known even in Ireland, to which Roman rule never penetrated, but to which raiders carried loot from some of their murderous incursions to places in Great Britain.

Antiquities of the period are frequently to be found wherever Roman soldiers or officials were stationed, wherever Roman civilians came to live, either for business or in retirement, and wherever Romanized Britons had their homes or their work. In such places we are likely to find a wide range of objects buried in the soil, and they are liable to be turned up by spade or plough.

In appropriate places we shall occasionally find parts of buildings of this period preserved. It may be in walls of churches or in such a case as that of the Roman lighthouse, the Pharos, in Dover Castle.

Some town walls preserve work, including that of gateways, which dates back to Roman times.

THE COMING OF THE ROMAN 105

Impressive examples of Roman masonry are to be seen in the ruins of many Roman military stations and civilian towns. These may sometimes still stand well above the ground, as at Viroconium in Shropshire and at Richborough in Kent, or be just under the surface so that they readily come to light when excavations are undertaken, as at Corstopitum (near the modern Corbridge in Northumberland) or at Verulamium (St. Albans). Taking it all in all, England is really very rich in examples of stone buildings of the period, and a visit to one or more of them will give you, at first hand, a lot of information which cannot be so well conveyed by description. Some examples of masonry may be mentioned, but, of course, it is

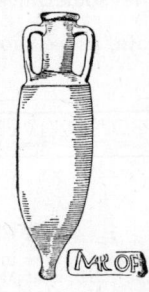

Fig. 71.—Roman amphora, a wine or oil jar. This example from Stanmore, Middlesex, is cylindrical, and is of sandy, brick-red coarseware, with stamp (either of the potter or of the manufacturer whose product it originally contained) MAROF, early first century. Height, 3 feet 6 inches. Stamp, scale ⅛.

From *Antiquities of Roman Britain.*

not wise to generalize when we are dealing with a subject which covers more than three hundred and fifty years, and which concerns the use of many different local materials in different parts of the country. Rocks like Carboniferous Limestone were used in some places; such materials can readily be cut into massive blocks. In other districts use was made of flint, hard it is true, but being nodular and in many different sizes and shapes, it is mainly suitable for use as rubble, because it is only with great labour that it can be reduced to regular shapes and sizes.

Roman masonry may consist of large blocks of stone, rectangular, laid in courses with or without mortar. In other cases the building material consists of almost cubical stones. The Romans were great users of concrete, and walls made of it might either be left unfaced or be covered in different ways, for example with stones either regular in shape or irregular or with bricks about one and a half inches thick (in modern times we should call such bricks tiles). Sometimes walls were of mortar and rubble, that is of stones, such as nodules of flint or pebbles, irregular in size and shape. The introduction of courses of bricks (tiles) into a rubble wall gives a striking and characteristic effect, but there are many Roman walls without bonding of this kind. In the identification of Roman workmanship a complication arises from the fact that Roman materials, including dressed stones and the bricks already mentioned, were much used in later building, especially in erecting churches in the succeeding Anglo-Saxon period.

The use in Roman times of mortar rendered pink by the inclusion of brickdust is sometimes a help in identifying Roman work.

Roman houses in Britain, as we should expect, are not all of

FIG. 72.—Product of Roman lead-mines in Britain. Lead pig, weight 184 lb., found at Hexgrave Park, near Mansfield, Notts. The inscription shown describes this as British lead from the Lutudarum mines (probably near Matlock), with the silver extracted; it gives the name Gaius Julius Protus. Scale $\frac{1}{12}$.

From *Antiquities of Roman Britain*.

one kind. There was the corridor type, in which internal corridors ran the length of the building. A row of rooms on one side opened on to the corridor. The floors of rooms were often supported upon a series of columns built of slabs of stone or of the tile-like bricks, so that there was a space beneath, through which hot air could circulate from a furnace in a special stokehold. Such a system of heating is called a *hypocaust* (meaning *under-burning*). Special tile-flues were frequently inserted in walls to give additional warmth. Floor decoration was sometimes executed in small cubes of stone or glass called *tesseræ*: these were arranged as a mosaic to form a pattern or picture. Some country houses had well-constructed bathrooms. The alterations and repairs that had occurred in many houses during the Roman period help to remind us of the long occupation of Britain by the Romans.

Internal walls were frequently covered with plaster ornamented with painted designs often rather crudely executed.

THE COMING OF THE ROMAN 107

Wells were lined with masonry or with masonry and timber. Roofs were frequently covered with tiles.

But we must not picture all the buildings of Roman Britain as being of masonry or brick. It is quite evident from the investigation of ruins that many buildings were largely of wood with tiled roofs: the wood has gone, the fallen tiles may lie in confusion. Sometimes walls were merely of earth, rendered on both sides with plaster. This method was used not only for internal partition walls but, surprisingly enough, even for exterior walls, as in one known case at Canterbury.

In the military towns accommodation was necessarily relatively cramped. If you are near enough to visit one of them, or if models are available in a local museum, study them

FIG. 73.—Roman carved stone sarcophagus, from the Minories, London. Length, 5 feet.

From *Antiquities of Roman Britain*.

or, failing all else, examine in your local library plans of some typical examples in books and reports on Roman antiquities. If you have a gift for drawing try to make a reconstruction of the buildings, and do not forget to put some human figures, soldiers, in your picture; let them walk about the streets, go into the shops and look out from the windows of the houses, because, after all, these towns were places where a military population lived and worked.

In towns that had evolved far enough to have a considerable civilian population, the area might be much greater, and there was more space for the houses, shops and public buildings, but there was a general similarity of plan about military stations and civilian centres. Could you, perhaps, construct a little model of such a place?

Burial was not permitted within Roman towns, and so cemeteries are found outside the walls, in the suburbs and beside the main roads. Conical burial mounds of earth twenty feet or more in height are sometimes to be seen beside main roads at a distance from the towns.

Shops and storehouses, such as granaries, deserve study, and the narrow streets, often with grooves worn in the paving-stones by wheels, and water-troughs with stone sides worn down by century-long scraping of buckets help us to people the towns, in our mind's eye, with a busy throng of men, women and children living an active civilized life and enjoying many of the amenities which we ourselves possess.

LITERATURE

For books about the Roman period see notes on Literature at the end of the next chapter.

CHAPTER ELEVEN

ROMANS REALLY LIVED HERE

GETTING A MENTAL PICTURE OF THE ROMAN CENTURIES

It is possible, by a careful study of the wide array of objects available, to get a very good idea of the state of Britain in the four and a half centuries of Roman influence.

Picturing Life in Roman Times

You will add greatly to the interest of teaching yourself archæology if you will constantly try to picture the employment of the objects with which you meet. Inside the northern gateway of the station of Borcovicus on Hadrian's Wall is a great trough made of upright stone slabs. I always relish the story of this told in Collingwood Bruce's *Handbook of the Roman Wall* about Anthony Place, one of the labourers on the excavations. He certainly used his imagination; for, with the usual prejudices of a Northumberland borderer, he gave it as his opinion that the Romans used the trough for washing their Scotch prisoners in. The simple labourer had learnt a lesson from which we all might benefit. To him the Roman soldiers were real people, and even if the actions he attributed to them were erroneous figments of his own imagination, at least to him the streets and stones were the stage on which he pictured living actors playing a part in real life.

Try to picture merchants, soldiers and shopkeepers, schoolchildren, artisans and farmers coming and going in all the din and bustle of the crowded thoroughfare and market-place or slipping into the cool of some tavern or visiting the heathen temple or the Christian church in response to the natural urge of religion.

The well-built metalled roads made in Britain in those early centuries, when taken as a whole are to be reckoned as the highest expression of Roman civilization in this country. They exhibit great engineering skill, and many of them are, of course, still in use. They were unsurpassed until the end of the nineteenth century and until improvement and construction of main arteries followed the introduction of motoring in 1895. In addition to the principal highways, there were many less important roads, some of them recently rediscovered for us. Close study will probably show that many more of these vicinal ways survive, although they are, at the moment, unrecognized. No doubt the Romans used and improved old roads as well as constructing new ones.

Many Roman roads are very straight, but they are not invariably so. Again, although the name " street ", an English (i.e., Anglo-Saxon) word, is often used for stretches of Roman roads, it is not to be taken as an indication that a road so designated is necessarily Roman. For example, in Kent the Stone Street is Roman, but the term is also applied to many hamlets in the North Downs unrelated to Roman highways. This seems to be true, for example, of Sole Street (in the parish of Crundale) and Hassell Street; these names indicate a few houses ranged along a straight piece of road, typically, but perhaps not necessarily, on both sides.

As you teach yourself archæology take a great interest in roads, remembering that men have always needed means of communication for defence, for social contacts and for exchange of goods. I once discovered a lost prehistoric settlement by noticing that several roads, without any apparent modern reason, led to a spot on a hill-top in wooded country. Close to the intersection of the ways the place was found and confirmed by excavation.

There is always a reason for the existence of roads and for the courses they take. Ancient roads are frequently sunken below the surrounding country, because in the days before they were properly metalled traffic wore them down, and because each winter the mud used to be shovelled off their surfaces and thrown up at their sides.

No fantastic ideas are necessary to explain road systems. Their common-sense study will often throw light upon local history and problems of the past. No one is better qualified to solve the hidden story of local roads than a well-informed observer living in the district.

We do not know a great deal about farming in this country during the Roman period, and here is an opportunity for some close study of present farms, roads and fields by an interested person who lives on or near one of the country farm estates called villas. I am a great believer in the continuity and evolution of many farms and fields in the countryside, especially in those parts of Britain that, soon after the Roman invasion, settled down to an industrious, peaceful mode of life. The introduction of new implements and new methods of farm-management would, of course, impose changes, but I see no reason to suppose that old arrangements of land and labour would be completely swept away so that a new start could be made. What reason is there to suppose that new Roman owners did not take over farms as they found them, sometimes, very wisely, improving them and altering them to increase efficiency, but certainly not destroying the whole

ROMANS REALLY LIVED HERE

system of management? In the fourth century there was an attempt to increase the output of farms in Britain. There was a ruthless insertion of corn-drying kilns on the country estates, and they were even put in where mosaic floors had to be broken up for the purpose; this suggests some form of government control or pressure at that time.

The Use of Letters

Because we use the same alphabet ourselves, the actual lettering of inscriptions of Roman age on altars, tombs and

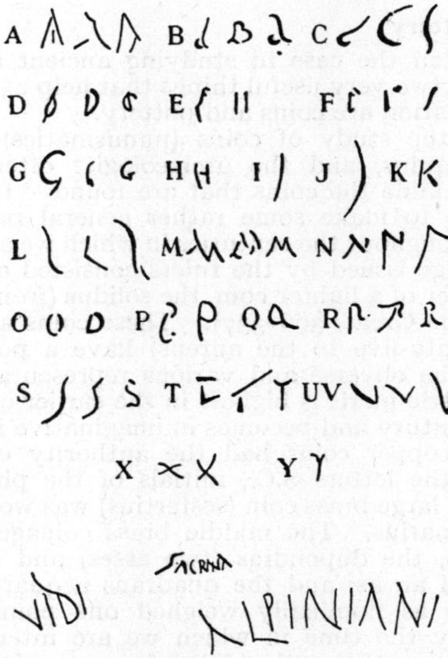

FIG. 74.—The written alphabet of Roman Britain, showing various styles of everyday writing such as we find scratched on fragments of pottery to denote ownership, or idly impressed upon the clay of tiles before baking. The inscriptions *vidi* and *alpiniani* are probably masculine personal names, the former from a rubbish pit of the second century at Canterbury and the latter from a burial near Folkestone. *Sacrina* is a feminine personal name found in a burial at Crundale, Kent.

Kindly compiled for me by Frank Jenkins.

other stones in this country is, generally speaking, easy to make out; but interpretation is somewhat hampered not only by the language difficulty but by the use of many conventional abbreviations which saved space and labour when the inscriptions were cut. However, many of these abbreviations are well known, so that with a little practice they present no further difficulty. Here again, then, we must study as many examples as possible, certainly in books, much better in a museum with examples before us, better still, of course, by handling and examining the stones for ourselves Generally speaking, a high standard of proficiency in lettering is exhibited by such inscriptions. Many Romano-Britons were literate, and this is well illustrated by the large number of inscriptions, called *graffiti*, scratched on potsherds.

Coins and Pottery

As is so often the case in studying ancient sites, for the Roman period two very useful things that help us to determine dates of occupation are coins and pottery.

Of course, the study of coins (numismatics) is a special branch of enquiry, and the archæologist often calls upon experts to examine the coins that are found. It is therefore sufficient here to make some rather general remarks about coinage. Throughout the centuries in which we are interested, the gold coinage issued by the rulers consisted at first of the aureus and later of a lighter coin, the solidus (from the reign of Constantine the Great, 306–337). These coins and the silver denarius (twenty-five to the aureus) have a portrait of the Emperor on the obverse and various representations on the reverse. Artistic merit is highest in the earlier coins, declines in the third century and becomes unimaginative in the fourth.

Brass and copper coins had the authority of the senate indicated by the letters S.C., initials of the phrase *Senatus consulto*. The large brass coin (sestertius) was worth a quarter of a silver denarius. The middle brass coinage was in two denominations, the dupondius (two asses) and the as. The semis was half an as, and the quadrans a quarter of an as. Originally the as nominally weighed one pound of twelve ounces, but by the time in which we are interested it had fallen to one-twenty-fourth of its former weight, and was nominally half an ounce in weight.

The dating of the coins is given after the name of the Emperor by some abbreviation of the phrase *tribunicia potestas* followed by a numeral to indicate the number of (annual) conferments of the tribunician power upon the Emperor, thus indicating the year of his reign.

The dating of pottery takes into account materials, shapes, rims of vessels, potters' marks and patterns and ornament. It is, of course, far beyond the scope of this book to indicate the details of this subject, but it is sufficient to say that with patient study of a large number of examples and with the growth of experience, the archæologist can build up a working acquaintance with a wide range of forms. Very large quantities of broken pottery are found in rubbish pits on Roman sites, and important conclusions as to date are possible upon the examination and study of such fragments.

Large quantities of red glazed ware called by archæologists Samian (or terra sigillata) was imported from Gaul; it looks like red sealing-wax. It is of a high quality, and at first it was moulded, but later on it was often ornamented *en barbotine* (see description of this under Castor ware, below). The potters' marks found upon it form a very long series, and the locations and dates of the factories and dates of the activity of a large number of potters are known.

Of course, there were many other kinds of pottery in use in this country during the Roman period, some native, some from the Continent. Belgic ware was imported; one kind is of a bluish-grey paste with a polished black surface, often with potters' marks.

Another kind of pottery is Upchurch ware. This is so called from its frequent occurrence in the neighbourhood of Upchurch in the Medway marshes of Kent. It is known that this was a local product both from the existence of kilns and the occurrence of spoilt pottery ("wasters"). The ware is black.

Pottery called Castor ware takes its name from Castor in Northamptonshire. This is interesting, not only for its own sake but because we can use it here to illustrate some of the refinements of manufacture. The pottery is of white paste, but it may have clay ornament added to it in a semi-liquid form (hunting scenes and the like) applied to the plain surface of the vessel with a funnel after the modern manner of icing a cake or by the use of a spatula or a brush. The raised pattern is called *barbotine* and this is also seen in the case of Samian ware. After the Castor ware had been treated in this way it was painted all over with a thin layer of slaty-coloured semi-liquid clay-cream. Clay of the consistency of thick cream added in this way either as a general cover or as patterned ornament is called *slip*, and pottery thus treated is *slip-ware*.

Mention may here be made of another variation from ordinary pottery; it is known as *rustic ware*. This was produced with the fingers by pressing them on to moist clay applied to the outside of a vessel and then withdrawing them at right angles to the surface, which, by this means, was pulled out into little projections.

There were pottery kilns in the neighbourhood of Sloden, Hampshire, in the New Forest. The pottery made here included hard reddish-brown ware with a metallic lustre and softer black ware, often with a white slip ornamentation.

If it be asked, "How shall we best recognize these different

Chronology of the Roman Emperors

	48–44 B.C.	Julius Cæsar, Dictator	
	44–31 B.C.	The Second Triumvirate	
	27 B.C.–A.D. 14	Augustus First Emperor	Cunobelin (Cymbeline) about A.D. 5–40, "King of the Britons".
Claudian emperors	A.D. 14–37	Tiberius	
	A.D. 37–41	Caligula	
	A.D. 41–54	Claudius	Aulus Plautius defeated Caractacus and conquered South Britain, A.D. 43. Ostorius Scapula, Governor of Britain, A.D. 47–52.
	A.D. 54–68	Nero	Suetonius Paulinus, Governor of Britain, A.D. 59–62. Boudicca (Boadicea), Queen of the Iceni, d. A.D. 61
	A.D. 68	Galbo	
	A.D. 69	Otho	
	A.D. 69	Vitellius	
Flavian emperors	A.D. 69–79	Vespasian	Agricola, father-in-law of Tacitus, Governor of Britain, A.D. 78–85. He beat the Caledonians at the battle of Mons Graupius, A.D. 84.
	A.D. 79–81	Titus	
	A.D. 81–96	Domitian	
	A.D. 96–98	Nerva	
	A.D. 98–117	Trajan	
	A.D. 117–138	Hadrian	Hadrian's Wall, A.D. 122.
Antonine emperors	A.D. 138–161	Antoninus Pius	Lollius Urbicus, Governor of Britain, built the Antonine Wall, A.D. 142.
	A.D. 161–180	Marcus Aurelius	A.D. 181, mutinies in Britain; attacks by Picts and Caledonians.
	A.D. 180–192	Commodus	
	A.D. 193	Pertinax	
Severan emperors (except Macrinus)	A.D. 193–211	Severus	A.D. 209–210. Campaigns of Severus in Britain.
	A.D. 211–217	Caracalla ("M. Aurelius Antoninus" in inscriptions) and Geta	After the murder of Geta, his name was obliterated from inscriptions by order of his brother Caracalla.
	A.D. 217–218	Macrinus	
	A.D. 218–222	Elagabalus (also called Heliogabalus)	
	A.D. 222–235	Alexander Severus	
	A.D. 235–238	Maximinus	
	A.D. 238	Balbinus	
	A.D. 238	and Pupienus	
	A.D. 238	Gordianus I	
	A.D. 238	and Gordianus II	

ROMANS REALLY LIVED HERE

A.D. 238–244	Gordianus III	
A.D. 244–249	Phillipus I and Phillipus II	
A.D. 247–249		
A.D. 249–251	Decius	
A.D. 251–253	Gallus	
A.D. 253–260	Valerianus	
A.D. 260–268	Gallienus	Many usurpers, called the "Thirty Tyrants," arose in the reign of Gallienus, e.g., Victorinus, Postumus, Tetricus.
A.D. 268–270	Claudius II Gothicus	
A.D. 270–275	Aurelianus	
A.D. 275–276	Tacitus	
A.D. 276–282	Probus	
A.D. 282–283	Carus	
A.D. 283–285	Carinus and Numerianus	
A.D. 284–305	Diocletianus	British "emperors" Carausius (A.D. 287–293), Allectus (A.D. 293–296). Constantius Chlorus slew Allectus A.D. 296. Fifty years of peace follow.
A.D. 286–305	Maximianus	
A.D. 305–306	Constantius Chlorus and Galerius	
A.D. 305–311		
A.D. 306–337	Constantinus I (Constantine the Great)	Christianity becomes the official religion of the Roman state.
A.D. 337–340	Constantinus II	
A.D. 337–350	and Constans	
A.D. 337–361	and Constantinus II	Picts, Scots, Attacotti, and Saxons attack Roman Britain.
A.D. 361–363	Julian the Apostate	
A.D. 363–364	Jovianus	
A.D. 364–375	Valentinianus I	
A.D. 364–378	and Valens (East)	
A.D. 367–383	Gratianus (West)	
A.D. 375–392	Valentinianus II	
A.D. 379–395	Theodosius the Great	Maximus (A.D. 383–388) made emperor in Britain. Civil war and intrigue.
A.D. 392–394	Eugenius (West)	
A.D. 395–408	Arcadius (East)	
A.D. 395–423	and Honorius (West	Stilicho, distinguished general, ruled during the minority of Honorius. Constantine, native "emperor" in Britain.

115

kinds of Roman pottery when we find them?" the answer is that examining and, if possible, handling sufficient examples beforehand will familiarize the student with the characteristics of the different kinds. It will be a poor museum that will not help you with any materials at its command when you are seen to be in earnest. Efficiency comes with practice.

FIG. 75.—Reconstruction of a Roman pottery kiln of the first century at Durovernum Cantiacorum (Canterbury). In order to be able to control the fire, the potter is seen standing in the stoke-hole. This was very large, because much fuel was needed to keep up the fire, which was placed at the entrance of the fire-hole. The heat within the kiln produced a draught, so that the fire was drawn through the furnace-chamber below the oven floor, and then by vertical flues into the oven itself, which was loaded with pottery. From thence the smoke escaped through a hole in the top of the temporary dome built of brickearth on a wicker framework. The dome was specially made to enclose the oven after the pottery had been put in position.

Specially drawn for this work by Frank Jenkins.

So, all over Britain, wherever the land was fully occupied in Roman times, among the relics of that age, products of the potter's art are to be found. Occasionally whole vessels have been preserved, but more usually you will find broken sherds as the only remains of a funerary urn or of some vessel ordinarily used that was shattered in the rough and tumble that still overtake the things we use in cooking and eating every day. Look, then, at such insignificant relics with understanding and try to hear the girl slave say to her mistress as

ROMANS REALLY LIVED HERE 117

she holds up the broken handle of a pitcher, " Decessa est in manu me', Domina!", "It come off in me 'and, Mum!"

Never let these fragments of pottery be mere objects. In your mind's eye fit them into a picture. Imagine them in their original setting; see the potter making them 1,700 years ago; think of them being brought to this country, put into a shop, sold, carried home, used, broken, discarded. Or if a prized piece was unfortunately broken, think of it as being riveted by the same method that we still use today. These long-forgotten scraps then become the means of lighting up a long-distant scene for us and making it real. So the clatter of domestic crockery being handled at the Roman meal rings for us down the centuries.

The Chronology of Roman Pottery in Britain

The principles only of this wide subject can be indicated here. Most Roman pottery was " thrown " on the wheel.

A. " SAMIAN " WARE, or more correctly *Terra sigillata*.

Fabric	Kind	Date	Origin
1. Pottery of good quality in soft yellow paste with friable yellowish-red matt glaze; often ornamented.	Arretine; uncommon in Britain, but widespread. Imported in pre-Roman times.	Late first century B.C.; first century of Christian era.	From Arretium (modern Arezzo, Italy) and other places.
2. Glossy, dark-red or cherry-red hard ware.	Products of southern Gaul; the usual best ware in Britain during the first century.	First century of the Christian era.	From La Graufesenque and other places.
3. Ware yellower than that from southern Gaul.	Products of central Gaul; the usual best ware in Britain during the second century.	From A.D. 40 to A.D. 260.	From Lezoux.

H. Dragendorff (in *Bonner Jahrbücher*, 96, 18-155, 97, 54-163) in 1895 and 1896 classified Samian ware and designated types by numbers which are still in full use and have been supplemented. Reference may be made to Walter's *Catalogue of Roman Pottery . . . in the British Museum*, 1908, and also (and especially) to R. G. Collingwood's *Archæology of Roman Britain*, 1930 (published by Methuen).

B. COARSE POTTERY

No work comparable with that of Dragendorff on Samian ware has been done for the coarse pottery, but it is dealt with by R. G. Collingwood in his *Archæology of Roman Britain*, 1930.

1. *Coarse Pottery from many manufactories*

Mortaria (large bowls for pounding food) and other bowls, dishes, flagons, jars, cheese-presses, wine and oil jars (amphoræ) can often be approximately dated by experts according to their form, and sometimes the name or mark of the potter is stamped on the ware.

2. *Castor Ware*
   Dates from the late second century to the end of the Roman occupation.
3. *New Forest Wares*
   Late third century : light pottery with incised ornament.
   Fourth century :   (i) characteristic hard pottery, with dark metallic surface, often has painted ornament; and
   (ii) rosette-stamped bowls with red surface (inferior imitations of Samian ware).
4. *Crambeck Ware* (*Crambeck is in Yorkshire*)
   Typically buff with ornament in reddish-brown paint, fourth century, particularly after about A.D. 370.
5. *Rusticated Ware*
   Popular in the North from late first century to A.D. 138 (death of Hadrian). Other varieties have been found in southern England.

Classical (i.e., Greek and Roman) Architecture

Classical styles were afterwards copied by the Italian architects of the Renaissance period, beginning in the fifteenth century; and later on their work and the modifications they made spread to other countries and contributed to the design of buildings in the British Isles and elsewhere. It is therefore opportune to make brief reference here to a few matters which influenced the pattern of English buildings as a result of this revival of Greek and Roman talent.

Greek architecture had three important styles or " orders ", the Doric, Ionic and Corinthian (see Fig. 76) each with a characteristic top, or capital, to its columns. The Doric is the earliest of these styles, its column is relatively stout, its typical height being about five times its diameter; the capital is simple. The Ionic style comes next in order of age; in it, the columns are slenderer and the capital has curl-like ornaments called *volutes*. The latest of these orders is the Corinthian, with a tendency to a still slenderer column supporting a capital having ornaments of conventional leaves of a plant called *Acanthus*.

The columns support the superstructure of the building, which is called the entablature. The origin of the various members used in the construction of the earliest existing Greek buildings is unknown, but there is a mixture of tradition and fanciful surmise to account for them. However, it seems certain that Egyptian sources provided some inspiration for Greece's early builders.

The Romans in their buildings adapted the arch, vault and dome from Etruscan sources, features unknown to the Greek styles just mentioned, and combined them with the column and entablature of Greek styles, and it is from the development of this modification of Greek architecture that Rome handed on to Western European builders of the earlier Middle Ages the styles generally comprised in the term Romanesque

ROMANS REALLY LIVED HERE 119

and to which Anglo-Saxon and Norman architecture in Britain owe their inspiration.

The Romans added the Tuscan and Composite orders to those of the Greeks. The Tuscan was a simplified form of the Doric, but it has a base which is absent in the Doric; the

FIG. 76.—The five orders of Classical Architecture. The columns left to right: Doric, Tuscan, Ionic, Corinthian and Composite.

Compiled by S. G. B.-B.

column is not fluted as that of all other orders is; the entablature is plain. In the Composite order the capital combines the features of the capitals of Ionic and Corinthian orders.

The Greeks had little building stone except marble. In Italy there was a wealth of geological materials, and brick and concrete were also used for building purposes by the Romans.

EXERCISE

Subjects for your study include the following: You can examine and draw objects in museums. Visit Roman sites if possible. Study road systems, especially the less-important branches of them. Can you detect probable parts of the local road system which have been degraded to farm roads, tracks and footpaths? Maps will help you (see the book by I. Margary under *Literature*). Roman coinage will interest many. Town-plans are interesting. Some will find pottery, potters' marks and inscriptions fascinating.

LITERATURE

It is an advantage to know the history of Rome and its language (Latin, which was also the language of all scholars in the Western World down to the nineteenth century). No attempt is made here to indicate particulars of the literature of this history and language.

Look at the appropriate references given in the paragraph on Literature at the end of Chapter Two.

A book for general reading on the period is *Roman Britain and the English Settlements*, by R. G. Collingwood and J. N. L. Myres (Oxford: University Press). For an account of the most beautiful silver treasure of the Roman period found in Britain see *The Mildenhall Treasure* (London: British Museum), and for one of the most important remains of the period consult the *Handbook of the Roman Wall*, by J. C. Bruce, revised by I. A. Richmond (Newcastle-on-Tyne: Reid). For pottery consult *An Introduction to Terra Sigillata Treated from a Chronological Standpoint*, by F. Oswald and T. D. Pryce (London: Longmans). Although it deals with a special area, you will find one book very useful in working out the course of hitherto unknown Roman roads; it is *Roman Ways in the Weald*, by I. Margary (London: Phœnix Press).

CHAPTER TWELVE

BRITAIN BECOMES ENGLAND

THE HEATHEN ENGLISH SETTLE HERE

Some account of the English invasion of Britain is given; the grave-goods of the pagan English show us what our heathen ancestors were like.

The Dark Ages

SOMETIMES the period that elapsed between the collapse of Roman power in Britain (shall we say A.D. 420) and the coming of St. Augustine and his companions (A.D. 597) is called "The Dark Ages". Dictionary-makers seem to use the Dark Ages and the Middle Ages (death of King Alfred, A.D. 901, to the death of Chaucer, A.D. 1400) as synonyms; but that does not alter modern usage, and you will find many writers speaking of the "Dark Ages" when they mean A.D. 420–597, or at least when they mean to include that lapse of years within the term. Another term that has been used (somewhat inaccurately as far as length of years is concerned) for A.D. 420–597 is "The Lost Century". At the end of this period one great source of information, the grave-furniture, ceases just as a new vehicle, writing, comes in to give us the records which, at first fragmentary and uncertain, eventually flow on into the full flood of chronicled history.

The Anglo-Saxon Period

The Anglo-Saxon period in England may be said to have begun in A.D. 449 and to have ended 617 years later with the

FIG. 77.—Silver penny of Offa, King of Mercia (A.D. 757–96), imitated from the denarius of continental moneyers. Diameter of original ⁴ inch.

Norman Conquest, a length of time as great as that which separates us from the reign of Edward III (1327–77). When we think of all that has happened since Wat Tyler's rebellion in the next reign (1381) or since the Black Prince won his spurs, it helps us to realize how much opportunity there was in those six hundred years, and more, of Anglo-Saxon influence, for changes in fashion and for developments in the arts of war and peace.

The English Come and Settle

If we want to obtain an idea of the mode of life of those of our remote ancestors whom we generally call the Anglo-Saxons, or the Saxons or, less usually perhaps, the English,

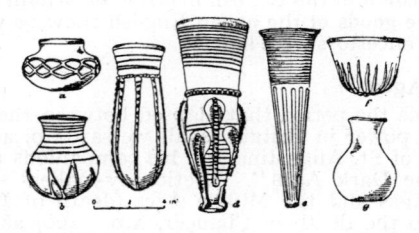

FIG. 78.—Specimens of Anglo-Saxon glass in the collections of the British Museum. Scale in inches, four inches in all.

we have as our principal sources of information goods and chattels that the people used, some of their later buildings and, for the later part of the period, written records.

The Saxons of our history books were fierce Teutonic raiders who swept down upon the coasts of this island in the later years of Roman rule, beginning in the closing years of the third century. At the same time they pillaged the opposite shores of continental Europe. Later on, after A.D. 417, when the Roman rule had gone, they came here, ostensibly to help the Britons to repel other enemies, and then themselves became real invaders and conquerors. Historians have alternated between acceptance and rejection of the story that the Anglo-Saxons had for their great leaders two brothers Hengest and Horsa, who landed in Kent in A.D. 449. Uncertainty exists, not only about names, dates and details in this tradition but also about the exact original homes of the first of our English ancestors who settled in this country in the fifth century. It can, however, be confidently affirmed that they came here rather from northern Germany than from Denmark. However, setting aside all uncertainty, we know that the first of our English forebears who came to Britain were a fierce, cruel and relentless wave of unlettered warriors.

For the purpose of this book we may assume that when, at last, the Teutonic invasion of this country was complete three main groups of immigrants were disposed in the following manner: Angles in the North-east, Midlands and East; Saxons in the South and South-west; Jutes in what are, today, Kent, Hampshire and the Isle of Wight.

The early fifth century was a time of great economic pressure in Europe, and tribes and peoples were much on the move. There was, no doubt, by conquest and migration, considerable intermingling of racial groups, and we must neither think of names like Angles, Saxons and Jutes as indicating races without any admixture of other blood nor of these people as coming from long-settled, clearly defined regions of the Continent. It would also be better to remember that these English came to this country as bands of warriors, united by their piratical purpose or war-like intent and yet probably incorporating numerous small parties of fighting-men who were little related in blood to the main body of the force or to one another. As they had moved about in the racial migrations of the immediate past, these peoples had had an opportunity of modifying their customs and language, their art and industry by the contacts they had thus made. Odd words here and there that have survived in records and in use, the evidences of patterns and styles in pottery and in jewellery, fragments of folk-lore, traces of laws and customs that have come down to our day must be used with caution, and although undue weight must not be given to them, we can certainly regard them like wisps of cloud in a summer sky that tell us which way the wind blows.

We may also assume that numbers of the Celtic inhabitants were slain in the invasions and that others fled to the regions in the west which remained as independent Celtic areas free from Anglo-Saxon rule. But we must also realize that the great bulk of the Celtic population was probably absorbed into the community of the invaders by menial employment and by marriage, and that thus blood relationship and some customs were perpetuated and a slight influence of the Celtic language continued to be felt, as, for example, in the Celtic names of Kentish streams today.

Let it be remembered that Christianity was already established in Britain during the days of Roman rule, and that it still remained the religion of the west, among the Celtic inhabitants, when the east of the country seems entirely to have fallen back to paganism.

Records of the Invasion and the Invaders

Reflection must convince us that to have been such successful invaders, special ability must have distinguished these persistent Teutonic immigrants, who were so rough and uncouth in outward appearance and manners and who still lacked the ennobling influence of the Christian religion. Since they were unlettered, the records of the invasions that have come down to us are not from contemporary Teutonic writings. Moreover, these records are fragmentary, and are liable to give us a general impression from conditions that obtained in a limited locality.

Gildas " the Wise ", a Briton, wrote about A.D. 545; he is naturally prejudiced against the English, enemies of his own race. He paints the sad plight of the people of the region around the Severn, but he does not give us a great deal of reliable history. For contemporary conditions, locally, he is authoritative, and the battle of Mount Badon, which he records, was, no doubt, within the memory of those then living; but for earlier events we must regard his record with suspicion.

The Anglo-Saxon poem *Beowulf*, composed in the north of England about A.D. 550, draws upon events occurring around the Baltic early in the five hundreds (sixth century) nearly a hundred years after the first settlement of the English in England, but it gives us some idea of the mode of life of the leaders among our ancestors. The poem was handed down by word of mouth for about one hundred and fifty years before being committed to writing in the early seven hundreds (eighth century).

Other records of the invasion were made at least two hundred years after it occurred.

The story of Hengest and Horsa is given in the *History of the Britons* written about A.D. 680 and edited by Nennius about A.D. 800. Bede, in his *Ecclesiastical History*, wrote down, about A.D. 730, the traditions of his race. His account does not always tally with the British (Welsh) records. The *Anglo-Saxon Chronicle* was not written up until about A.D. 890, in King Alfred's reign. It takes a good deal from Bede. This is not the place to discuss in detail these early narratives that have come down to us, for they are especially the concern of the historian. Nevertheless, this is the sort of ground on which the archæologist and historian meet.

We should not, of course, slavishly follow any of these ancient writers; we should, however, treat such authors as Bede with respect, and not be too inclined to throw over accounts preserved for our day, of events which were at least twelve hundred years more recent when they were recorded than they are now. Especially where the historian feels uncertain, the wise archæologist will weigh against the written word the evidence of the soil revealed by plough and spade.

Pagan Burials

For the early period of the English settlement in Britain, while our ancestors were still pagan, there is one very important source of information. In different parts of the country there are both individual burials and cemeteries of this date.

Even from the earliest Anglo-Saxon times bodies were buried unburnt in Kent. This practice, called inhumation (Latin, *humus*, " the soil "), was followed by the Jutes. They buried the body fully extended, and it was provided with the things that friends thought would be needed by the deceased in the next world. Elsewhere than in Kent at the beginning of the Anglo-Saxon period interment was preceded by cremation.

The vessel in which the ashes were placed is called a cinerary urn (Latin, *cineris*, " of ashes "). These urns were moulded by hand and not made on a wheel. From their shape and ornament, their style can be traced back to the Continent to the area now called Saxony. A little caution is necessary in the interpretation of this fact. Remember that the presence of Dresden china in a modern English home does not mean that the family came from South-east Germany. It does, however, look as though the folk who used these burial urns in England had either come themselves from Saxony or had had very close relationship, perhaps that of trade, with people who had lived there. Sometimes unburnt objects of domestic use were also placed in the urns with the ashes, but there is rarely any wealth of this kind of material with these burials. Cremation continued in the Midlands and North up to A.D. 600. It gave way to inhumation in the Anglian and Saxon areas of the East, South and South-west.

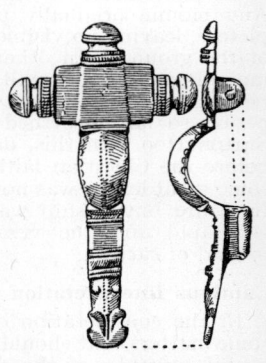

FIG. 79.—Anglo-Saxon long brooch, with side view, from Malton, Cambridgeshire, showing the English tendency to broad, flat forms. About first half of sixth century. Scale ½.

The objects intended, in pagan burials, to be useful to the departed included arms and equipment such as had been used in this life. Though the clothes in which the dead were buried have perished, brooches and other jewellery have survived, often in very good condition. Plain flasks or cups of black or dark-brown pottery were quite usually placed in the graves. It is generally supposed that they originally contained food and drink. In the long list of objects found in Anglo-Saxon graves in England, some may have been made specially for interment, but most of these things were not. Because most of these goods were in daily use by the living as ornaments, weapons or utensils, they throw light upon the tastes and habits of their owners, and are good evidence for the conditions of home life during the period. Often being of local origin, they indicate the skill of English craftsmen at the time. Goods occurring with burials are termed *grave-furniture* by archæologists.

The nature of the grave in Anglo-Saxon times was different in different cases. In many instances the burial was in a cemetery with many others of the same kind, and there was as little disturbance of the ground as in a modern cemetery. Any mound originally present may have disappeared completely, leaving no visible sign of the interment on the surface of the ground. In other cases the burials are marked with mounds or tumuli, small or great, and the form of these may be circular or elongated. The most magnificent burial of the period so far unearthed in England was the ship-burial at Sutton Hoo. In this, dating from the seventh century and before the Christian faith had been accepted in East Anglia, some great leader was not only provided with the usual grave-furniture but a ship was fitted out for him (perhaps as a cenotaph) and the vessel was then covered with a great mound of earth.

Cautious Interpretation

In the consideration of Anglo-Saxon antiquities there are some matters that should be borne in mind; they also serve as useful examples of the caution that ought to be observed in examining relics of ancient times.

1. Roman coins are frequently met with in Anglo-Saxon graves. This coinage had survived the upheaval and was used by early Anglo-Saxon jewellers.

2. Funeral customs were different, at one and the same time, in different parts of the country. The Angles and the Saxons, when they first came to live in this country, cremated their dead and placed the ashes in urns (see page 125). The Jutes, however, as we have seen, did not cremate their dead (see page 125).

3. In days before the Conversion, crosses and cruciform objects were in use and are found in graves; they were probably not derived from Christian sources. But such a subject as Daniel in the lions' den may be found depicted in pre-Christian ornament, because there was an infiltration of Biblical lore into those early pagan communities. Such designs (and perhaps the *history* of Daniel) may have been introduced by traders, a likely source of ideas, as well as of materials, from distant places.

Value of the Commonplace

The rarity of an object found among grave-furniture gives a special thrill to the finder, while the discovery of anything intrinsically valuable results in a wave of popular interest when news of the find appears in the Press. In striking contrast with these thrills and excitement, the trained archæologist realizes that there is a particular value in the occurrence of classes of objects so common in use that they are associated with a high proportion of burials, for it is in this way that familiarity with forms and patterns is attained by the student of the past. By the discovery of large numbers of an object he can compare one example with another and see the

FIG. 80.—Anglo-Saxon gold ring with runes, from Kingmoor, Cumberland. The runes read ÆRÚRIUFLTÚRIURIThONGLÆSTÆPON and (inside) TOL. The meaning is unknown. Scale ⅔.

course of development in form and design over the years, so that he is able to use these features as criteria for dating the finds with which such objects occur. It may be added that broken pieces of a vessel, fragments of an ornament, a spear in the last stages of decay, may be evidence as valuable as perfect specimens in establishing the date of an interment or in providing some clue to the occupation of an early site. It may be that the enquiry in hand will be facilitated by the discovery of charred wood from a fire on a primitive hearth, tiny scraps of pottery, filled-in holes where posts once stood (these postholes mark the position of the supports of a primitive building), oyster-shells or meat bones from an ancient feast.

EXERCISE

It yours is a pre-Conquest place you are well situated to study it. You are on the spot, experts are not. When holes have to be dug examine the stratification, especially if it is on a site long occupied. What layers can you identify?

People will get to know you are interested, and will show you things they discover. Always thank them and tell them anything you *know* about their finds. Explain that nobody can know all the answers, and never be ashamed to say you will refer something doubtful to an expert. Submit it to the curator of the local museum; he, in turn, may need to take further advice. In this way you will: (i) interest other people; (ii) get further specimens from the finders to examine; (iii) add to your knowledge; (iv) add to archæological information about your area.

The local schools may be interested. They might make a model of the place in Anglo-Saxon times.

LITERATURE

For books about the Anglo-Saxon period in Britain see note on Literature at the end of the next chapter.

CHAPTER THIRTEEN

THE ENGLISH CAME TO STAY

THE PERIOD THAT LASTED SIX HUNDRED YEARS

We ought to emphasize the great length of the Anglo-Saxon period. In it great changes were possible, and it covers subjects of absorbing interest. The archæologist still has many problems to solve for us.

Anglo-Saxon Art

AMONG things often found in graves (the so-called *grave-furniture*) of the Anglo-Saxon period are brooches; these were used with the clothing of both sexes. The considerable range of brooches has enabled the development of design and construction to be closely followed, and they are

FIG. 81.   FIG. 82.   FIG. 83.

FIGS. 81-3. FIG. 81.—Bronze-gilt saucer-brooch, from Leighton Buzzard. Scale ½. FIG. 82.—Bronze "applied" brooch, from Fairford, Gloucestershire. Scale ½. FIG. 83.—Cloisonnée "keystone" brooch in silver, from Faversham, Kent. The term "keystone" refers to the shape of the principal garnet settings. Scale ½.

therefore of great value in estimating the approximate dates of interments.

Among their different shapes some are round, some elongate. Of the round brooches the so-called saucer brooch is solid and has a self-explanatory name. It is simply a bronze disc with a curved-up margin, and its flat area in the middle has different ornamental designs in so-called chip-carving (see page 129). The design was cast and then tooled and gilded, and a hinged pin was added at the back, as in many modern brooches. Saucer brooches exhibit designs which are survivals of Roman

128

art: geometrical designs, egg-and-dart, cable patterns, running scrolls and a star. Animal motifs which are typically Teutonic also occur. Another kind of round brooch consists of two pieces, one applied to the other (Fig. 82).

The Anglo-Saxons were influenced, long before they settled here, by an art which came from southern Russia. One of its characteristics was the use of animal forms for ornamentation. Another was a great love of colour effects. Often a patchwork of glass fragments and sliced stones, such as garnets, was applied to a metallic surface in an expanse of very small adjacent shallow metal boxes or cells (French, *cloisons*, hence

FIG. 84.—Bronze plate with lions and "chip carving". This example was obtained in Rome, and is dated about A.D. 400, and shows *animals woven into a pattern,* which was a characteristic of early Teutonic art as distinct from the Classical idea of rendering a representation of the animal—" a portrait rather than a pattern". Scale ⅔.

FIG. 85. — Sword-pommel, from Crundale, Kent, early seventh century. The pair of elongated animals are worked into an interlacing pattern, typical of Teutonic art. Compare this with Fig. 84. Original in the British Museum. Scale ½.

the term *cloisonnée*). Sometimes uncut polished convex fragments of gems (called, in French, *cabochons*) were secured to the flat surface by frames of metal. From this treatment we have the term *en cabochon*.

In England we find the early use of a technique called *chip-carving*, imitated from wood carving, in which the pattern is produced by V-shaped incisions. The chip-carving in this country is characteristic of the first half of the five hundreds (sixth century) and the animal motif remained simple.

There followed fifty years in which animal patterns degenerated; they were applied to flat surfaces without regard to anatomy. The next stage (seventh century), not well represented in England, is fantastic interlacing of the animal form. The silver coin, the *sceatta*,* ornamented with quadrupeds, birds and vine-scroll and other devices, was current from the end of the sixth to the beginning of the eighth century.

With the coming of Christianity cremation entirely ceased,

* Pronounced "scatta".

grave-furniture (see page 121) was no longer needed, but monumental slabs and crosses, some of great beauty, came into use. Moreover, the manuscripts of the Christian Church provided a new field for artistic ability There was much interchange of ideas between monks of different nations, and this resulted in intermingling of styles.

The Vikings

Scandinavian influence was especially important in the British Isles during part of the Anglo-Saxon period, namely from the middle of the eighth to the middle of the eleventh centuries. This influence began in 753 with the sporadic attacks of the Norse and Danish Vikings, and increased until Scandinavian power became so great that we had Danish Kings, Knut (Canute) 1016–35, Harold *the first*, 1035–40, and Hardicanute, 1040–42. In the reign of Knut the whole of Scandinavia and much of Britain were united under the one king.

Vik in the Old Norse language meant " a creek ", and so we may translate *Vikings* to mean " men of the creek ". They were fierce, skilled sea-raiders from Norway and Denmark; their first recorded attack upon our island was earlier than that given in our school-books, which obtain *their* story from the *Anglo-Saxon Chronicle*. As Dr. Gordon Ward has pointed out they raided the Isle of Thanet in the north-east of Kent in 753. We owe our knowledge of this fact to a writer of the fifteenth century called Thomas of Elmham, whose account is authenticated by historical evidence. This raid was evidently unknown to the tenth-century compiler of the *Anglo-Saxon Chronicle* and, because it did not appear in the *Chronicle*, it was not passed on to the early historians. This Viking attack of 753 never seems to have been common knowledge in England from the days when general English histories were first written for use in schools. It is a strange thing to find this general ignorance of the first plundering expedition of the Vikings to England, even in eminent historians (as you will see from reading standard works and the encyclopædias).

If the round towers of Ireland and Scotland built close to monasteries were not actually intended as protections for men and goods against the Vikings, they certainly were of very great service during Viking raids as places of retreat from the predators and for the safety of property.

The round towers are stoutly constructed circular stone buildings about 120 feet high, and when complete are surmounted by a conical roof. One at Glendalough, co. Wicklow, which I saw recently, is in a very good state of preservation.

The first recorded Viking raid on the *West* of England was that of three ships from Hörthaland in the reign of Beorhtric,

King of Wessex (786–802) and, from that time on, the attacks are matters of history.

There are, naturally, Scandinavian burials of the Viking Age in Britain. An old man was interred in a mound on the Isle of Barra, Hebrides. With this burial were two fine tortoise-shaped bronze brooches about four inches long. These are ornamented with a fine design of bosses and interlacing lines, into which run the limbs of a lion-like conventional animal. A bone comb with angular interlacing ornament and an iron comb were found in the same grave, which was surmounted by a standing stone. There was also a sword in the grave. Objects from the interment are preserved in the British Museum.

The Northmen of the early raids were, of course, pagans, and were users of the Runic script, which is dealt with in Chapter Nineteen.

The Anglo-Saxon Pagan Religion

We know that our heathen ancestors worshipped many gods; to take those in order which are commemorated by our names for the days of the week. Sun and Moon need no comment. Tiw, incorporated in Tuesday, also has his name perpetuated in the words Teuton, Dutch and Deutschland (the German name for Germany); he was the traditional ancestor of the Teutonic peoples, a human hero worshipped as a god after his death. Woden was the god of war, corresponding with the Roman Mars. Thor, whose name is preserved in Thursday, was the god of thunder. Friga was the god–goddess of peace and plenty, love and amity. Saeter, often identified with the Roman god Saturn, was perhaps the god of travellers and the god of political unity and of freedom.

There is remarkably little indication of the nature of the worship of these deities by our forebears. One temple in Kent where King Ethelbert (A.D. 560–616) worshipped an idol before he accepted the Christian faith is supposed to have been converted afterwards into the Christian church of St. Pancras, Canterbury. You can still see the building, in ruins, but, of course, we do not know its original pagan form. Perhaps many idols of this time were of wood; they may have been carved to represent deities, but none such are known to us. Not far away from Ethelbert's temple is an uncarved monolith (stone pillar) which may have been the idol the King worshipped.

From Bede we know there was a priesthood and a belief in magic. King Ethelbert received St. Augustine in the open air because he thought magic might be practised upon him if they met in a building. The classical Anglo-Saxon poem *Beowulf* mentions supernatural beings which had bodily form, but these should only be regarded with reserve as part of the religious *belief* of our ancestors; they may have been inventions of the story-teller.

Belief in an after-life is indicated by burial customs (see page 17). The account in *Beowulf* of the last voyage of the warrior King Scyld and the ship burial at Sutton Hoo, Suffolk (see page 126), are examples of rites indicating a very material view of life in the next world. Scyld was sent off to sea in a ship richly provided with costly armour and other splendid treasures.

There is reference to pagan deities in some English placenames, sometimes it is very obvious, in other cases there is doubt about the derivation. Examples about which there can be little doubt are Tuesley (Surrey), from *Tiw*; Woodnesborough (Kent), from *Woden*; Thunderfield (Surrey), from *Thunor*.

Land Tenure and Land Use

As far as the occupation of land is concerned, I picture the invading English taking over the farm-lands of the conquered people as going concerns, often employing the same labour as before and introducing little more than those improvements which in view of their Continental experience they thought expedient. It has often been said that the Britons lived on the heights, while the Anglo-Saxons settled in the valleys. I think that archæology is showing that this is a wrong impression. In some places where Britons occupied high land which became derelict when the English came, their occupational sites have never been inhabited again, nor have their fields ever been turned again by the plough. On the other hand, where the English took over farms and lands and managed them much as they had been managed for years, the cultivation then continued has gone on ever since, and there has been a continuous process of the loss of the evidence of the earliest periods of land-use. Every time land is ploughed, every time farm-buildings are rebuilt or replaced, something of the past is obliterated and, so, lost to future observers. In this way the evidences of British occupation of their sites may have been completely obscured by subsequent continuous use. From time to time, some exceptional circumstance or extremely careful observation may reveal the fact that the long history of the farm has its roots, not in Anglo-Saxon times but in the preceding period. This is where an archæologically minded observer on the spot who notices a sherd of ancient pottery thrown out from a post-hole, or even when digging or ploughing, can add an important quota to the knowledge of his parish history from evidence which an expert at a distance can never hope to see.

THE ENGLISH CAME TO STAY 133

I remember an incident which well illustrates this point. I was standing in a farm-house garden, talking to one of the sons of the house, an Army officer on leave, about some antiquarian subject which interested us both. His father, approaching, overheard some snatches of our conversation, and jokingly remarked that anyone could pick up ancient pottery. Suiting his action to the word, he stooped down and took up a fragment of what I suppose he believed to be a piece of plant-pot. I looked at the sherd, remarked that it was in fact ancient, that I was going the following day to the British Museum and would get my surmise confirmed. The expert at the Museum to whom I submitted it, dated the piece of pottery at about 500 B.C.! The farm-house is close to a river. Roman pottery has been found close at hand, and the land was farmed in Anglo-Saxon times. The parish is mentioned in Domesday Book, and its mediæval and later records form a long and interesting series. So there is continuity for you, and a good archæological lesson.

Writing and Architecture

The archæological story of Anglo-Saxon times is incomplete without reference to the use of the written word (see page 168)

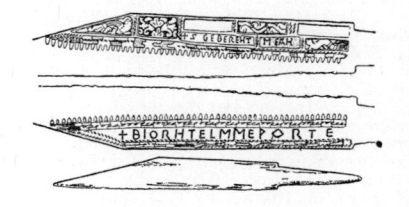

FIG. 86.—Anglo-Saxon Scramasax, or sword-knife, from Sittingbourne, Kent. On the front is inscribed, +S GEBEREHT M EÂH (or ME ÂH), which probably means *Gebereht* (or *Sigebereht*) *owns me*. On the reverse is +BIORHTELM ME WORTE *Biorhtelm made me*. The rune *wen*, which looks like the letter P, is used for W. The date is probably between A.D. 850 and 900. Scales ¼ and ⅛.

and without mention of the churches in timber and stone which were erected in various parts of the country and of the other buildings which were in use at this time (see pages 140 and 153). There may be some documents of pre-Conquest date which mention the town or village where you live (see page 171).

EXERCISE

Your Own Work on Anglo-Saxon Archæology

Make a map of your town and/or parish today, showing Anglo-Saxon features. Then draw a map of your own parish or neighbourhood in Anglo-Saxon times; it may be largely conjectural. Begin with natural features. (Which of these would be exactly the same as they are today?) Indicate water-supply, woodland, supply of building materials (wood, stone). Add roads, the church, principal dwellings, smaller dwellings, farm-buildings. Indicate the arrangement of lands. Were there any industries? (quarries, a pottery kiln). Christian burials were probably around the church; was there a pre-Christian cemetery?

Examine any local antiquities of the period.

A few months' careful study of Anglo-Saxon might suffice, especially if the student already knows German, to obtain a useful working knowledge of this interesting language.

Improve your background of the period by reading as much as possible of the original sources of information—*Beowulf*, Bede, Gildas, Nennius and the *Anglo-Saxon Chronicle*.

It is amazing how few people have read Beowulf, but the other day someone told me he had read it at school before he was fourteen and that was an elementary (primary) school.

LITERATURE

For some points, books recommended at the end of Chapter Two are very valuable.

Beowulf and the Finnesburg Fragment, a translation into modern English prose, by John R. Clark Hall, revised by C. L. Wrenn (London: George Allen and Unwin), is recommended.

For reference *The Arts in Early England*, 6 vols. (1914–1930), by G. Baldwin Brown (London: Murray), will be found useful, and *Anglo-Saxon Jewellery*, by R. F. Jessup (London: Faber, 1950) gives an excellent modern account of some treasures of the period.

A general review is provided by *A History of the Anglo-Saxons*, by R. H. Hodgkin (Oxford: University Press (3rd ed., 1952).

The subject of the Vikings is dealt with briefly in a book long out of print, *The Vikings*, by A. Mawer (Cambridge: University Press, 1913), and fully in *A History of the Vikings*, by T. D. Kendrick (London: Methuen, 1930). Dr. Gordon Ward's paper, to which reference has been made in this chapter, appeared in *Archæologia Cantiana* (the periodic publication of the Kent Archæological Society), Vol. 63 for 1950, pp. 57–62, and is entitled " The Vikings Come to Thanet ". A local study which throws a good deal of light upon the settlement of one of the English tribes in England is *Pre-feudal England: the Jutes*, by J. E. A. Jolliffe (Oxford: University Press, 1933).

The Beginnings of English Society, by Dorothy Whitelock (Harmondsworth, Middlesex: Penguin Books, 1952) is an account of the life and thought of the Anglo-Saxons. A select bibliography (which will be found useful by those who wish to go deeper into the subject) is included.

The Sutton Hoo Ship Burial: A Provisional Guide (London: British Museum, 1947) gives a finely illustrated account of the ship-burial excavated in 1939.

CHAPTER FOURTEEN

THEY KNEW HOW TO BUILD

ARCHITECTURE: ROMANESQUE (ANGLO-SAXON AND NORMAN) AND GOTHIC (EARLY ENGLISH, DECORATED AND PERPENDICULAR)

> Here we have the story of the earlier periods of our architecture (up to 1500). The subject is not so difficult as it is often thought to be. A little concentration will give the student a good working knowledge upon which to build further detail.

Architecture: Why we Begin with Churches

WHEN we come to the question of recognizing styles and dating English ecclesiastical, military and domestic architecture there is one very good reason for beginning with churches: they are well-distributed throughout the country and are therefore available for local study. Having been in continuous use for worship from the day of their erection, perhaps as far back as Norman or even earlier times, they often exhibit a series of styles. Also, for churches there are more general books on the subject of architecture than for other buildings. Again, many churches nowadays have admirable guide-books dealing with the individual building.

The subject is a big one and the technical details complicated, so it is best to begin with very simple matters which will soon help us to get a grip of general principles.

Look first at windows and the principal arches, and get clearly in mind the shapes of these that are typical of each of the post-Conquest styles before 1600. These we can name (and date *approximately*) as follows:

Norman before 1200; Early English 1200–1300; Decorated 1300–1400; Perpendicular 1400–1500; Tudor (Early Renaissance) 1500–1600.

Norman arches are massive and rounded (not pointed). The windows are generally small, consist of one light and have rounded tops—a character which is not met with again until the Later Renaissance which followed the Tudor style.

Early English is the first " Gothic " style, the first pointed style. The arches are still rather massive, though less so than those of the Norman period. The arches are pointed. The windows are single lights pointed and lancet-like (hence they are often called lancet-windows).

Decorated is the second pointed style. In this we begin to have a number of lights included in the same window, each light separated from that adjoining it by an upright stone bar called a mullion. But the mullion does not, in this style, continue straight up to the top of the window, but stops short or rather passes into a design of geometrical or leaf-like stonework which gives that decorated character to the window and the name to the style.

The *Perpendicular* style or third pointed is characterized by windows in which the mullions run right through from the bottom to the top. Decoration of the windows, especially in their upper parts, is often complex.

Tudor. This is a debased style; the tops of windows become depressed. Arches are still pointed, but there is generally a poverty of design, a certain clumsiness and a deterioration of craftsmanship.

One good way to begin the serious study of church architecture is first to familiarize yourself with the main characteristics of the different periods of English architecture and then with a good guide-book in hand to visit one of the great cathedrals which exhibits most of the styles and at your leisure take careful note of the main features of the succeeding styles. I remember that when first I wanted to master the subject, I took Lincoln Cathedral as a building for study, but any of our ancient cathedrals will provide a good deal for you to examine, even if the whole range of styles is not exhibited.

I intend here to give sufficient information to put you on the right track. Your part will then be to visit the cathedral of your choice, to find the dated examples mentioned in your guide-book and to check them against the fundamentals that you have already taught yourself.

Of course, there are other ways of learning the same lesson. You can study in detail some local ancient parish church or a series of ancient churches. For the Anglo-Saxon period, your lessons in the cathedral should be supplemented by visits to one or more of our famous Anglo-Saxon parish churches, such as Bradford-on-Avon in Wiltshire, Sompting in Sussex or Halstead in Essex, to familiarize yourself with this very early style of church architecture.

The earliest parish church in England at present in use is St. Martin's, Canterbury, where Queen Bertha was already worshipping when St. Augustine came to preach Christianity in Kent (A.D. 597). It had been a Christian church in Roman times, but had been in ruins until Ethelbert, King of Kent, gave it to his Christian queen on their marriage. The edifice still retains certain features of Roman architecture, but they are too slight to teach us much about Roman work, beyond

THEY KNEW HOW TO BUILD 137

indicating the exact nature of Roman bricks, which were largely re-used in later building here.

First steps in the study of Roman architecture are difficult to obtain in Great Britain, and only bit by bit can you hope to piece together anything like its complete story. Some indication of how this can be done you will be able to learn from Chapter Ten.

Our Anglo-Saxon ancestors brought in with them from Europe a tradition of building with timber, but later on in this country they began to use stone, and both Anglo-Saxon and Norman church architecture owe their main characteristics, when stone was used, to the persistence of the Roman tradition of building, which was natural when we remember that Christianity came from Rome.

They retained the rounded arch and rounded pillar, and combined them with a simplicity of ground plan in the building of churches.

Mouldings

Much more difficult than the examination of windows and arches is a fascinating subject and a very enlightening one if you wish to become a real expert on architecture; it is the study of mouldings. These are the continuous lines of alternate recesses and projections worked on the edges or surfaces of masonry by cutting away part of the stone. In a book of this compass the question of mouldings cannot be fully considered, but you can teach yourself by proper observation and the use of books specially written about the subject, and we can say here enough to indicate the lines upon which you should work.

It will be well to mention a few terms right away. You will want to make drawings of mouldings as you study them, and a sketch that represents the outlines of the recesses and projections is called a *section* or *profile*. A single hollow or projection is called a *member* or *moulding*; members which fall naturally together are called a *group*. If you stand under an arch and look up you see its underside or undersurface. This is called a *soffit*, and the plane in which it lies is called the *soffit-plane*. It curves down and eventually reaches the ground. The side of the central stone in the same arch is, of course, in the same plane as the wall above the arch; this is the *wall-plane*; it, too, comes down to the ground, by way of the limbs of the arch.

A sharp (right-angled) edge or *arris* between the soffit-plane and the wall-plane may be cut off (or chamfered), generally at 45°, to produce a surface called a *chamfer*. This is the *chamfer plane*.

A Saxon or Norman arch is typically *segmental* (i.e., the

segment of a circle in form), often semicircular, and its simplest form will have a single soffit-plane and a single wall-plane. But often such a structure is not quite so simple, it consists of arches within the main arch, in other words it consists of recesses exhibiting successive soffit- and wall-planes, so that an arch of two or more *orders* is produced. The main arch is one order, each sub-arch is another.

If each arris is chamfered we also have a series of *chamfer-planes*.

Another way of dealing with the arris, instead of chamfering it, is to round it off so that a cylindrical *roll* or *round* (also called a *bowtell*) is produced. Remember, the result is achieved by *cutting stone away*: it is important in studying mouldings to bear this fact in mind: nothing can be *added*. Sometimes small projections called *fillets* are left on or near the roll.

In the projections and recesses of the mouldings masons of the different periods produced a number of forms which help us to date work.

A frequent recess is the *hollow* which may be quite shallow or extend to three-quarters of a circle. If the hollow is extremely wide, as it sometimes is in the Perpendicular style, say four inches or more, with projecting mouldings on either side, it is called a *casement*.

The *quirk* is a small acute channel which is often found between members in moulded work.

The projections are produced by cutting away unwanted stone, and this generally leaves the most prominent part of the projection as a survival of the original surface of the dressed stone. By regarding the successive projections in a moulded feature as part of a surface we can reconstruct for ourselves the original outline of the dressed but unmoulded stone, and in this way, of course, we can identify *soffit-plane*, *wall-plane* and *chamfer-plane*, even in a very elaborately moulded piece of work.

An early member is the *roll-and-fillet*, a flat bead set as a rib on the surface of a cylindrical bowtell.

With the invention of the pointed arch the *pointed bowtell* came in.

An *ogee* is an S-shaped curve in architecture, so when two rolls-and-fillets are conjoined at their bases so that their respective fillets are at right angles to one another the whole feature is called a *double ogee*; it is also called a *double-ressant* or *brace* (a brace is a printer's sign, and this ⌒ is the shape that results). When ogee curves are still further repeated a *compound ogee* or *wave moulding* is produced.

Scroll-moulding is often found in the Decorated style; it owes its name to its likeness to a roll of stout paper in which the visible end of the roll stands off from the inner part so that it is a cylinder with its under half standing back a little behind the upper.

Craftsmanship in Wood and Stone

In the next chapter we shall review, in order, the styles of architecture with which you may meet, especially in parish churches, as you teach yourself archæology. The more magnificent examples you will see in the richer cathedrals and greater monastic churches.

Where features in wood and stone can be compared, similarity in design was followed by contemporary craftsmen. Early woodwork, wherever it occurs, will well repay study; the more architectural features include screens, in which you will often be able to make close comparison with stonework. Fine carved bench ends and misereres (brackets on the undersides of tip-up seats) provided ample scope for the skilled craftsman to express himself in representations of foliage, animals, human figures and heraldic devices. Testers (flat table-like canopies) and other canopies of tombs worked in wood also provided scope for the wood-carver, and some fine examples remain to us from the fourteenth and later centuries; they also reflect the architectural fashion of their day. Being embellishments of elaborate tombs, such canopies are to be regarded as individual expressions of the art of the period to which they belong, and they will often repay lengthy study when you have reached a stage of great proficiency in archæology.

LITERATURE
Will be considered at the end of the next chapter.

CHAPTER FIFTEEN

GLORIOUS BUILDING

ECCLESIASTICAL ARCHITECTURE

This chapter shows how you can recognize the different periods of English architecture. Mason's marks are mentioned.

Anglo-Saxon (before A.D. 1066)

ANGLO-SAXON masonry consists largely of rubble (unworked fragments of stone). Roman bricks are sometimes included. Stone used in an Anglo-Saxon church may have come from a local Roman site and be of Roman workmanship. Ashlar (dressed stone) is often placed alternately flat and on end (this is called long-and-short work); it is used this way in quoins (corner stones) and in the jambs of openings such as doorways. Strips of ashlar embedded in the rubble of walls suggest a survival of a timbered style from earlier days.

Pillars are supported on clumsy blocks of stone, and the impost, or support for the arch above, is a simple rectangular slab, without any moulding (see pages 137–9).

FIG. 87.—Anglo-Saxon belfry-window

Arches are semicircular, and generally without moulding, though there may be rough and coarsely cut moulding, generally semicylindical. Arches may be constructed with tile-like bricks from Roman ruins or with thin stones. Sometimes small openings, such as doors or windows, have pointed heads made with two straight stones placed obliquely on end on the imposts and meeting one another in an angle at the top. Windows are small and if splayed have as much, or nearly as much, splay externally as internally. Windows, especially belfry windows, may be of two lights separated by a pillar and impost, with imposts in the outer jambs. The pillar is often baluster-like (Fig. 87).

Norman (1066–1200)

The Norman style is one of the easiest to recognize by its semi-circular arches, its massive, generally round, pillars and thick walls.

GLORIOUS BUILDING 141

The massive masonry is frequently of rubble with ashlar for vaulting, quoins, jambs and arches and, in cathedrals and other great churches, for external and internal surfaces of the walls as well. There is an absence of "long and short work" which we find in the earlier Anglo-Saxon churches. The Norman tooling of ashlar is characteristic; the stones were dressed with a chopper, and this produced a series of straight and almost parallel lines on the finished work. This tool went out of use at the end of the twelfth century, and if this kind of tooling is seen on ancient masonry we can be sure it was dressed before 1200.

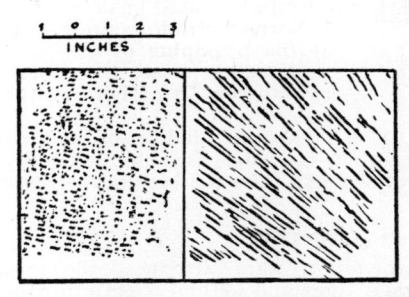

Fig. 88.—Dating masonry by the tooling. The claw, widely used after 1200, made a characteristic kind of tooling throughout the thirteenth century, as seen here on the left. Norman tooling (*right*), produced with a chopper, consists of nearly parallel straight lines. These have a slightly fan-like arrangement, due to the fact that the mason held the stone between his feet and worked the stone by repeated blows with his tool. In Kent in 1200 the chopper was superseded by the claw.

Drawn by S. G. B.-B.

Arches are semicircular. Pillars are round, but some are polygonal. In the Anglo-Saxon style we noted that the member upon which the pillar rests (base) and that which crowned the pillar (impost) were both very crude. The base now consists of two parts, the square plinth standing on the ground and the base mouldings, which fit the pillar to the plinth. The impost is now of dressed stone, and may be merely a simple slab square edged above, perhaps with a shallow groove for ornament cut in its vertical face, which is chamfered below, and the stone is then shaped to fit the pillar upon which it rests, or it may be a quite well-developed capital already showing parts which will be fully described when we come to speak of Early English capitals.

The moulding of the base is usually very slight, and often consists of a concave upper curve and a convex one below.

As mouldings in general in Norman work tend to be few in number, they also tend to be of large proportions. The mouldings are often broken into zigzag lines, which gives a very characteristic appearance. The important moulded surfaces are the soffit- and wall-planes (see page 137), and the chamfer-plane remains unmoulded; in these respects the Norman and Early English styles agree, but, of course, the nature of the mouldings shows differences. Ornament of this period can be studied from a well-illustrated book on architecture.

Norman windows are round headed, and at the beginning of the period were proportionately small, becoming larger in the twelfth century. There is a wide internal splay.

FIG. 89.—Norman window.
Drawn by S. G. B.-B.

Circular windows of the period occur.

Buttresses, when they are used, are generally broad, and do not project as much from the building as those of the later styles.

Early English (1200–1300)

This style of architecture introduced the pointed (Gothic) arch for the first time, and we find it both in arcades (series of

FIG. 90.—Early English single-lancet window.

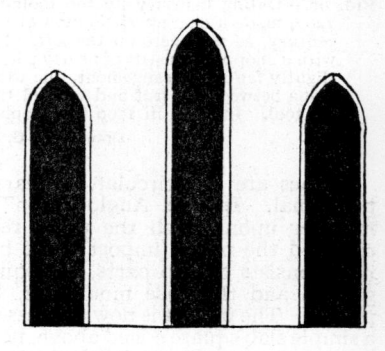

FIG. 91.—Early English triple-lancet window.

Drawn by S. G. B.-B.

arches supported by pillars) and in such openings as windows and doorways.

Masonry generally is lighter than in the Norman period.

The tool used for dressing stone was a claw, and the ashlar often exhibits characteristic parallel bands of tooling, each about a quarter of an inch wide and broken up by the action of the claw into rectangular scars (Fig. 88).

As in the Norman period, the important moulded surfaces are the soffit- and wall-planes, and the chamfer-plane again remains unmoulded. The deep, bold mouldings consist of rounds and fillets and hollows often three-quarter rounds. The result is a strong contrast of light and shade.

Arches are generally lancet shaped (like the blade of a penknife), and the long, narrow windows of one light are used singly or in twos, threes, fives or sevens.

Plain octagonal or circular pillars are usual in smaller churches, but in cathedrals small shafts are often arranged round a large central pillar.

The capital can now be seen to consist of three parts: (1) the *abacus* upon which the arch rests; (2) the *bell*, which is somewhat basin-shaped, becoming narrower below than at the top; and (3) the *neck* just above the column.

The square Norman abacus had a square upper edge. In the Early English style both upper and lower edges of the abacus are rounded, and the whole capital is generally circular, as it is shaped to the column upon which it rests. The abacus often remains plain, but may be strongly undercut by a rounded hollow giving a fine effect of light and shade. The bell may have a double or single set of mouldings, its lower part remaining smooth.

In Early English bases the plinth is square or polygonal, and the mouldings are of two kinds:

> (i) the so-called "water-holding base", consisting of two rolls (rounds) with an intervening downwardly directed hollow, cut in a three-quarter circle, separated from the rounds by fillets;
>
> (ii) two or three spreading rolls without any hollow—when there are three the intermediate one is generally smaller than the others.

In great churches ornament often consists of boldly executed foliage much undercut and rather stiff.

Roofs are high pitched.

Buttresses are often large.

Decorated (1300–1400, end of the Middle Ages)

In the Early English period windows of lancet shape had come to be closely associated with one another, sometimes under a common hood. Between the top of the lancets and the arch of the hood was a plate of masonry, sometimes pierced by a small light.

This led eventually to the development of the Decorated style, in which there was a window of two or more lights separated by mullions. The upper part of the window above the mullions was filled with tracery consisting of circular, triangular and quatrefoil forms. This stage is appropriately termed Geometrical. Later development produced shapes more like foliage: this is called Curvilinear.

English Architecture.

Fig. 92.—Plate tracery. (Transition from Early English to Decorated.)   Fig. 93.—Bar tracery (Decorated).   Fig. 94.—Tracery with soffit cusps (Decorated).

From *English Church Architecture*, by W. H. Riley.

The window arches tend to become flatter as the style develops, and some window heads are quite flat.

There are circular windows in this style.

A weather moulding generally occurs over windows and other openings and, even in country churches, may be terminated in foliage or the carving of human heads.

In addition to the forms of moulding already mentioned, there is an additional kind found already at the end of the Early English period, but generally regarded as especially characteristic of the Decorated style. It is the scroll moulding. It is cylindrical, but the lower half of the cylinder is slightly withdrawn behind the upper half. Also fillets tend to be broader in Decorated work than in earlier styles. Mouldings may occur on any of the three planes, soffit, wall or chamfer, and are not so large as in previous styles, and therefore the members tend to be more numerous, and they are very varied. Decorated moulding is not so deeply cut as that of the Early English style.

In great churches pillars are elaborate with clustered engaged shafts, but in less ornate churches the pillars are octagonal or circular. Capitals and bases (including the plinth) commonly conform to the shape of the pillar. The abacus has the scroll moulding. The bell seldom has double mouldings. The neck generally has scroll moulding. Decorated bases are often stilted, that is, they are raised above the floor, the plinth being divided into stages.

Equilateral, lancet or drop arches occur, which means that they may be formed on equilateral, acute-angled or obtuse-angled triangles.

Ornament of the Decorated style includes beautifully and naturally carved foliage.

Buttresses are generally constructed in stages, and often have carved decoration.

Perpendicular (1400–1500)

As the name denotes, long vertical lines in windows and mouldings are very noticeable features of this style. The mouldings are shallow and often widely spread.

At the end of the fourteenth century the tracery of windows began to take on a simpler form, and the mullions were run up vertically to the tops of the windows. Window heads, when arched, became flatter, and transoms (cross-bars) were often introduced into windows.

Some of the change was no doubt due to the rising cost of labour, but very beautiful work resulted.

At the end of the period the characteristic English feature of fan vaulting was developed in the more important buildings.

There is a rectangular arrangement of the mouldings over doorways so that a spandrel (a nearly triangular corner space) is produced on each side above the arch, and this is generally decorated.

Panelling of the walls is usual in large churches, both internally and externally.

The four-centred arch is in general use in Perpendicular architecture.

Pillars in the Perpendicular style exhibit considerable diversity. They are often oblong or parallelogramic in plan, with the long direction north and south. A plain octagonal pillar may also be found. The bases of Perpendicular columns are also found to have great variety. There is usually a bell-shaped spread in the upper part, and this often rests on a cushion-like member. The plinth, which is usually octagonal, whether the upper part of the base is or not, is formed by graduated stages.

Perpendicular capitals are generally plain, the neck being of the same form as the pillar. If the pillar is round, the neck will be the same, and perhaps also the moulding above it, and yet the rest of the capital may be octagonal. Sometimes the capital is entirely absent, and the mouldings of the pillars are

ENGLISH ARCHITECTURE.

FIG. 95.—Decorated window, Merton College, Oxford.

FIG. 96.—Decorated window, St. Mary Magdalen, Oxford.

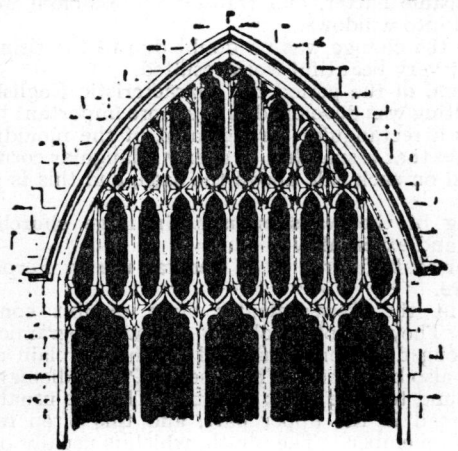

FIG. 97.—Perpendicular window, Swinbrook Church, Oxfordshire.
From *English Church Architecture*, by W. H. Riley.

uninterruptedly continued into the arch above. In any case, the typical shallow mouldings are sufficient to indicate the style. Sometimes the moulding of an arch includes a very broad, deep hollow, called a casement. Most of the moulding is on the chamfer-plane.

Early Renaissance (1500-1600)

Italian influence began to make itself felt in the sixteenth century. Italian architecture had developed from the Roman, and had been very little influenced by the Gothic styles, which had evolved not only in England but also on the Continent of Europe. In our churches it is particularly noticeable in the classical designs which begin to be used for monuments.

As far as church buildings are concerned, the tops of windows become much flattened, and there is less delicacy in the general design. There is a tendency for the stonework to become heavier or clumsier or, as we say, debased.

After the Reformation building almost ceased for a time, and it is only in alterations and repairs and in tombs and monuments that much workmanship of the later sixteenth and earlier seventeenth centuries is to be found.

Later Renaissance (1600-1700)

In the church building of the seventeenth century the full influence of classical models was felt. Already in the reign of Charles I, Inigo Jones had designed the Church of St. Paul, Covent Garden, on a Roman model. Reconstruction after the Great Fire of London in 1666 provided an opportunity for the exercise of the talents of Sir Christopher Wren, who designed more than fifty London city churches to take the place of those that had been burnt. The greatest of them all, of course, is St. Paul's Cathedral. The study of the work of the great architect Andrea Palladio (1518-80), the recognized Italian authority on the revived classical style, established much more rigid standards for architectural design in England.

Georgian (1700-1800)

George I came to the throne in 1714, but the architecture of the eighteenth century is generally described as Georgian, although Queen Anne lived on into the second decade of the century and George IV did not die till 1830. In the eighteenth century the classical styles imposed by the circumstances and tastes of the latter part of the seventeenth century had become established. A well-known church of the Georgian style is that of St. Martin-in-the-Fields, Trafalgar Square (1722). Birmingham Cathedral was built as a parish church between 1711 and 1719.

The classical forms are now dominant, and Gothic styles are, of course, entirely forgotten. It is a complete victory for the invading style from Italy.

The Return of Gothic (1800–1900)

At the beginning of the nineteenth century the Classical styles were supreme, and St. Pancras Church, London (1819–22), is an example built upon Greek designs, but in 1820 St. Luke's Church, Chelsea, built upon Classical models, incorporated Gothic details, and from that time on the two styles were followed, side by side, by a succession of distinguished architects of the Classical and Gothic schools respectively. It has been called the Battle of the Styles.

From the middle of the century many churches were built in the revived Gothic style. This is especially true of towns where the population was rapidly increasing, but it is seen also in the country.

Contemporary (Without Systematized Style) 1901 Onwards

The present century has been able to use the experience of past failures and successes. The great work of Liverpool Cathedral uses the Gothic tradition without slavish attention to detail, and this is, perhaps, an indication of the freedom of design which has been won by the experiments of the nineteenth century.

Architects are free to design churches in accordance with the needs of the parishes, and new materials, especially concrete, are now available for use. There is a tendency towards boldness in design and a restrained use of ornament.

Masons' Banker-marks

You will sometimes see cut on the surface of a stone in an ancient building, a clear, well-executed, simple design, such as a triangle surmounted by a cross, or an arrow, or one of the letters of the alphabet, or a bell, or indeed one of hundreds of incised figures. These were cut by the stonemasons at their benches (or banks) to identify their work, and are called Masons' Marks or more correctly Banker-marks. Mr. Charles C. Elam of Canterbury has collected hundreds of different marks in Canterbury Cathedral alone. Salzman, in *Building in England down to 1540*, illustrates a bargain for the purchase of stone in 1536 attested " with three masons' banker-marks in place of signatures or seals ".

The marks are interesting enough, but are of little use for dating; for example, the same mark, "a dumb-bell" or double triangle, ⋈ (which is the latest face mark known to Mr. Salzman, dating from 1630) occurs in Canterbury Cathedral

GLORIOUS BUILDING 149

repeatedly, and at approximately the following dates: 1096, 1100, 1166, 1175, 1180, in the period 1184–1220, 1405, 1423,

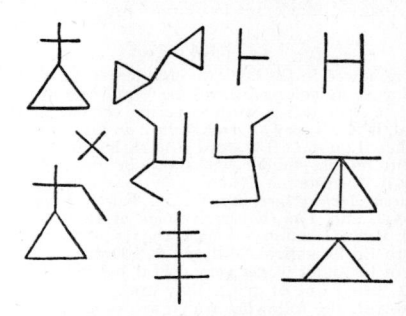

FIG. 98.—Masons' marks. Banker-marks, i.e., marks made on the bank or bench, Biddenden Church, Kent.

Drawn by S. G. B.-B.

1439, 1448 and 1500. Mr. Elam tells me that in Canterbury Cathedral there are a few types of marks which occur only at certain dates:

Bow and Arrow . . 11th–12th centuries
Pennants . . . 12th–13th centuries
Halberds . . . 13th–14th or 15th centuries

Marks that are closely similar, occurring on the same work, Mr. Elam thinks, were those of people either related in blood or of two men working on the same job together.

Banker-marks are known on the face of stones almost throughout the whole period of English masonry, certainly from 1090, or so, to 1630, but when they are used today they are generally put on the bed of the stone so as not to be seen as a disfiguration when the work is finished.

Since the marks were put on the stones on the bench, the same mark may occur upright, sideways or upside down.

EXERCISE

Make your own note-book of architecture. Begin with easy features. You can make your first drawings from books, but aim to see and draw (however poor an artist you may be) the different features from actual buildings. Window openings are best to begin with. At first draw only *typical* examples. Difficult cases will come later; they are very interesting, but they are too puzzling and discouraging for the beginner.

When you have mastered the first principles go on to more advanced stages, the shapes of pillars, the nature of mouldings (this is most fascinating). At first avoid cases that do not seem typical; tackle them when you understand the usual forms well.

Look out for banker-marks made by masons.

LITERATURE

The subject reviewed in the last two chapters has a vast literature. The articles in the larger encyclopædias will be found useful. A comprehensive, well-illustrated, authoritative work covering secular architecture, as well as ecclesiastical, is *A History of Architecture on the Comparative Method*, by Banister Fletcher (London : Batsford (the 14th edition appeared in 1948)). Among many interesting smaller works may be mentioned *How to Study an Old Church*, by A. Needham.

English Church Architecture, by W. H. Riley (London : Hodder and Stoughton, 1951), and *The Observer's Book of British Architecture*, by J. Penoyre and M. Ryan (London: Warne, 1951). Although a small book, the latter deals with Ecclesiastical, Military and Domestic Architecture.

I find many of the older works very useful, especially those that are well illustrated, but, being out of print, they are generally difficult to obtain. I mention, however, the following which are sometimes to be seen offered by second-hand booksellers :

A Glossary of Terms used in Grecian, Roman, Italian and Gothic Architecture (Oxford : Parker). (This work was first published in 1836. Later editions were enlarged.)

A Manual of Gothic Mouldings, by F. A. Paley (5th ed. revised by W. M. Fawcett) (London : Gurney and Jackson, 1891).

CHAPTER SIXTEEN

MAN MUST HAVE A HOME

EARLY DOMESTIC BUILDINGS (UP TO THE FOURTEENTH CENTURY)

Domestic architecture is a more difficult subject than ecclesiastical architecture, but you will see here that with a little application you can fit yourself to make valuable original observations.

Man Must Have a Home

WE conjecture what the homes of Palæolithic men were like. It is often said in a general sort of way that these remote inhabitants of our country lived in caves. Perhaps some of them did, permanently; but this was, of course, only possible in certain areas, especially in limestone districts,

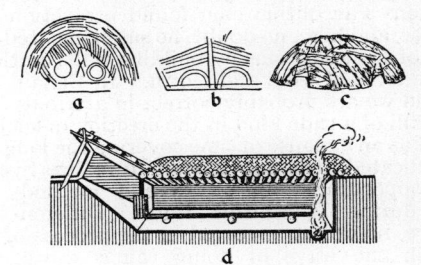

FIG. 99.—Palæolithic dwellings.

a, b, Magdalenian paintings of summer huts (?), Font-de-Gaume (Dordogne). Scale $\frac{1}{24}$.

After Breuil.

c, Communal bark-roof hut of aborigines, North Queensland; height 7 feet.

After D. F. Thomson.

d, Reconstructed section of underground dwelling (rectangular pit, length, about 30 feet, roofed with logs and earth); Upper Palæolithic, Timonovka, Russia.

After Gorodzov.

From *Man the Toolmaker*, by Kenneth P. Oakley.

where natural caves frequently abound. It seems likely that caves might be used only seasonally or temporarily in times of stress or perhaps on hunting expeditions, at least in some parts of the country. It must also be borne in mind that we are speaking of the whole Palæolithic period, an almost incredible expanse of time, not less than five thousand *centuries*, perhaps a great many more; while the whole of man's existence upon the earth since has totalled no more than some 200 centuries, so that any general statement that we make on this subject must indeed be an extremely broad generalization.

In any case, we can be fairly certain that the homes of Early Man were simple constructions in which the materials locally available determined, then as always, most of the characteristics of their primitive building. However temporary cave dwelling may have been, it provides us, at least for the later part of the period, with useful information about the contemporary fauna. The bones of animals now extinct are found associated with Man's rude stone implements, and some caves on the Continent provide, through wall paintings of surprising merit, records of the animals that he met with near his home. (See Fig. 12, page 40.)

From the discovery of implements we are also able to attribute certain rock-shelters, open-air sites protected by natural rock walls, to this remote period of Man's prehistory. In such situations Palæolithic men found protection from inclement weather, and here, no doubt, he supplemented the natural advantages of such positions by building walls on the open side to break the force of wind and storm. In Britain the climate was cold, and we are probably correct in attributing gradually increasing skill of a rude kind in the erection of such dwellings.

Looked at as an expanse of time covering the long period that has been indicated, it is not difficult to realize that there was plenty of opportunity for styles and methods to change repeatedly during Palæolithic times. Different races and cultures were, no doubt, involved in the process of advance in ideas and in the ways of doing things during the whole Palæolithic period and in the Mesolithic times which followed. Man was not yet a farmer, and his mode of life was to some extent responsible for less-permanent homes than are needed by people whose preoccupation with the soil increasingly binds them to a settled life where crops can be won by close attention to the cultivation of a plot of land. As we turn this over in our minds we shall teach ourselves how little we ought to expect that we can really generalize (as we so often do) for the different races represented and for the different geographical and climatic conditions involved, especially in view of the different heights of skill attained by Man during the vastness of Palæolithic and Mesolithic times.

Neolithic Homes

The association of Neolithic implements with dwelling-sites enables us to assert that while some Neolithic peoples lived rather like the present-day Sea-Dyaks of Borneo, others had a village life of hut dwellings comparable with East African villages in the present century. Moreover, there is sufficient evidence to show that the round huts of Neolithic Man in Britain, grouped to form the village, differed very little in general form from those of the peoples that followed right down to the coming of the Romans.

Romans Brought New Standards of Building

When the Romans swept into this country as conquerors in the middle of the first century of the Christian era they brought with them methods of home-making already known to those inhabitants of Britain that had crossed and recrossed the Channel as traders, or messengers from tribal leaders and councils, to their kinsmen and friends on the opposite shore. In Gaul, where the Roman rule had long made itself felt, these travellers from our island had, no doubt, been impressed by the well-constructed homes, shops and public buildings of Roman towns, and already to some extent this knowledge had influenced the tastes of those from this country who had experienced the comfort and comparative luxury of this Roman way of life. Be that as it may, the establishment of Roman control over the country was accompanied by the building of homes that brought a completely new standard of construction into the country. It was the imposition of something never before seen here, a complete break with the past. These things were, at first, for the conquerors and their dependants alone, but it cannot have been long before the most highly placed Britons began to copy the methods of their conquerors.

This influence was important until the sudden break of political and military contact between Rome and Britain in the fifth century.

The Englishman's Home

When the English came soon after Roman influence was withdrawn, they brought with them from north-west Europe ideas that were entirely alien to all that Rome has given to this country. They neither understood nor cared for the high standards of domestic architecture that had been attained here during the Roman period.

In the latter part of the fifth century complete ruin, resulting from violence or neglect, had evidently overtaken large places—it is certainly true of Canterbury, for example—and when in later Anglo-Saxon times building was resumed, ignorance of the original Roman layout of the town might be sufficient (as it was at Canterbury) to result in the new streets having a different alignment from those of the forgotten

Roman city over whose dust and rubble the English might erect dwellings five feet or so above the Roman foundations.

From literary sources, and especially from *Beowulf*, the Old English poem which every Englishman should know, we can picture the kind of home in which the nobility lived. Here and there in England, barns of the fifteenth century have come down to us, wonderfully preserved; students of the Anglo-Saxon period are agreed that these wonderful old timber structures preserve for us the kind of building used by great Anglo-Saxon notables, from the earliest days of the English invasion in the fifth century, as household halls, where the lord with his family and retainers lived. No doubt they spent

Fig. 100.—Interior of a typical English barn, built at Godmersham, Kent, in or about 1486, on principles that had been in use from Anglo-Saxon times. Drawn by Sydney E. Castle, F.R.I.B.A.

most of their time out of doors, but here they ate and drank, here they feasted and entertained their friends, here, in poem and song, were recited records of the prowess of bygone days and the stories of the heroes of their race. It was a rough life but it had its compensations, at least for a fortunate few. More than one authoritative modern book seeks to give an impression of the household hall of an Anglo-Saxon noble by depicting the fine and large rectorial tithe-barn, new in 1486, which still stands in the parish where I write these words. If the great houses of Anglo-Saxon leaders really were like fifteenth-century barns, being built of wood, they were no doubt replaced in later times by stone buildings, probably upon a closely adjacent site a little farther from the parish church, for the original building in wood would most likely immediately adjoin the churchyard. This is one of the things to be investigated by archæologists in the future, and most intriguing problems are presented by our present scanty knowledge of these early homes. The common people, outside the circle of the greater lords and their families, lived in insignificant dwellings about which a little more will be said later, page 163. They often worked hard on the land. It is always easier to picture the conditions of the rich than those of the poor in ancient times, because the stouter construction and better workmanship of the wealthy man's possessions have more frequently resulted in survival; incidentally, for the same reason, it is possible to form an entirely wrong and much-exaggerated opinion of the excellence of the achievements of past generations, because the best of their possessions have stood the greatest chance of survival for our admiration, while work of inferior materials and poorer craftsmanship have generally perished. So right down the centuries, beside the better work that is known to us from the relics that time has spared, we must imagine that there have been huts and hovels in the country, and perhaps just outside the cities, which have left little trace of their widespread existence. The cities themselves were too well planned to have slums in very early times: they came later.

Castles

The general conditions of life in the country and the organization of local society at any particular period determine the form, strength and situation of the dwellings of the principal inhabitants and the way in which their immediate dependants and their neighbours are grouped near them or dispersed in the district.

In the earliest times caves and earthworks provided protection in times of local or national danger, and when the Romans came to Britain those were the conditions for defence that they found among the inhabitants. The Romans brought a new organization, and the country became dominated within and protected along its boundaries against any enemies outside by military and naval power. Wherever necessary, strong garrison towns were brought into being, and for nearly four hundred years such centres of military organization were to be found wherever there were frontiers to be defended. Such towns were naturally established in strategic positions; their characteristics were determined by the system of government, and they were, naturally, strong points for the control of the civilian population of the area. In neighbourhoods of peaceful development town-planning took place in the first and second centuries after the Roman invasion, and the street-plan of civilian towns was set out and gradually developed. At the beginning of the third century of the Christian era alarm began to fill the minds of the authorities; they feared for the safety of their urban populations, and so the principal places, even those remote from the areas of disaffection, were encircled by protective walls and, at least to this extent, became strong points. That this fortification was rather hurriedly undertaken may be inferred from the fact that only those parts of towns and cities that had been built up and developed were enclosed by the walls; adjustments of roads were sometimes necessary, and the results were not as orderly as many of us would envisage in thinking about Roman precision and the geometrical exactitude that is to be seen in the plan of Roman military stations.

When at last the military domination of Rome came to an end through the pressure of the northern barbarians upon the Empire and the consequent removal from Britain of the Roman legions, there was no intentional break of relationship between Rome and this country. Thus, no doubt at the beginning of that obscurity which began about A.D. 420 and lasted until A.D. 597, the ordinary men and women of Britain still felt they were Romans and had some pride in their status.

When the English came in the middle of the fifth century they no doubt brought with them features of their own Continental civil administration and laws. How far these importations were influenced and modified by the survival of customs and legal forms from Roman times, both on the Continent and here, we can only surmise. There was no written language in the country at that time, so we have no record to which we can turn. Later on, there was obvious Roman influence in the English institutions, but perhaps all or nearly all of this arose from the mission of Saint Augustine and his fellow monks which arrived in this country in A.D. 597. In the years that followed we find, for example, that the Roman rule of burying the dead outside the cities was observed: this was probably a re-introduction with the Christian missionaries from Rome and not a survival through the Romano-British inhabitants of the late fifth and the sixth centuries.

In this country building in stone during the Anglo-Saxon period was influenced by Roman architecture, and the same was true on the Continent for the builders in Normandy. Thus when Norman architecture was introduced into this country in the eleventh century it bore very strongly the marks of its classical origin, especially in the form of its arches and vaulting and in the details of its ornament. The shape and form of churches sprang from the same origin.

But to go back again to the fifth century, as we ought, the end of the dominance of the central authority of Rome led to the break-up of the community in Britain into small local units not unlike the old tribal organizations of pre-Roman times, and we know from subsequent history how weak it rendered the inhabitants and how prone they became to attack from without. The English (Anglo-Saxons, if you care to call them that), when they came, were a warlike people, but they were subjected to external pressure and, at long last, after six hundred years of development in this country they were overcome by military power from without in the best-known year of English history, 1066. Then were established, once more, dominating centres of great armed strength, comparable in function with the Roman garrison towns. These armed centres were the Castles, which gave new security to the nation, now organized under the feudal system introduced from the Continent by William the Conqueror and adapted by him to the special needs of his new realm.

Never again has England been successfully attacked by a Continental power in nearly nine hundred years.

Castles secured internal order in the country, and they were obviously very necessary for the subjugation of the English after the Norman invasion. But they were not only fortresses, they soon became homes. In many ways they were inconvenient as homes and not very comfortable; nevertheless, they had to serve as homes to meet the war-like hazards of that age.

There is more, historically speaking, in the saying that " an Englishman's home is his castle " than the usual recognition of our right to live our private lives free from outside interference, for in the castle we have a stage in which the military leader's home had to be incorporated into a stronghold. What we see of domestic arrangements in the central building of the castle, generally called the *Keep* by modern writers, was a modification for purposes of defence of the houses of Anglo-Saxon and early Norman days. Although the form of the *hall* in the keep tells us what Norman homes were like, this situation in the vertical building was of the nature of a temporary expedient born of the warlike nature of the times.

It is true only in a limited sense to say that the great mansions of the nineteenth, eighteenth and even earlier centuries, but also the humblest of modern English houses, are direct descendants of the mediæval castle. Perhaps it would be better to say that the castle was a temporary offshoot from the main line of descent followed by Man's home in its development from the Anglo-Saxon hall down to the lobbied suburban house of the twentieth century.

What were castles like ?

They began as strong points which could be defended, and they were places from which attacks could be made upon the enemy. In their simplest form they were towers, often of wood, built upon natural or artificial rising ground. A mount might be thrown up for the purpose (it was called a *motte*), but it would, naturally, not be a very large earthwork. The precincts of such a castle, called the *bailey*, could be protected by a timbered palisade.

The hastily constructed castle of this kind served its purpose during the heat of war, but when subjugation and supervision of a district was necessary afterwards, a more permanent structure had to be built. This consisted of a series of protective earthworks and protective curtain walls enclosing a bailey of sufficient area to accommodate both the personnel and stores required to exercise effective surveillance over the neighbourhood and to withstand attack by any enemy advancing into the district. The numerous buildings within the protecting walls were arranged according to the requirements and ability of its military commander.

The *donjon* (now usually called the keep) was a tower of several storeys. The living-room was the hall. Above it and below it were other rooms required for the business of defence and for sleeping.

The other buildings of the castle and the curtain walls around the whole enclosure were important in their way, but the keep remained the home of the family. As soon as military conditions allowed it, a real house was again built. This contained the hall, which was not only found as the principal room in the keep but had also been the outstanding feature of the house that preceded the castle. When the time came for building a home with dwelling accommodation on the ground floor, the house was generally erected within the castle precincts. Now, as before, the hall, for eating and sleeping, was the main part of the dwelling.

In the wealthy Englishman's home of the thirteenth century there was usually a haphazard arrangement of the auxiliary rooms, many of them as separate buildings. This seems to have resulted from the fact that in the twelfth century there had been plenty of space within castle walls for numerous buildings to meet the different needs of the inhabitants, and there had been no compelling circumstance to set up a rigid plan for the disposition of these buildings in any particular order. In the new homes of the thirteenth century the former irregular disposition of the accommodation was instinctively followed, and the different rooms or buildings were placed as seemed most convenient at the time. But the hall was the essential building.

As a result of experience a greater regularity of arrangement evolved, and by the fourteenth century there is usually a well-defined lofty hall in the middle of the house, with most of the other rooms forming wings at either end. Cooking was recognized as dangerous, for fat is especially liable to take fire and blaze up, so kitchens were normally kept apart from the main building, especially in the case of timber-framed houses, which were very usual in well-wooded parts of the country, especially if stone was not readily available. The fire for heating the house was built upon a stone hearth in the middle of the hall, and smoke escaped through a hole near the centre of the roof. So there was no other fire-place and no chimney.

The protecting wall around the whole area of occupation was retained as long as foes from outside were any real threat to the peace and welfare of those who lived in the house. Entrance to the precincts was obtained through a gatehouse, and the great doorway was closed by strong doors, while foot-passengers could be admitted through a small (postern) gate at the side of the main gateway or by opening a small hinged section in the main door. Outside the wall there was often a moat, in which case a bridge had to be provided opposite the gatehouse. The bridge could be hauled up from within. Additional protection was often provided by a metal grille called a portcullis, which could be let down in front of the gate. From a projecting platform over the entrance, and especially through holes in its floor, men inside the gatehouse could drop missiles and molten metal upon anyone making a determined assault on the entrance.

EXERCISE

The Homes of the Ancient Past

As you teach yourself archæology you can get an excellent picture of the disposition of the homes of the people fifteen hundred years ago, or for that matter a thousand years or five centuries ago. Go out from city or town to some unspoiled spot in the countryside. If you live there, all the better; close your eyes, as it were, to the modernity of buildings in your neighbourhood, obliterate from your mind the mechanization of agriculture and bring back into the picture the primitive wagon and the eight-ox plough. Replace the modern highway's sharp outlines by the irregular margins of an ill-surfaced, stony road. But keep in the picture the wandering stream, the alternation of woodland and pasture; retain the meadow and the waste. Unless some great development has taken place since Roman times, say the establishment of a port or the building of a monastery, and disregarding the construction of a canal or railway or the building of an arterial road where once all was undisturbed farmland, the present farms are not unlikely to be the sites of prehistoric holdings. Why not? For good soil has always been the best place for productive arable, and our early ancestors were not without a discerning eye! The roads that lead today from farm to farm served an ancient purpose, and we are not unlikely to be able to form a good impression of the disposition of the homes of our fifth-, tenth- or fifteenth-century forerunners by this process of blurring the modern detail and modifying the landscape of our own time, only by those means that I have indicated.

Draw sketch maps to indicate your conclusions.

LITERATURE

For notes on books, see end of next chapter.

CHAPTER SEVENTEEN

CHANGES FOR THE BETTER

HOUSES ATTAIN GREATER COMFORT (FROM THE FOURTEENTH CENTURY ONWARDS)

There is great variety in domestic architecture, due to differences of materials used and to the different social positions of the people whose homes we study. There is great opportunity here for local observation and research.

The Story of the Hall

By the end of the fourteenth century the hall-house (that is to say the house in which the hall we have mentioned was the most prominent architectural feature) was well established as an English type of home. The hall itself was much what it had been in the castle or indeed as it had been in the old Anglo-Saxon days. At one end was the raised platform or dais for the family. Below, on the floor of the hall, were the tables for the retainers. In the centre of the hall was the stone hearth. The windows were like those of the churches of the period. Two doors opened into the hall, one at the front of the house, one at the back; there was a passage-way between them across the end of the hall remote from the dais and its high table. This passage was hidden from view of the family by a wooden screen running across the hall. The screen was pierced by doors, so that, though there was ready access and much coming and going, those within were sheltered to a great extent from the draughts which the main doorways behind the screen admitted. In such a hall there was little privacy, and the principal evolution that took place in the fourteenth and fifteenth centuries was towards greater comfort and more seclusion of the family and an increase of privacy for members of the household. The principal room to which the family could retire was typically placed as a second storey over the room adjacent to the dais-end of the hall. In addition to external windows it generally had one that opened into the hall, so that those below were under the eye and control of the family. The sleeping-quarters of the servants were either in the hall itself or at the end of the house opposite to that occupied by the family. Since the hall with its upper part reaching to the roof intervened, there was no internal communication between the upper storeys at the two ends of the house (Fig. 101).

CHANGES FOR THE BETTER

As years passed, an increasing amount of accommodation was provided outside the hall-house, and eventually many of the servants became more and more detached from the common life of lord and retainers, and many of them were accommodated in homes of their own, separate from the manor house. Then there were fewer people to feed in the hall, and so it became less important. As the years passed modifications of the original arrangement were made. One change

FIG. 101.—House at Shorne, Kent, as it was when first built. Reconstruction by Mr. R. W. Schultz. This is a "hall" house. In the front elevation the door is seen at the "lower" end of the hall. The hall (see also ground plan) occupies the middle of the house from floor to roof, and there is no chimney. Scale in feet, 40 in all.

which produced an important effect was the introduction of a chimney to take the place of the open hearth and the vent in the roof. This chimney was proportionally very large, and was typically introduced within the hall, so reducing its size considerably. It was generally built against the wall which separated hall from wing.

New houses, with more servants living out, needed and had smaller halls, and eventually in the sixteenth century the principal entrance was provided in the centre of the frontage, taking the place of the front door leading into the passage behind the screens. Also a porch was usually provided for this new central front door. This was the beginning of the end of the hall, for the time soon came when it shrank so much as to be more a part of the entrance than anything else and its last stage of all is seen when it has become a mere passageway as it is in small houses today. It is then a tiny relic of the great hall of early times.

Ideas from the Renaissance

By the time of Elizabeth I there was little fear of armed attack upon a great house, and so large windows could be provided even in walls that were externally exposed.

But another change had been taking place ever since men's minds had been re-awakened to the greatness of ancient Greece and Rome. This interest embraced the writings of classical authors, the sculptures of the ancient artists and the design and erection of buildings. As far as architecture was concerned, although the builders (architects or craftsmen) of the fifteenth century had begun to use classical features, the wonderful principles which the Greek builders had evolved from long experience were not understood at all. The Greeks had learnt to build the perfect temple, they had found out essential principles to make a success of construction and design, using the materials at hand in Greece, which included extremely large pieces of stone, and building for the particular climate of southern Europe. They were very accurate in their building.

The Romans had modified the ideas of the Greek architects, and had added dome and arch to produce the bigger buildings they required.

In the Renaissance (the re-birth of classical ideas and principles) of the fifteenth century Continental architects had taken Greek and Roman edifices as models, and from this new Continental development of the old in design and erection some ideas had spread to Great Britain.

There were two outstanding first steps in the acceptance of classical models by Englishmen which I shall mention, use of ornament and the production of symmetry. This was a time of increasing prosperity; people were beginning to be rich, and so they were able to vie with one another in putting up bigger and better buildings in the grand manner: something that money could buy. They had done it in building churches. They did it also with their great houses. A striking feature of Greek and Roman buildings (which you will see at once if you find and look at a good range of pictures of the architectural masterpieces of the classical age) is their symmetry, and this very obvious feature was quickly appreciated and applied. So the sixteenth century is notable for the symmetrical plan in the buildings that were erected.

The buildings of the sixteenth century were still essentially Gothic, and the embellishment that was lavished upon them was something in imitation of the faintly appreciated riches of the classical age. This imitation gave a readily recognizable character to these early Renaissance buildings.

Palladian Principles

From 1605 onwards the great architect Inigo Jones (1573–1652) introduced into England the use of the accurate principles which governed classical architecture. Inigo Jones had closely studied the work of the great Italian Renaissance architect Andrea Palladio (1518–80), who, in his turn, had designed his Italian buildings in the restored classical style, only after the most painstaking study of original work of the classical period, measuring the buildings of ancient Rome so as to obtain absolute accuracy in applying the principles of antiquity.

The Banqueting House, Whitehall, London, was the first building in London designed by Inigo Jones in accordance with Palladian principles, and it began something entirely new, in complete contrast with Jacobean architecture, which was itself a continuation of the Elizabethan style. In the work of Inigo Jones and his successors there is a combination of strict symmetry with variety in detailed treatment. Bold and severe, when compared with Gothic styles that preceded it, this restoration of classical principles was the beginning of an era which was only interrupted by a revival of Gothic styles in the nineteenth century. In town and country we can trace the way in which the new kind of architecture dominated the erection of all kinds of buildings for upwards of two hundred years.

A great architect who applied the Palladian principles introduced by Inigo Jones was Sir Christopher Wren (1631–1723), whose masterpiece is, of course, St. Paul's Cathedral, London.

The great buildings of the Renaissance period exhibit flat masses of masonry enlivened by columns and restrained ornament, especially carved festoons and, over windows, pediments and cornices.

The Humbler Homes

The earliest humble homes still remaining frequently show us low timber-framed buildings of simple construction not very different from that of the central hall of the manor-house, but retaining perhaps less of the architectural planning and more of the individual whim of the builder.

It is a fascinating study to work out the style and dating of the smaller homes. We meet with many puzzles, but we can at least recognize certain characteristics of the various periods which will help us to make determinations as to date.

One feature of smaller houses which undoubtedly is very useful as a check upon our own identifications is the dated house tablet; but in this connection we must remember that such dated plaques may sometimes refer to alterations or additions, and also it is well to remember that such alterations or additions may greatly modify the appearance of old houses, as for example when an old house is timber framed (shall we say built in the sixteenth century) but has been encased with brick to increase warmth and resistance to rain and snow.

Timber Houses and Cottages

In districts that were well wooded and yet lacked any considerable supply of stone for building purposes you will find the houses and cottages of the fifteenth, sixteenth and seventeenth

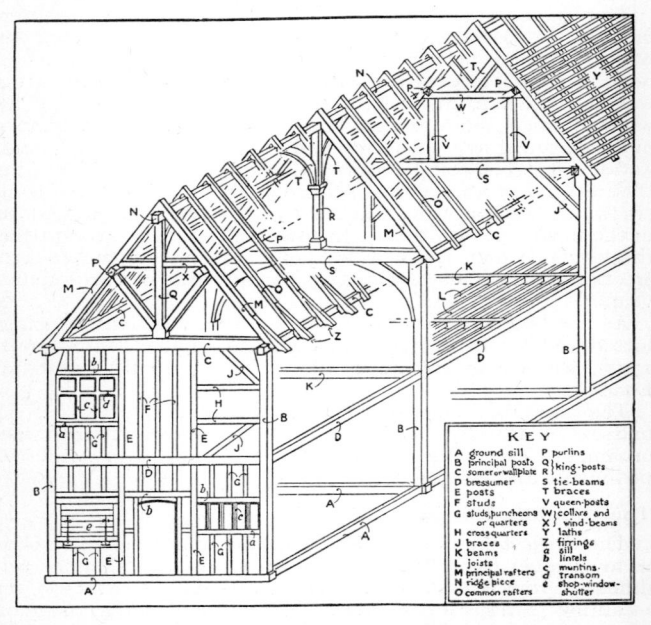

FIG. 102.—Diagram of the construction of a timber-framed house.

Reduced from the original in L. F. Salzman's *Building in England down to 1540* Oxford: Clarendon Press 1952) by kind permission of the author.

CHANGES FOR THE BETTER 165

centuries built largely of timber. These timber houses are built as a framework and skeleton of stout wood filled in with plaster; but the lowest timbers, which form sills (like extended window-sills, running the whole length of the building), often rest upon a low wall of irregular stone-work (called *rubble*) or, in late work, upon brick.

Remembering always that some reconstruction may have taken place in an old house, indications that the work is early in the three centuries mentioned include: a steep roof, less than 60° at the ridge; projection of the upper floor (called a *jetty*) not only at the front of the house, but at the sides and/or at the back as well; stone foundations generally visible below the sill of the building for a foot or more from the ground.

Among details which deserve attention are the door-frames (sometimes the Tudor style with spandrels gives a clue to the date), the brackets on the corners of the house (early ones are solid) and the glazed windows (those not more than 22 inches high are generally early).

Tiles, Bricks and Roofing

Tiles, bricks and roofing materials, including slates, shingle and thatch, deserve study; the plaster-work on walls, often surviving even from Roman times and sometimes still exhibiting crudely painted formal patterns, may also come occasionally under our notice when we visit ancient sites or museums. We may say a few words here about tiles and bricks, leaving you to investigate for yourself the other things and any additional special local materials, including, for example, any slabby stones used for roofing in different parts of the country.

Tiles of ornamental design and of a high standard were used for flooring in churches in the fourteenth century, and they had been preceded by plain tiles which were sometimes glazed. In Roman times building was sometimes carried out in bricks which we should describe today as stout tiles; they were of no standard size, or perhaps we should say there were different standards; we find them $7\frac{1}{2}$ inches square and $1\frac{1}{2}$ inches thick, $16\frac{1}{2}$ inches square and $2\frac{1}{4}$ to $2\frac{1}{2}$ inches thick and 1 foot 10 inches square and $2\frac{3}{4}$ inches thick. These bricks were often re-used by Anglo-Saxon builders in England, which is a tribute to the excellence of the Roman product. Pavements in Roman times were often tiled, and sometimes they were carried out in small cubes of stone and manufactured substances such as brick and glass, giving the craftsmen and artists who made the pavements a wide range of colours to work with. The cubes (or *tesserae* as they are called) were often arranged with great skill to form pictorial designs or formal patterns.

In the Middle Ages bricks were imported to England from Holland, and this implies that the art of making them had been lost after the end of the Roman period, although it is obvious that since tiles of good quality were produced, bricks also could have been made.

The modern standard size of English bricks was limited by statute in 1625. A tax was formerly levied on bricks, and those larger than standard paid at a higher rate.

For mediæval bricks there was no standard size, and in this they can be contrasted with modern bricks of standard dimensions, namely $9 \times 4\frac{1}{2}$ inches by a nominal 3 inches which includes the joint; thus in Victorian times there were always *four courses to the foot* in the best ordinary brickwork. There is a little difference, I believe, in different parts of the country in the thickness of the actual brick; it is being made in Kent today $2\frac{5}{8}$ inches thick. To produce these modern measurements ($9 \times 4\frac{1}{2} \times 2\frac{5}{8}$ inches), the brickmaker has to set his dies and cutting wires according to the different shrinkages that occur when burning different brickearths and clay-mixtures.

English bricks about 1500 were often longer and broader than those of today but generally thinner. I cite measurements (given by L. F. Salzman, *Building in England down to 1540:* Oxford: Clarendon Press (1952)): $10 \times 5 \times 2$ inches (Little Saxham, 1505) $9\frac{1}{2}$ inches in length " or more " (Westminster, 1496) $10\frac{1}{2} \times 5\frac{1}{2} \times 2$ inches and $10\frac{1}{2} \times 5 \times 2\frac{1}{2}$ inches (Beverley, about the same time). The average is said by N. Lloyd in his *History of English Brickwork* (quoted by Salzman) to be about $9 \times 4\frac{1}{2} \times 2$ inches, so that it is the *shallow* nature of the brick that contrasts it with the modern one (after 1625).

EXERCISE

Checking Your Results

When you have studied domestic architecture a little, you will be able to test your progress and be your own examiner in a little test. Walk along one of the main thoroughfares of an old city or town and a little ahead of you, on the opposite side of the road, note the finely proportioned house. Take the details in. There is some lettering on the house, and probably a date over the front door. The inscription is still too distant to be deciphered. As you approach keep looking at the building and try to decide upon its date. " Eighteenth century! " you say. " About 1750! " Now you are opposite the house; you can read the lettering easily enough. There it is. Yes you were right, " A.H. 1755 ". You do not expect to get the exact year, and after all the *exact* year is not important; 1755 just happened to be the date of the inscription, and presumably of the building. What is of interest is the fact that we have here, as already mentioned with a caution (page 164), a sure way of checking our advancing knowledge of domestic architecture and of assuring ourselves, by an examination we devise and conduct ourselves, that we really are making progress.

Of course, we can also look in books at pictures of dated houses and, by covering the captions (descriptions) below them until we have decided on a probable date, can check our increasing proficiency in our subject.

Another interesting check may be provided by actual records. You look at a house and form an opinion of its date. Later on you find that the house was built for some public man and that the date of its erection is accurately known. Your deduction was correct within a few years, and you are encouraged by that confirmation of your own ideas.

LITERATURE

In addition to books already mentioned in this chapter, special attention may again be directed to *History of Architecture on the Comparative Method*, by Banister Fletcher (London : Batsford), and to books listed at the end of Chapter Two.

The Growth of the English House, by J. A. Gotch (London : Batsford), and other books by the same author will be found useful.

You will find many articles dealing with local examples of houses in publications of the archæological societies.

CHAPTER EIGHTEEN

THE WRITTEN WORD

LEARNING TO READ ANCIENT RECORDS

The study of early writing is useful to the historian; skill in reading old records is mainly a matter of patience.

We Want to Read Manuscripts

THERE is a great variety of reasons for wanting to read the written word of our ancestors, and I use the phrase in its widest sense to include inscriptions on coins and monuments, pottery marks, lettering in stained glass and on jewellery and other works of art, including tapestry and paintings, all in addition to the normal written word of charters, registers, manor rolls, letters and other documents. We may wish to read writing of the past to understand the history of our own family or of a parish or manor. We may be making an enquiry requiring comparison of modern practice with that of earlier centuries, say in some economic subject. We may want to make a transcription of parish registers or other records or wish to consult monetary accounts or legal records in local or national collections.

Many national manuscripts are at the Public Record Office, and there are many documents in the libraries and archives of private owners, of cities, towns and colleges throughout the country; most of these documents are open for study by duly accredited persons, such as serious students, if proper application to consult them is made to their owners or custodians.

The Story of Writing

Writing, or penmanship, as we know it today is very obviously a natural development from the written word as we see it in England in parish registers going back to the sixteenth century and in national and local records of the thirteenth to fifteenth centuries and still farther back in the Domesday Book (A.D. 1086) and in Anglo-Saxon charters, the earliest of which date from the beginning of the seventh century immediately after the re-introduction of Christianity. It is also very obvious that the alphabet in use today is the same in most respects as that used in this country in inscriptions made here in Roman times and still preserved for us on altars, tombstones and coins. The history of writing goes back a great deal farther, of course,

THE WRITTEN WORD

and it is not necessary here to go into the origin of alphabets and writing.

The exact form taken by words and letters in writing depends upon the nature of the implement with which the inscription is made. With a modern fountain-pen the letters of a word often run on from beginning to end, and there is even a tendency to write two words without removing the pen from the paper. This flowing style of writing is called cursive (Latin *cursum*, " to run ").

As we trace our writing back we find that from the beginning of the eighteenth century to the present day writing looks familiar, and can generally be easily read by educated people, but before that time the written English alphabet was sufficiently different to present some difficulties.

Let us take some examples; a neatly written sheet lies before me, it is dated 1904. I can see no difference between the form of the letters and those in use today. I next open a book of churchwardens' accounts beginning in 1736 and ending in 1842. The last entries are not very well written, but I can make them out easily enough. The capital *c* goes below the line; the letter *s* is sometimes long. I turn back to 1800; the writing is better and has almost the same peculiarities as that of 1842, but I notice that the final *d* has a backward flourish. Let us look at 1750: yes the writing is quite like a modern hand and still very easy to read. The first page for 1736 has some additional peculiarities: most noticeable is the form of the letter *e*; it is rather like a modern *o*, and final *s* is in some cases little more than a stroke. Nevertheless, the somewhat faded writing is easy enough to decipher.

I pick up next an overseers' account book which runs from 1651 to 1699. In 1699 there is not much to distinguish the writing from that of 1736. The capital *t* is unfamiliar, and capital *a* is uncrossed. The first page (for 1651) begins to present some difficulties to the modern reader. Capital *f* is written like two small *f*'s. Capital *c* is quite unfamiliar; several small letters are unlike ours: *e*, of course, and *k*, *p*, *r*, *s*, and *x*; but when you have solved these letters there is no further difficulty.

I next pick up a beautifully written manuscript about twenty years older; the form of some of the letters is still more difficult; there are also abbreviations which are unfamiliar. So, altogether, the manuscript cannot be read without considerable care. However, the alphabetical peculiarities can soon be mastered.

The next manuscript I have before me is a good deal older, actually it is part of a court roll of the fourteenth century (22 Edw. III). It is a good deal faded, many of the letters are quite easily recognized, especially the following: *a*, *b*, *c* (sometimes), *f, g, i, m, n, o, p, q, s* (sometimes), *t, u, x, y, z.* The capitals as before are not easy. However, *learn the alphabet*, and the transcription of the roll is not too difficult. It is written in Latin and Anglo-French.

My next piece of writing is of the twelfth century, about 1160. It is part of a page from the book of Leviticus, and is, of course, in Latin. It is a beautiful piece of work; the letters are very clearly written, and that is one reason why it is easier

FIG. 103.—Writing in Parish Registers. Examples of seventeenth-century letters collected by the Society of Genealogists.

to read than the fourteenth-century writing already mentioned. Here, again, once the alphabet is mastered, the rest is easy.

I turn now to a facsimile of Domesday Book, and among all the writings of earlier times none is perhaps of such great importance and wide interest for students of English history and archæology as Domesday Book. The original is preserved, and can be seen, at the Public Record Office in London. It contains in concise form, in abbreviated Latin, a survey of the greater part of the property liable to taxation at the Norman Conquest, and was compiled in 1086. A number of these facsimiles have been published, generally county by county; in some cases there are also translations published, with notes, and yet it is surprising how frequently local people know nothing of the particulars given for their own parish in Domesday Book. With a little practice it is easy to read and translate this record. It has, of course, certain peculiarities, but in the main its interpretation does not present too formidable a task.

I possess a photostat of an Anglo-Saxon charter in which I have a special interest and, once again here, although the script was written in A.D. 824, it is a bright and clear piece of writing, and it can readily be made out after a little study.

The moral of all this is that you can teach yourself to read these writings if you have the necessary perseverance. The great thing is to learn the alphabet carefully and then apply your knowledge.

There are explanatory books dealing in detail with the peculiarities of the different hands used for different purposes, and these are important for students wishing to go deeply into the matter.

Books, Coins, Inscriptions

Early printed books may interest you, countless inscriptions on buildings, pottery, coins and tombs exist, and I remember

FIG. 104.—Gold coin of Philip II of Macedon. This was the kind of coin imitated by moneyers in Gaul and Britain in the Early Iron Age. In copies, the various features of the original become greatly distorted until they are hardly recognizable (see Fig. 105). Scale ½.

that quarries worked in Roman times sometimes provide inscriptions cut into the rock to commemorate the work of military quarrymen. Again, as a result of trade, Gaulish coins came into use in the south of Britain before the Belgic invasion

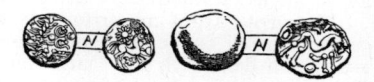

FIG. 105.—Two uninscribed British gold coins, found at Aylesford, Kent; Copies of coins such as that illustrated in Fig. 104. Note the distortion. Scale ½.

of about 75 B.C., but these coins were uninscribed, and the first inscriptions known are those of Tasciovanus the father of Cunobelin (the Cymbeline of Shakespeare) on gold, silver and copper coins struck at Verulam (St. Albans) a few years before the time of Christ. From those days onwards coins tell a tale of their own. Official and monumental inscriptions provide us with scraps of information about affairs in the Roman period, and the same is true of metallic military diplomas, the stamps impressed by potters on their wares and the odd scribblings (*graffiti*) scratched on tiles and pottery.

Thus we can patch together just a little of the story of the years when Rome ruled our island. Information gleaned in this way can be read in conjunction with similar information gathered from other parts of the Roman world and with actual historical records written by classical authors, the best known of whom was Julius Cæsar, the first Roman invader of Britain in 55 and 54 B.C., who in his *Gallic War* gives us his own account of his military operations in this country.

A list of places in Roman Britain situated on the roads occurs in a document called the Antonine Itinerary, an imperial route-book believed to have been compiled in the reign of Caracella (A.D. 211-217).

The fragmentary inscriptions of Roman times ceased here when the Roman Empire began to break up and the best Roman troops were withdrawn from Britain in the early part of the fifth century (about A.D. 410). The permanence of the break only made itself felt as the years passed and the Romanized Britons and any Romans who were left in this country naturally still regarded themselves as part of the Roman Empire. There was no constitutional withdrawal corresponding to the withdrawal of British rule from India. Our scanty knowledge of the events of the next one hundred and eighty years or so is more a matter for the historian than for the archæologist, but the archæologist ought to have as much knowledge as possible about authorities for such an obscure and difficult period.

The contemporary historian of the Dark Ages, as the years 420-597 are often called, was a British monk, Gildas, who wrote about A.D. 540. No reliance can be placed upon his account of what happened immediately after the close of the Roman period. He wrote from an erroneous oral tradition more than a century after the events of those years. The other early works which deal with the Dark Ages are : (i) the History of the Britons (written about 685 and edited with later additions by Nennius in the ninth century); (ii) the scholarly Ecclesiastical History of the Venerable Bede (written about 730, and incorporating material from Gildas, his own ancestral tradition and some other sources); and (iii) the Anglo-Saxon Chronicle (of which the part covering the Dark Ages was compiled at the very end of the ninth century, largely from Bede but supplemented by traditions).

Christianity was already established in Romanized Britain by the time of Constantine the Great A.D. 306-337, and there were almost certainly some Christians in Britain about a hundred years earlier. But we have no record of the continuance of the Christian religion in those parts of Britain that were invaded by the English in the middle of the fifth century. In the Celtic unconquered regions the Church was still active.

LITERATURE

For reference you can turn to *English Court Hand* A.D. *1066 to 1500*, by Charles Johnson and Hilary Jenkinson (Oxford: Clarendon Press, 1915).

CHAPTER NINETEEN

SOME QUEER CHARACTERS

MAINLY ABOUT RUNES AND OGHAM

This chapter deals mainly with two early forms of writing which occur in this country side by side with the alphabet we all know. These strange letters are Runes and the Ogham script. A short account of some unfamiliar alphabets is added.

Runes

THE Roman alphabet was not used by the Scandinavian peoples until their conversion to Christianity about the year 1000. For many centuries before that letters called rune-staves or runes were used by the Northmen. How ancient this form of writing is is a matter of conjecture, but it was

FIG. 106.—Runic characters. The two letters at the bottom of the last column resemble *gifu*, G and *queorth*, Q. Other letters are shown in the list (pp. 175–6).

employed for thousands of surviving inscriptions on stone in Denmark, Norway and Sweden in the eleventh and earlier centuries, certainly as far back as the fifth century and possibly as early as the first. From the Scandinavian area its use spread in very early times, probably as far back as the second century, to other parts of Europe, including Germany and the British Isles. Some of the letters are like those of Greek and Roman writing, and they probably had a very ancient common source, being brought as an early form of Greek script to Baltic lands by traders. But the usual form of most of the runes is very different from the letters of the Roman alphabet. (See Figs. 80, 86 and 106.) Some Scandinavian manuscripts as late as the fifteenth century were written in these characters.

The "alphabet", which begins with the six letters *f*, *u*, *th*, *o*, *r* and *c*, is, for that reason, called the *futhorc*. It consists of three series of eight letters each, with some extra runes.

Spreading, as this mode of writing did, and being in use for many centuries, it is not surprising that there is a great variety in the forms of some of its runes.

In early times the inscriptions were retrograde, that is to say they were written from right to left. The futhorc influenced the Anglo-Saxon alphabet, and some of the runes were employed with Roman letters in Old English inscriptions. The letters thorn (*th*) and wen (*w*) long remained in use in English alongside the letters of the Roman alphabet, and even survived in English after the date of the Norman invasion. In fact, thorn still survives as the first letter of the sign "Ye olde tea shoppe". That letter is not *y* at all, but *th*.

In the British Isles runic inscriptions on stone exist in Orkney and in the Isle of Man, in Dumfriesshire, Cumberland and Kent.

Objects inscribed with runes include gravestones or monumental stones, coins and personal possessions, such as weapons, brooches, rings and other ornaments. The famous Franks casket (named after Sir Wollaston Franks, who gave it) in the British Museum dates from about A.D. 700, and has a number of inscriptions in runes upon it. Also in the British Museum is a sword-knife (scramasax) of about A.D. 800 on which a futhorc is inscribed. The cross at Bewcastle in Cumberland has a notable runic inscription upon it; it is a memorial to Alcfrith, son of King Oswy of Northumbria in the seventh century. Among other inscriptions in runes may be mentioned that on the Ruthwell Cross in Dumfriesshire.

The Futhorc

Here are runes arranged in the three first groups with some of their names and equivalents:

I. 1. Feh.   F   ᚠ
   2. Ur.   U   ᚢ
   3. Thorn. Th   ᚦ

4.	Os.	O	ᚾ
5.	Ræd.	R	ᚱ
6.	Cen.	C	h
7.	Gifu.	G	ᚷ
8.	Wen.	W	ᚹ
II. 1.	Hægil.	H	ᚻ
2.	Næd.	N	ᚾ
3.	Is.	I	ᛁ
4.	Gær.	G (*y* consonant)	ᛄ
5.	Ih.	I	ᛇ
6.	Peorth.	P	ᛈ
7.	Ilcs, Calc.	A	ᛉ
8.	Sigil.	S	ᛋ
III. 1.	Tir.	T	ᛏ
2.	Berc.	B	ᛒ
3.	Eh.	E	ᛖ
4.	Man.	M	ᛗ
5.	Lagu.	L	ᛚ
6.	Ing.	Ng	ᛝ
7.	Dæg.	D	ᛞ
8.	Oethil.	Œ	ᛟ

Additional letters include

ᚪ, *A;* ᚫ, *Æ;* ᚠ, *Y;* ᚥ, *Q;* ᛘ, *St;* ᚸ, *G.*

The Ogham Character

I am greatly indebted to the late Professor R. A. S. Macalister, D. Litt., F.S.A., of Dublin, upon whose work this account of the Ogham script is based. (Incidentally, *Ogham* is pronounced " Ohm ".)

Ogham is not itself a language; it is merely a form of writing in which an alphabet of twenty-five letters was used to set down inscriptions in the oldest known form of Old Irish. Twenty of the twenty-five letters are indicated by combinations of from one to five parallel strokes set in various positions with respect to a central stem-line; the remaining five letters are more complex in form, but are rarely used. Knowledge of the script was preserved in the Irish folk-memory down to the first half of the nineteenth century, but apart from this, the alphabet is recorded in MS. sources (the best-known rendering is contained in a grammatical tract in the MS. known as the Book of Ballymote), and the bilingual (Latin–Irish) inscriptions in Wales provide useful confirmatory evidence. The normal form of the alphabet is:

```
       H D T C Q
 ┬┬┬ ┬┬ ┬┬┬ /  //  ///  ////  /////  ·  ··  ···  ····  ·····    X   0   /X\   6   ≡
 B L V S N        M G NG Z R     A O U E I         K  TH  P   PH   X
```

The letters *h* and *z* have not been found in Irish inscriptions, and the letter *v*, though always called *f* in the mediæval MSS., is transliterated *v* in the Welsh bilingual inscriptions.

The grouping of the various letters shows that the inventor of the alphabet was able to distinguish not only between consonants and vowels but also between broad and slender vowels. He was able to see that *d* and *t*, and *c* and *q* were phonetically related consonants. Formation of the letters by means of strokes (or scores as they are usually called), ranging in number from 1 to 5, suggests that the signs may have been invented for use as a "manual alphabet", the five fingers held in different positions having been used to denote the letters in much the same manner as the modern deaf-mute alphabet is used today. But whether this be so or not, it is evident that Ogham had in its background another literary alphabet. So sophisticated an invention would hardly have been possible otherwise.

Linguistic scholars have put forward various suggestions as to what this literary alphabet may have been. In his most recent publication [1] on the subject of Ogham, the late Professor Macalister held that it was the Chalcidic form of the Greek alphabet. On the other hand, Professor Marstrander had earlier held that the Ogham script should be derived from one or other of the Runic alphabets, while Thurneysen in 1937 made a strong case for the Latin alphabet as the most likely origin, though he admitted the force of Marstrander's arguments. The last word has not yet been said on this difficult question.

The date of invention of the script is not known, but it is generally held that the "Ogham period" lies between the second and the seventh centuries A.D. Neither is its place of invention known. It is not found anywhere on the European

---

[1] R. A. S. Macalister, *Corpus Inscriptionum Insularum Celticarum* (Irish MSS. Commission, Dublin 1945), Vol. I, p. vi.

mainland. The distribution of the extant inscriptions suggests the south-west of Ireland. County Kerry contains 121 inscribed stones; Co. Cork eighty-one; Co. Waterford forty-seven; Co. Kilkenny twelve.[1] This distribution suggests that Ogham originated in Kerry and that it spread eastward across the south of Ireland, eventually reaching Britain through Irish contacts across the Irish Sea.

As given in the mediæval MSS., the Ogham scores are positioned above, below and through the horizontal stem-line, and the words are read from left to right as in Irish or English at the present day. When the inscriptions are found on stones (as are the great majority), one vertical arris of the standing stone forms the stem-line, and the consonant scores are then cut horizontally on the two adjacent faces of the stone. The inscription is read from the ground to the top. If it is long it may continue over the top of the stone and down the opposite arris.

The inscriptions are in the main very brief, and rarely contain more than a personal name with a reference to his ancestry. No inscription contains a verb. The following formulæ are those most usually found:

1. A single name usually in the genitive case. The word "stone" or "monument" is to be understood before the name. Example at Ballyvourney, Co. Cork:

L A C A V A G   N   I

(Lacavagni)

2. Single name in the genitive case with the word ANM prefixed. ANM = AINM which is the modern Irish word meaning "name". Example at Ballyknock, Co. Cork:

A N M   M E D D O G E N   I

(Anm Meddogeni)

3. Name of person commemorated and of his father, in the formula A MAQI B. The word *maqi* is an early form

---

[1] *The other Irish counties are:* Kildare 8, Mayo 8, Wexford 5, Wicklow 5, Carlow 4, Clare 3, Limerick 3, Roscommon 3, Antrim 2, Cavan 2, Meath 2, Tipperary 2, Armagh 1, Dublin 1, Fermanagh 1, Galway 1, Leitrim 1, Derry 1, Tyrone 1. Total in Ireland 315 inscriptions.

In Britain: Pembroke 15, Brecon 8, Carmarthen 7, Cardigan 4, Glamorgan 3, Denbigh 2, Caernarvon 1, Cornwall 5, Devon 2, Hampshire 1. Total 48.

Isle of Man: Five inscriptions.

of the Old Irish *maic*, genitive of mac = son. Example at Ballyknock, Co. Cork:

G R I LAG N I MAQ I S C I LAG N I
(Grilagni maqi Scilagni)

In this formula the word *maqi* is sometimes doubled. In this case the second maqi is part of the following name. This is shown by some of the Welsh bilingual inscriptions such as that at Cilgerran, Pembroke. The Latin inscription there is TRENEGUSSI FILI MACUTRENI HIC IACET and the Ogham is: TRENAGUSSU MAQI MAQI TRENI. The word ANM is sometimes prefixed to inscriptions in this form.

4. Name of person commemorated and of his grandfather or more remote ancestor. The form is A AVI B. AVI is an early form of the Old Irish *Aui*, from which comes the modern form Ua, as in the modern Irish form of the name O'Kelly = Ua Ceallaigh. Example at Faunkill-and-the-Woods, Co. Cork:

MAQ I DEC C EDDASAV I TUR AN I AS
(Maqi Decceddas avi Turanias)

5. Name of person commemorated and of his uncle in the formula A NETA B. NETA is an old genitive of *nia* meaning nephew. The word NETA sometimes forms an intrinsic part of the first name. It occurs in both senses in the inscription at Castletimon, Co. Wicklow:

N E TACAR I N E TACAG I
(Netacari neta Cagi)

6. Name of person commemorated and of his patron in the form A CELI B. CELI is genitive of Cele meaning follower or devotee. Example at Kilmartin Lower, Co. Cork:

U D DME N SAC E L I N E T TAS LOG I
(Uddmensa celi Nettaslogi)

7. Name of person commemorated, with reference to a remote ancestor or founder of his family in the form A MAQI MUCOI B. MUCOI is an old gentive of MACCU

meaning descendant. Example at Coolmagort, Co. Kerry:

D E G OMA Q I M U C O I T O I C A K I

(Dego   maqi   mucoi   Toicaki)

8. Name of person commemorated and of his father and of a more remote ancestor in the formula: A MAQI B MAQI MUCOI C. Example at Coolmagort, Co. Kerry:

MAQ I T TALMA Q I VOR GOS MA Q I M U C O I T O I CAC

(Maqittal   maqi   Vorgos   maqi   mucoi   Toicac)

Apart from the inscriptions on stone there were others on waxen or wooden tablets (they are mentioned frequently in the ancient Irish Sagas), but none has survived to the present day. The inscriptions show phonetic forms of great antiquity, many of which had gone out of use by the time that Irish began to be written in the Latin alphabet introduced by the early Christian missionaries. It may be that these archaic forms were deliberately used so as to make the written words more mysterious to the uninitiated. The inscriptions are of great importance for philological studies in early Irish.

Charters

With the re-introduction of Christianity to England by the preaching of St. Augustine and his companions in and after A.D. 597, the art of writing came back to the eastern part of this island.

Of great interest in Anglo-Saxon times are the numerous documents of a legal nature, often referring to grants of land and drawn up at gatherings of various kings with their clergy and nobles. The general term for a document of this kind is *charter*.

The very earliest charters no doubt dated from the years immediately following the arrival of the Christian missionaries, but many of the earliest have only survived as copies made into the *registers* of their religious houses by the monks. These ancient charters, whether originals or copies, throw a good deal of light upon the meaning of place-names by providing us with early forms of names often subsequently corrupted. Boundaries of ancient parishes are often written in these charters, and they also preserve large numbers of personal names. These very early documents have been succeeded by others, right down to the present day, which have told the same kind of story for the period to which they belong.

Many charters have seals which are a study in themselves; and are, of course, frequently of heraldic interest.

Various Alphabets

In addition to the kinds of lettering already mentioned, inscriptions upon monuments, coins and personal possessions occur in some other alphabets which have followed to some extent changing fashions adopted by those who wrote with a pen.

There are obviously two kinds of letters: large, called *Majuscules*, and small, called *Minuscules*. Large letters are of two kinds, *Capitals* and *Uncials*. In *Capitals* the letters have an angular appearance, and curves occur only where they cannot

FIG. 107.—Mediæval inscriptions. From above, downwards: (1) From the tomb of King Henry III, 1273. (2) From the tomb of Queen Eleanor, 1291. (3) From that of King Edward III, 1377. (4) On the tomb of Alianore, widow of Thomas of Woodstock, 1399. (5 and 6) From King Richard II's tomb, 1399. All are in Westminster Abbey.

From Boutell's *Manual of Archæology*.

be avoided in the letters, *b, c, d, g, j, o, p, q, r, s, u*. *Uncials* avoid angles wherever possible, and the letters are generally large, rounded characters. *Minuscules* were developed from large letters to save space.

From Anglo-Saxon times, Roman capitals, from which our capitals descend, were used. For example, they occur upon the Franks casket in the British Museum; this also has inscriptions in runes; it is dated about A.D. 700. But some of these Roman capitals were modified in form. About A.D. 800 uncials began to appear, and thereafter became more usual and continued till about 1350. The complete uncial alphabet, which is generally called Lombardic, was only in general use for about the last century of this period (i.e., 1250–1350). The Lombardic (Gothic majuscule) was superseded in northern Europe by the Gothic minuscule about 1350. This kind of lettering is generally called black-letter (or, popularly with us, Old English). It is, of course, the type used for much printing in Germany down to the present time.

With the revival of classical learning, from the end of the fifteenth century, Roman letters began to come back, the capitals first.

EXERCISE

Methods for teaching yourself to read old writing, ancient inscriptions and to decipher what is written in stone, wood and metal have been indicated already to some extent in the course of the last two chapters. You must make your own opportunities, and you can always begin (although it is not so thrilling as working with originals) by working out facsimiles.

Perseverance is the greatest factor in making you successful.

LITERATURE

As far as Runes and the Ogham Script are concerned, perhaps the best references are to be found in encyclopædia articles. (In addition, of course, to the work mentioned at the foot of page 177.)

CHAPTER TWENTY

THE LANGUAGE OF SHIELD AND JUPON

SOME PRINCIPLES OF HERALDRY

In this chapter we touch upon the subject of HERALDRY which is of considerable interest to archæologists.

Heraldry

HERALDRY is of considerable archæological interest and may help, for instance, to identify the builder of a church tower by a coat-of-arms exhibited upon it, or may indicate, by a shield preserved over the door of an ancient house, a former owner. Heraldry may throw light upon family history. It must, however, always be borne in mind that,

FIG. 108.—Arms of Knight: Vert a bend lozengy or i.e., a green ground with a bend of gold (or yellow) made of lozenges. These arms should be compared with those of Thomas Knight seen in Fig. 109.

FIG. 109.—Arms of Thomas Knight, he was Knight by adoption, not by descent, so his arms are "differenced" by adding a silver cinquefoil to the original Knight arms (see Fig. 108): Vert a bend lozengy or, in base a cinquefoil argent.

although there are strict rules of heraldry, they are not always observed by individuals, and too much reliance must not be placed upon the significance of arms shown upon buildings, monuments or personal possessions.

The details of heraldry are intricate and its language technical, but anyone can quickly learn enough of the rudiments of the subject to be able to use them in the study of archæology. Every educated person ought to know enough about heraldry to take an intelligent interest in any coats-of-arms with which he meets. There are many books on the subject, and articles on heraldry in the best encyclopædias give good elementary information about its principles.

In the Middle Ages the adoption of a device by which the leader of his men in battle could be seen and recognized must have been a matter of great advantage. Such was the origin of heraldry, and from simple beginnings the whole code of rules regulating the form and use of heraldic achievements developed.

Knightly Equipment

Consider the equipment of a knight in the later Middle Ages. He wore armour, which included his metal helm or helmet, the top or crest of which could support the representation of some chosen distinctive object, such as the head of an animal (this is the *crest* of heraldry). Part of his knightly equipment was a jupon or coat, on which could be depicted, in their correct colours, a field or background and superimposed charges. Charges were devices or objects by which his friends knew him when his face could not be seen. This jupon or coat-of-arms was a fine, well-made garment. The body of it consisted typically of a linen foundation with back and front alike, each with a covering of correctly coloured padded cloth such as velvet. The linen, the padding and the cloth covering were often quilted together. On separate pieces of cloth the embroidered charges could subsequently be stitched down over the quilted surface of the garment.

FIG. 110.—Arms of Lewkenor: Azure three chevrons argent. Three silver (white) chevrons on a blue ground.

Sometimes the jupon was sleeveless, but if it was provided with short sleeves they also might be adorned back and front with separate representations of the same design as the front and back of the body of the jupon.

The knight also had a shield or escutcheon. This might be of metal (either of gold, or gilded; or of silver) or be covered with the skin of some animal or animals or be painted. This ground of metal or colour was the field upon which the charges could be superimposed either by being cut out and applied or by being painted upon the shield. The shield corresponded in design with the jupon, and it may be mentioned that the metal gold could be represented by yellow and silver by white.

The cloak or mantle was typically of the colour of the principal charge, with a lining of the same colour as the shield and the ground or field of the jupon.

All these things were useful in battle and in the sport of the tournament, for by them the knight's friends and followers could instantly recognize the wearer's nobility.

It was from these: the *helm*, the *crest*, the *coat-of-arms*, the *shield* and the *mantling* that the recognized present-day achievements of arms have been derived.

Blazoning and Tricking

We cannot, in a brief space, go far into this subject, but we may say something to indicate a few important points.

THE LANGUAGE OF SHIELD AND JUPON 185

In describing arms the first thing mentioned, logically, is the colour of the field of the shield followed by the description of the position and nature of the charges and their colour.

This can be done in English, or we may use conventional Anglo-French terms.

When coats-of-arms are described with or without illustration they are said to be blazoned; when they are drawn or painted they are said to be tricked.

Metals, colours and furs in heraldry are called tinctures, and metals and colours are described as follows:

Gold, Or (tricked gold or yellow); Silver, Argent (tricked silver or white); Red, Gules; Blue, Azure; Black, Sable; Green, Vert; Purple, Purpure.

When arms are tricked in black and white, a *modern* convention indicates colours as follows : *or*, by dots (grains of gold); *argent*, left plain; *gules*, by vertical lines (blood runs down); *azure*, by horizontal lines (lines of the sky's horizon); *sable*, by lines vertical and horizontal (the darkest effect possible with lines); vert, by oblique lines (NW–SE.), parallel to the *first* limb of V (for *vert*.); *purpure*, by oblique lines the other way (NE.–SW.). The two furs *ermine* and *vair* are conventionally depicted (*ermine* by black tails on a white ground, *vair* by an alternation of blue-and-white areas, the shape of squirrel skins).

FIG. 111.—Arms of May: Gules a fess between eight billets or—i.e., the ground is red and across its middle is a horizontal gold (yellow) band, above and below which are the gold billets (oblong, perpendicular figures).

FIG. 112.—Arms of Brodnax: Or two chevrons gules; on a chief of the second three cinquefoils argent. On a gold (yellow) ground are two red chevrons. "The second" (colour mentioned) is red; so the "chief" (transverse strip at the top of the shield) is also red: on this are three silver (white) cinquefoils.

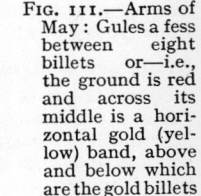

Positions on a shield or coat-of-arms are always described from the bearer's point of view, *dexter* (right) being on the observer's left, and *sinister* (left) being on the observer's right. Other technical terms of position include *chief*, top, and *base*, bottom.

The least complicated charges are simple geometrical figures, of which the best known and very frequently used is the *chief*, which is a strip one-third of the height of the shield placed across the upper margin of the escutcheon.

From what has been said about a knight's equipment it will be easy in teaching yourself the principles of heraldry first to imagine the shield of metal (gold or silver), unpainted or painted, wholly or in part, in one or more of the heraldic colours (tinctures) or covered with fur of squirrels (vair) or of stoats in their winter coats, with their black tails on the white pelts (ermine). Then to this surface (*field*) are attached *charges*. Some of these are mere strips of coloured material, or they may be geometric figures or conventional or common objects. Some charges like the *chief*, already mentioned, are simple enough to support other charges; such simple charges are called *ordinaries*. If the charge is still of simple design but not suitable to support another charge, it is called a *sub-ordinary*. *Common charges* are conventional or ordinary objects, such as griffins, lions, roses, suns, garbs (wheatsheaves).

Arms are Informative

Marshalling is said to take place when the particulars indicated upon one coat-of-arms are added to those upon another. Marshalling is carried out in a variety of ways. For example, when a marriage takes place the particulars of the arms of the bride's father can be added to those of her husband by *impaling* the two coats, that is by placing them side by side on one shield, the husband's on the dexter, the wife's on the sinister side.

Another way in which arms are marshalled is by quartering. This is seen in the arms of Her Majesty the Queen, where the first and third quarters exhibit the arms of England, the second and fourth those of Scotland and Ireland respectively. In the days when the sovereigns of England claimed the title of King of France the lilies of France were included in the quartering.

Privileged persons, especially peers, have supporters, generally animal or human figures standing on either side of the shield.

Ladies did not go to war in the Middle Ages, so they had no shields. The place of the escutcheon was taken in their case by a diamond-shaped plaque called a lozenge.

There was a custom which died out in the nineteenth century of placing a board painted with the arms of the deceased person upon the front of his house before the funeral; afterwards it was put up in church. These "hatchments" as they are called (an obvious corruption of *achievements*) are still preserved in many churches.

Coats-of-arms on tombs and public buildings and on funeral hatchments in churches often tell an interesting story to those who can read the language of heraldry. On book-plates, signet rings and silver plate, coats-of-arms or even full achievements occur.

There was a fashion many years ago of inventing coats-of-arms for famous people of the days before heraldry was employed, and so you will sometimes see in churches coats-of-arms of such Anglo-Saxon saints as St. Edmund and St. Hilda. Although serious suggestions have been made that coat-

THE LANGUAGE OF SHIELD AND JUPON 187

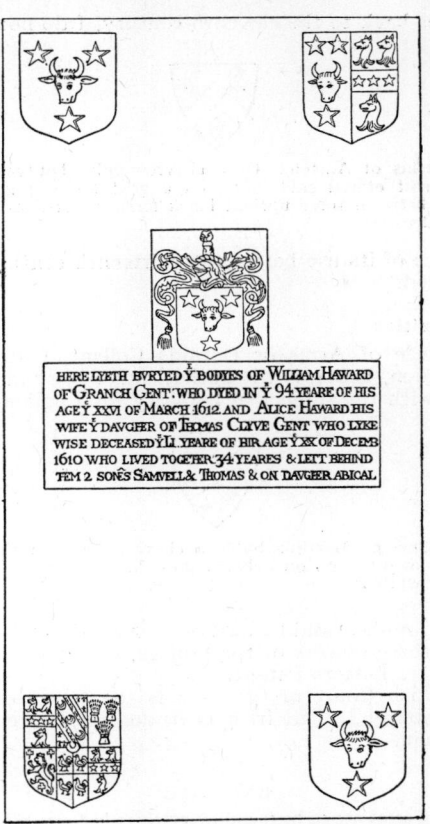

HERE LYETH BVRYED Ỹ BODYES OF WILLIAM HAWARD
OF GRANCH GENT: WHO DYED IN Ỹ 94 YEARE OF HIS
AGE Ỹ XXVI OF MARCH 1612. AND ALICE HAWARD HIS
WIFE Ỹ DAVGHER OF THOMAS CLYVE GENT WHO LYKE
WISE DECEASED Ỹ II. YEARE OF HIR AGE Ỹ XX OF DECEM̄B
1610 WHO LIVED TOGETHER 34 YEARES & LEFT BEHIND
TEM̄ 2 SONĒS SAMVELL & THOMAS & ON DAVGHER ABICAL

FIG. 113.—Ledger stone with six brasses. The monumental inscription commemorates William Haward and his wife Alice, daughter of Thomas Clyve. The first brass is the escutcheon of the Haward family; the second gives the coat of arms of the married couple, the bearings of the Haward and Clyve families *in pale* (the dexter side (right) the husband's, the sinister (left) the wife's). Over the inscription is the achievement of the Haward family: shield, helm with crest on a wreath, and mantling. The shield at the bottom left is the fully marshalled escutcheon of the Clyve family. The other families represented here are Huxley, Stuche, Wronkeslow and Broughton. The small crescent in the centre of the shield is a mark of cadency (order of descent in a family), and indicates the second son of the family: to his branch the bride belonged. The last shield is a repetition of the first.

armour goes back to the eleventh century, I do not know that

FIG. 114.—Arms of Austen: Or a chevron gules between three lions' jambs erect erased sable—i.e., on a gold (yellow) ground, a red chevron between three upright black forearms of lions, cut off with jagged edges.

any instance of its use before the thirteenth century has been authenticated.

The Authorities

The College of Arms or Heralds College, Queen Victoria Street, London, E.C.4, is the authoritative body in all matters concerned with the subject of heraldry for England and Com-

FIG. 115.—Arms of Martin: Sable a chevron between three doves or martlets argent—i.e., on a black ground, the chevron and birds in silver (or white).

monwealth families, and by authority delegated to them by the Sovereign, three officers of the College, called Kings of Arms, grant arms by Letters Patent.

The Scottish Court of Chivalry is the Court of the Lord Lyon, Edinburgh. The Irish Genealogical Office is at The Castle, Dublin.

EXERCISE

Examples of arms are to be found everywhere in town and country. A good way to teach yourself is to visit a building where there are many coats-of-arms which are correctly described in local books on the subject. An example is given under Literature, page 189. Read the blazon and look at the shields. Repeat the descriptions as you look at the shields without reference to the book. Check and re-check. Read and re-read. You will soon know and understand. The language is technical, but it is accurate. It soon becomes intelligible. After that, it soon becomes easy. Try it.

Blazon arms in your note-book. Trick them too. Learn to use the reference books.

THE LANGUAGE OF SHIELD AND JUPON

LITERATURE

Some very fine books upon Heraldry are long out of print, but such books can generally be consulted in public libraries, usually perhaps in the reference department. Mention may be made, in this connection, of a work generally called Berry's *Heraldry*, 3 vols., about 1828, but undated. The title of the work is *Encyclopædia Heraldica*, or *Complete Dictionary of Heraldry*, by William Berry (London : Sherwood, Gilbert and Piper).

The articles in the best encyclopædias give a good deal of information in a short space.

An example of the kind of book referred to in the Exercise is *The Heraldry of Canterbury Cathedral*, Vol. I. *The Great Cloister Vault*, by A. W. B. Messenger (Canterbury : Friends of the Cathedral, 1947). (This includes an explanation of terms used (most useful) with clear, simple (and more complicated) illustrations ; an inventory of arms occurring in the cloisters, illustrated by photographs ; the armorial ; ordinary of the arms and two pedigrees.)

CHAPTER TWENTY-ONE

WHAT'S IN A NAME?

PLACE-NAMES AND SURNAMES TELL THEIR STORY

Sufficient information about Names of men and places is here laid before the student to fit him to make his own way into the strange byways of the subject.

The Archæologist and Place-names

PLACE-NAMES often throw a good deal of light upon the early history of a parish, hamlet, farm or field. It is important to remember that all place-names have a meaning, often it is quite an obvious meaning (the name of Battle in Sussex, for example), and if the name is not English its translation may make its significance *quite* clear. (I have in mind Ballintubbert in co. Kildare, which I visited recently. The *t* at the end seems to be a modern addition. In Irish *Baile* is *town* or *townland*; *tobar* is *a well*. Baile-an-tobar is the town (or village) of the well. The church at Ballintubbert is dedicated to St. Brigid, and local tradition connects the well in the churchyard with the saint who is said to have visited the place.) Yet however obvious a name appears, the older forms of the name should be sought in ancient records, manor rolls, registers, charters, Domesday Book and so forth, because place-names often become corrupted and greatly transformed when their original language has ceased to be the common speech of local inhabitants. Such a name is Honeychild, in Kent, meaning "Huna's spring". The personal name Huna is forgotten, and the Anglo-Saxon word *celde*, "a spring", had already in the twelfth century become *child*.

Many place-names have two parts, especially those of English (Anglo-Saxon) origin. The affix or ending of the name often being some object that may be possessed, such as an estate (*ham* = home, the Continental *heim*) farm (*ton, wick*), open stretch of land (*field*), house (*stead, sted*), wood (*wood, holt, hurst*), swine pasture (*den*), valley (*dale, den* or *dene*), enclosure (*ham, tigh*). The former part of the name, its prefix, may be descriptive and relate to some peculiarity, especially of its form or position (topographic), its value, use, history, colour or other condition. The following actual examples, all within a few miles of my own home, will illustrate the point:—*Winch-combe*: here the oldest form (in A.D. 824) has *wincel*, meaning "crooked". *East*well, which is self-evident, especially in conjunction with the next parish *West*well. *Love*town: this field adjoins my garden. The name goes back to the Middle Ages, and I interpret the first element to mean "low", for indeed this field is low-lying, close to the River Stour; a very appropriate designation. *Len*acre: *len* or *lin* is "flax" (we have it in our word "linen"). *Nack*holt: the *n* is perhaps a survival of *in*, i.e., "in ackholt". *Ack* is "oak" (as in *ac*orn). *Bough*ton: the old form is *Boc*ton, and *boc* is sometimes "beech-tree" and sometimes "book" (i.e., charter), the place, in this case, having been granted by charter. The name of the owner, frequently corrupted, may indeed be appended (Boughton *Aluph*, Boughton *Malherbe*, Boughton *Monchelsea*). *Yal*lands: this is the name of a local manor, and there are several ancient forms of this name. The form *yal* evidently means "old". *Bower*land, with an early form *Burlonde* (1275): the name of a small manor (of about seventy acres) in East Kent. The prefix here very probably means "peasant". *Fel*borough, "dun coloured". *Thorn*hám (i.e., accent on the *ham*) "thorny". *Ollan*tigh, "holly". *Hassell*-street: ancient forms show that the first part of the name of this hamlet is a corruption of words meaning "harts' sole": *hart* is "a deer", *sole* means "a small (generally muddy) pond". The meaning of the prefix in some of the foregoing examples may be open to discussion, but at least they illustrate the principle I have indicated. All over the British Isles, and indeed almost everywhere in the world, place-names have been built up in a comparable manner. In Wales and Ireland, where the names are mainly Celtic and the original language still understood by many people of the present generation, educated people ought easily to be able to give an explanation for most place-names.

Another possibility about prefixes in place-names is that they may indicate personal ownership. This is seen in names of places like *Shepherds*well, which is, however, not quite what it appears to be. Ancient records show that the first element has been corrupted and that its early form is *Sibberts*. Also the suffix was formerly *wold*. Some prefixes are open to either the personal or the topographic interpretation (e.g., *Bods*ham, where the first syllable may be either a personal name or a reference to the elevated position of the place meaning something like "top" or "head").

Of course, there are many other possibilities of origin when we consider place-names as a whole, the dedication of churches (St. Albans) the existence of some famous object or structure. (Stonehenge; Chester, i.e., "the Military Headquarters") or an event in national or local history: *Baldock*, Hertfordshire, is an Anglo-French form of Bagdad, and commemorates the Crusades; *Battle* is an obvious example. In other cases, especially with languages which have long gone out of use in a district, the origin of the place-name may be obscure, and this is particularly noticeable with Celtic names in England, like Dover (from *dwvr*, Celtic " water ", a reference not to the sea but to the small stream upon which Dover stands).

This whole subject is full of interest, and will provide many links between local history, topography, archæology and family history. The use of good Anglo-Saxon and Celtic dictionaries and perusal of the interesting and authoritative publications of the English Place-name Society will provide much information for those who wish to pursue the subject.

EXERCISE

Take a local map; write down the names of twenty of its villages. How are these names constructed? How many of their prefixes contain: (*a*) topographic; (*b*) personal elements? Can you see the meanings of their suffixes? [Remember old records may show that the names of these places have been corrupted in spelling and apparent meaning with the long lapse of time.] Can you find any Celtic names on the map? [River names are often still Celtic when all the names of villages are English.] If you have a farmer friend ask him to show you his farm map. Study the field-names. Relate all this to local history as far as you can; a history of your parish may have been written, or there may be a good account of it in an authoritative county history. The parish registers, if ancient, and churchwardens' accounts (which often go back many years) should give additional particulars if you can get the privilege of consulting them. The tithe-map and its schedule of field-names, if in existence and available, will often give valuable and fascinating material for study.

Family Names

If you delve into local records you will come across surnames which are no longer represented in the neighbourhood, but others still occurring, perhaps widely, in your locality will also meet your eye.

Although capable of much more detailed classification, there are four principal kinds of surnames : (1) Names of trade, occupation or profession, often ancient callings: Barber, Baker, Turner, Tanner, Bowman, Franklin, Scrivenor, Fletcher. (2) Names indicating place of origin: York, Derby, French, Hall, Bridge, Linacre, Atwood, de Trafford. (3) Parental names sometimes abbreviated or the personal name perpetuated: Widdowson, Richardson, Richards, Robbins, Hewison, Wills, John, George. (4) Nicknames or personal descriptions: Armstrong, Redhead, Catt, Wild, Strong, Bold, Grace (anciently meaning " big "), Fox.

If you take a directory or voters' list and run through it you will find that there are many names you can readily classify but others, from strangeness of form or obscurity of meaning, will be puzzling.

WHAT'S IN A NAME?

EXERCISE

The study of Place-names, Family-names and personal names depends largely on books. You have a name in which you are interested, you seek out its meaning in such works as those mentioned under Literature, below, and it becomes part of your knowledge. You may care to make a card index of the names you determine, and as time goes on it will grow. A knowledge of Anglo-Saxon and French is a help to the solution of some problems.

LITERATURE

As far as place-names are concerned *The Concise Oxford Dictionary of English Place-names*, by Eilert Ekwall (Oxford: Clarendon Press (first published 1936)) forms a good foundation for study, and contains a long list of works consulted. The publications of the English Place-name Society are of great importance; special mention may be made of *Introduction to the Study of English Place-names* (Cambridge, 1924) and *The Chief Elements used in English Place-names*, by A. Mawer. The Society is publishing works on the place-names of the different counties.

For Ireland *Irish Names of Places*, by P. W. Joyce (Dublin: Phœnix Publishing Co.) will be found very useful. References to other Irish works are included.

A good many books on surnames have now appeared, but an important place is still held by *A Dictionary of English and Welsh Surnames*, by C. W. Bardsley (London: Frowde, 1901), already mentioned; it contains a valuable list of references.

Patronymica Britannica, by M. A. Lower (London: Smith, 1860), although published so long ago has much matter of interest, including the derivation of many Irish and Scots names.

The Oxford Dictionary of English Christian Names, by E. G. Withycombe (Oxford: Clarendon Press, 1946), may also be mentioned.

CHAPTER TWENTY-TWO

THE PATCHWORK OF THE PAST

ARCHÆOLOGY COVERS MANY SUBJECTS

This book cannot cover every branch of Archæology, but it can point out the lines upon which the student may teach himself far more than the subjects indicated by the headings of the foregoing chapters.

Many Facets

THE study of archæology, in the sense in which we mean it, is so wide in its interests that it encompasses every phase and facet of Man's changing skill and fortune. Where Man has advanced, archæology seeks to trace his steps. To take one instance of many, that of Man's implements; from his first rough-fashioned tool in stone through stages of increasing skill to the polished product of the New Stone Age; from stone to bronze, from bronze to iron, the archæologist seeks, studies and appraises. Where Man fell back, archæology notes cause and effect. In agriculture, art and architecture the student of the past sees the principles of trial and error applied right down the centuries. He sees the rough being trimmed, the simple becoming elaborate, the ideal becoming flamboyant, the flamboyant passing into degeneracy, the degenerate decaying. And so he tempers his judgment of the present by his experience of the past, and often sees better taste in comparatively simple and adequate designs than in something more elaborate and pretentious. Thus archæology is a subject of wide vistas, and to those who study it, it soon returns ample dividends of enjoyment and appreciation.

Sometimes the archæologist may be saddened when he looks upon the magnificence, restraint and genius of some late-fourteenth-century English monument, reflecting upon the over-elaboration that the fifteenth century brought and upon those succeeding changes which the Renaissance effected. On the other hand, with that same Renaissance came again those classical motifs that had been lost for centuries: these may please the eye and take one on, in mind, to the glory of those masterpieces of great architecture which graced the latter part of the seventeenth century. But then the thought of decadence returns and we picture some of the drab work that finally succeeded the days when gentlemen paid great attention to their country houses and built " temples " in their pleasure grounds. It is a fashion to decry the "Churchwardens' Gothic" of the second half of the nineteenth century, but we ought to be grateful to those who, after another period of debased design, stirred once more an enthusiasm for something better and if, at first, they failed to find it, were at least pioneers in a quest which in the present century has freed architecture from some of the bonds of indifference and shackles of mediocrity.

In past excellence the archæologist perceives good examples for today; in decadence or failure he sees warning for the present. The wider his experience and interests, the more certain will he be that Man's past has suggestions for planners in every department of our present-day reconstruction and advance.

Life Has Always Been Complex

The earlier pages of this book have dealt with a variety of topics concerned with the past activities of Man in these ancient islands of ours. The topics have been dealt with one by one in a sequence dictated by a desire to make the rather complicated subject as clear as possible. For example, the Roman period is, as seems natural, in its proper chronological position. We turn to it *after* a discussion of the Early Iron Age and *before* we talk about life in Anglo-Saxon times. But, of course, in actual practice we may occasionally want some information about all three of these periods at one and the same time, as when an Early Iron Age settlement afterwards became a Roman city and then later still became a place where our Anglo-Saxon ancestors made their homes. In our study, today, of such a site we shall want some information about things belonging to each age from 500 B.C. to the Norman Conquest.

It is true, of course, that you may set out one day to visit a world-famous monument of antiquity, like Stonehenge, and limit your excursion for that especial occasion to that particular item of interest, but, generally speaking, you will find with regard to the information you have built up for yourself that your observations on an ordinary day of archæological visits will not be restricted to the relics of one particular age nor to one particular group of objects. The hard lines of chapters in this book will melt away, and you will find yourself flitting from age to age and topic to topic as you investigate your surroundings. On a visit to a new place you may notice the arrangement of the streets, and you may find in that some evidence of early settlement. Winchester, Caerwent, Canterbury, for example, all exhibit some signs today of the plan that determined the layout in Roman times. Even the roads and lanes of remote country places may have a wonderful story to tell of more than a thousand years of Man's coming and going.

The shops and houses may exhibit their relics of bygone centuries. Public buildings, such as a town hall and the market, may bear the evidences of their age; there may be town walls and gates. Monuments and inscriptions, paving-stones, the bricks and masonry all around you, streams and bridges, water fountains and pumps, old fire-insurance signs on buildings, these and many another feature, small and great, will certainly come to your notice in town and country, and studying them will add much to your enjoyment. It will be especially gratifying if you have really taught yourself archæology. And as you look around you at such things as have just been mentioned you will rely upon your knowledge of many periods and many types of object. You will draw the threads of your studies together from many sources, and you will weave them into a real picture of the past. If you add churches and cathedrals, castles and museums, manuscript collections and libraries to your visiting list, you will further extend the range of your enquiries and pick up more threads of study to be woven into the pattern of your fabric.

Of course, it will not be long before you meet with some object of antiquarian interest which has not been mentioned at all in this book, because it is impossible to devote space here to the discussion of every topic which is likely eventually to come to your notice.

Here are some ideas for your archæological note-book, set down, without regard to chronology, as suggestions which may provide you with pleasant tasks for many hours, in some cases extending into months and years.

Study the place-names of your area (see page 190), take every opportunity to trace the earliest form of the name and any corruptions of it as the centuries rolled by; and do not forget the local names for fields and roads, for pits and posts and stumps and stones. Here are a few names I know in my locality: the Witch's Pool, the Damson stone, Lambsley, Stump's Lane, neolan mere (this in an ancient charter), Spider's Castle Jacket's Field, Mosewell (i.e., ? Moses' well), Coneyearth Wood.

Examine local words and collect local proverbs and allusions. Always remember that *you* are singularly well placed to study such things in your own immediate neighbourhood. Daily contact with people, casual conversation may reveal items of interest that nobody else in the wide world, however clever, can have such a good opportunity to add to the sum of human knowledge.

Listen to old people talking about their schooldays and their childhood: they may remember local customs and beliefs that are almost forgotten. They may tell you of old songs and of stories handed down but never committed to writing, of

THE PATCHWORK OF THE PAST

traditions attached to families, persons and places. All these things are well worth jotting down in your note-book.

Then, again, surnames are of great interest: there is your own surname, what does it mean? It must have a meaning (see page 192).

Witchcraft may still linger in out-of-the-way places; it certainly was practised in the younger days of men and women still alive, but advancing education will dispel such mists of superstition, and unless you record any instances that are mentioned to you they may be lost for ever. Old-time cures and recipes come into a similar category.

But there are also many things that are common knowledge today that will be uncertain in the future if we do not trouble to record them: what our village people did towards winning the two World Wars, the dates of modern buildings; the present activities of local government; the making of new roads; land-use, today, including the crops grown; the cattle raised in our area; unusual occupations in our district, surviving crafts and workmanship; the standards of living; the dress of men, women and children at work and at play, their leisure pursuits: all these things and many more, if duly noted now and deposited for preservation, may be of extreme interest in a hundred years. Individuals or local history groups or societies might compile a record book of some of the things that have just been mentioned.

Roads and Byways

One of the most fascinating studies in archæology, and one that is linked with a good many other facets of our ancient past, is concerned with the old routes by which Man moved from place to place on his lawful occasions for purposes of trade, pilgrimage and defence.

If you will take a small-scale map, say one inch to the mile, and find upon it your own district and your own main roads, you will see at once, the general plan of your local communications. In the study of highways, (and byways, too, for that matter), two things are necessary, common sense and imagination. Picture the past and the needs of those who used the roads in bygone centuries. What did they want the roads for? First, there was the link between the first settlement in your parish and the great world outside. Was this link part of a way between two great centres, or was it of no use at all to any but the inhabitants of the immediate neighbourhood? If it was of general use to the community, what established that use and at what period of history or prehistory?

To take simple examples: there is a way north from the salt-producing areas of Cheshire. If you live near it look at it on the map and work it out for yourself. From east to west across Northumberland and Cumberland run the roads which are part of the defensive system which has its most spectacular and very well-known feature in Hadrian's Wall, a magnificent monument to the military might of Rome. Roman roads form an important part of modern communications in many parts of England, but it is also true that in some places former Roman highways have either sunk to the status of lanes or field paths or have disappeared altogether and are only to be recognized now by very careful investigation. From Winchester to Canterbury runs the so-called but very problematical "Pilgrims' Way", in many places a mere track running on high ground in a continuous line roughly from west to east. How much this route was ever used by pilgrims going to the shrine of St. Thomas Becket at Canterbury we do not know, but there is other evidence of its extreme antiquity.

Whether employed for religious or military needs or for purposes of trade, there is no doubt that many roads in our countryside date back much farther than is generally recognized.

One feature of very old roads, especially in remote districts, is the depth below the surface of the surrounding land to which they have been worn by use. This is often most marked where the road passes over the brow of a hill, because, in olden days before the roads were well metalled, the surface was apt to be washed away by rainstorms. In other places the mud was scraped up and thrown out when the weather in winter made the road almost impassable. Occasionally you will find evidence of parallel tracks, where, owing to the bad condition of a road in the past, a diversion to right or left has been made and a new track established where the surface was firmer and better. Occasionally diversions will be found to avoid pits or settlements, and where this is the case the settlement must obviously be older than the diversion.

I know a case where a road passes between two systems of ancient fields. The boundaries of the fields are related to the road, and are not continuous across the road, showing that the outlines of the fields as we see them today were established after the road was in use; or to put it the other way the road is older than the existing field outlines.

LITERATURE

In addition to works mentioned in the discussion of Literature at the end of Chapter Two, mention may be made of *Stonehenge Today and Yesterday*, by Frank Stevens, now out of print, I fear (my copy is dated 1924, price sixpence) (London : H.M.S.O.). The British Museum *Guide to Mediæval Antiquities and Objects of Later Date* (London : B.M., 1924), which you may be able to consult in your public library, deals with a very wide range of objects of archæological interest.

CHAPTER TWENTY-THREE

A COMPLEX PICTURE

TEACH YOURSELF BY TAKING A WIDE VIEW OF THE PAST

There must be an end to a book like this, but the topics we could talk about are not exhausted. The author hopes you will be encouraged by this chapter to go on teaching yourself. Archæology has a beginning, but it never has an end.

Studying Inscriptions, Sculpture, Carving and Engraving

TOMBS, monuments and monumental inscriptions are useful in throwing light upon national, local and family history. Care is, of course, required in transcribing the peculiarities of spelling, the obsolete words, the Latin and other foreign languages and in the blazoning and tricking of arms.

The styles of different centuries are fairly easy to learn, because so many of the inscriptions are dated and, having learnt the style from a profusion of examples in which the dates are given, it becomes easy to recognize undated examples. Of course, a good way to check your growing knowledge, is to examine a piece of work, first without reading any inscription on it, decide what you think its approximate date is and then, if a date is actually given in the epitaph, either you are delighted with your own proficiency or assured that you need more practice.

A class of monument which has long received a good deal of attention is the *sepulchral brass*. The metal of which these memorials are made (brass) is often called *latten*. Many books about these important objects have been written, some general, some local.

The earliest brasses in this country are late thirteenth century, and for nearly 300 years they provide good material for the study of costume, arms, armour and weapons. There is sometimes a touch of humour about some of the inscriptions on brasses as there is about many other epitaphs. The little girl who is reputed to have asked " Mamma ! where are the *bad* people buried ? " was asking a wise question. At Wye in Kent is the multiple memorial to Thomas and Alice Palmer and Alice's first husband John Andrew and to the children of her first marriage. No doubt it was erected by one or more of these children, the second marriage apparently having been childless. The first husband (father of the children) is described

Fig. 116.—Brasses provide us with valuable evidence about costume in the centuries represented by these memorials, many of which reach a high standard of craftsmanship and art. Here is a military brass; it is the oldest brass surviving in England, and commemorates Sir John D'Abernon, died 1277 and is to be found in the Church at Stoke D'Abernon, Surrey. The knight is in complete mail with the exception of the knee pieces, which are leather. He wears a surcoat over his armour. He has a sword and a shield; the shield is charged with his arms, *azure a chevron or* (a gold chevron on a blue ground). A small pennon on a long spear is charged with the D'Abernon arms. The marginal inscription is in Lombardic letters. The scale below the brass is 1 foot in length.

From *Transactions of the St. Paul's Ecclesiological Society*, 1895.

on the brass as *iustus*, " good ", their stepfather was *venustus*, " good-looking ". Comment is superfluous, but it may be added that both husbands " departed from the world and were laid in hard marble " (indicated by a grammatical error in the Latin) " and their wife Alice suffered a similar fate ".

A simple method of copying a monumental brass is to brush the metal carefully free from grit and dust with a soft brush and lay upon it a sheet of thin paper. The tougher the paper the better, but it must be thin. Even newsprint will do; nor need the paper be white. Weight this down into position with books or other small objects. Then, with a piece of heel-ball, wax which you can obtain from any cobbler, rub the impression of the brass carefully through and on to the paper, beginning at one end of the monument and working systematically towards the other, rubbing only in one direction. This last point is very important, and if you do not observe it, you will fail to get a clear impression.

The best way to learn how to do this is perhaps to watch someone else the first time and then try it yourself. But there is no doubt that with a little patience you can teach yourself and get excellent results.

You can use your ingenuity afterwards in mounting the rubbings on stouter paper or upon cloth, and perhaps you can get some hints about this from looking at collections of rubbings. It may be that your local public museum has such a collection. There are also, of course, privately owned collections.

Incised slabs are not so common as brasses, but they give much the same kind of information. They are best copied by laying a weighted sheet of thin paper on the slab and tracing out carefully, with pencil, the lines that have been engraved in the stone. The copy can subsequently be lined in with Indian ink and checked against the original. It is a laborious work but well worth doing, and a fine reproduction of the original can be obtained by this method (Fig. 117).

Bas-reliefs, that is pieces of sculpture in which the figures represented project less than half their true proportions from the surface, can be successfully copied in plaster or in concrete. It is, however, only safe to attempt this when the work is in sound condition without any crumbling of the stone, otherwise much damage may be done to the bas-relief (Fig. 118).

Begin by covering the whole work with thin brown paper which has been thoroughly soaked in water, using a fairly stiff paint brush to make the paper fit the sculpture. As the paper spreads over the irregular surface of the stone it will tear in a good many places, and the stone will not be completely covered. Never mind, cover the rents with patches of wet paper. When all the tears have been covered in this way and the patches well brushed down you will not be able to see the stone anywhere. Now, as evenly as possible, apply a second layer of soaked paper, dabbing the paper into every nook and cranny and patching wherever tears occur. There is sufficient size in the

FIG. 117.—Incised marble slab in Crundale Church, Kent. The inscription is worn. The memorial is to John Sprot, Rector, died 1466. He is depicted wearing Mass vestments and holding the Chalice. 6′ 9″ × 2′ 9″.

Drawn by S. G. B.-B.

paper to make the second layer stick firmly to the first. Do not forget to brush the paper smoothly down on to the first layer. Now add a third layer of your wet paper and go on, layer after layer, until there is a thickness of paper nearly as thick as your little finger firmly adherent to the bas-relief. Now leave the paper to dry; it may take three or four days. When it begins to peel take the paper carefully off the work and

FIG. 118.—A bas-relief in Purbeck marble. In such a treatment less than half the depth of the subject is represented. When half the depth is depicted the work is in mezzo-relief. When more than half is modelled it is a high relief. The original is in Godmersham Church, Kent, 2 feet 8 inches high; it represents St. Thomas Becket and is not later than A.D. 1200.

Drawn by S. G. B.-B.

get it quite dry. This is your mould; paint the surface that has been against the stone with oil until it ceases readily to absorb more.

Then lay the mould, moulded side up, on a bed of sand spread on the floor and press the paper well into the sand so that there is support everywhere for the different irregularities of the mould. Be careful not to get sand on the moulded surface.

Having next erected a frame of wood or bricks around the mould to prevent the escape of plaster or concrete, mix sufficient plaster of Paris or Portland cement and sand (according to your own fancy for a light permanent or for a heavier cast) to fill the mould and pour it carefully in, avoiding air bubbles and leaving it to set thoroughly. With large subjects it is best to reinforce the cast by putting wire-netting (supported, if necessary, by string) into the liquid plaster or concrete.

If you remove the mould carefully it can be used again.

It is a good plan to begin with a very small piece of work.

For small sound carvings in wood, a modification of this method can successfully be employed, but the mould can then be made in modelling clay, and it will be necessary to oil the woodwork before applying the clay, to prevent sticking.

It is hardly necessary to remind you that every care must, in all cases, be exercised to avoid damage to objects copied in these various ways and that permission from owners or custodians must always be obtained before attempting the work of rubbing, drawing by tracing or making a mould of paper or clay.

The study of brasses and of other monuments will give interesting information about heraldry and family history and provide many examples of early dress—ecclesiastical, military and civilian—and the study of armour, as represented in these memorials, will provide an introduction to the study of real armour.

Two small points about brasses and other tombs. It used to be said that the crossed legs in effigies of knights indicated that the warrior so shown had been on a crusade; it was also affirmed that the representation of a pastoral staff with the head turned *inwards* indicated the internal jurisdiction of an abbot and that when the head of the staff was turned *outwards* it showed the external rule of a bishop. Such views are not now held.

Stained Glass

If you live in an area where there is a wealth of ancient stained glass, or if you have the opportunity to visit such a neighbourhood, you will find yourself well rewarded by studying it.

The stained-glass artist of the Norman period (1066–1200) had a bold drawing of his subject to work from. He produced his design with pieces of glass, each of a separate colour. With reference to his drawing, he cut each to a required shape, such as that of a head or a foot or an arm or the red part of a garment. These pieces were fitted together to make the picture.

A COMPLEX PICTURE

It was mainly a design of coloured glass. Black pigment was used with a minimum number of bold strokes to indicate the features of the face, the fingers of a hand, the folds of a garment. These were painted as an enamel on the glass, which was then "fired" (heated in the furnace enough to fuse the black lines with the surface of the glass and make them permanent). The pieces were then fixed together with strips of grooved lead so that the metal tended to emphasize the bold design. Slight differences of thickness in the glass produced slight differences in the intensity of colouring. The differences of colour were produced by using different substances, mostly oxides of metals; for instance, copper gave red (ruby), cobalt gave blue.

The glass was "pot-metal", that is to say the substance to produce the colour was mixed in with the molten glass, so that it stained it right through. An exception was ruby glass, because if this was stained throughout, too much light was cut off. So the craftsman hit upon the expedient of "flashing". He applied to the white glass a thin layer of molten ruby glass, so that the two were fused together.

Lettering could be provided by covering white glass with black pigment; the pigment could then be scraped away to form letters of the Lombardic alphabet. Subsequent firing of the glass left the inscription permanent as white letters on a black background.

The panel-maker of the Norman period did not try to show too much detail; his work when viewed from the proper distance gives a bold, clear picture. Single subjects, such as a standing or sitting figure, almost filling a whole panel are typical. They have a rude vigour which would have been spoilt by the introduction of greater detail. In the unique and famous figure of Adam digging, which is incorporated in the West window of Canterbury Cathedral, the artist boldly indicates activity; Adam is really at work; yet there is no great detail, and the panel is meant to be seen from a little distance (Figs. 119 and 120).

In the thirteenth century (the Early English period of architecture) stained glass was still a mosaic, and the predominance of one colour gave character to the window. Greater detail was attempted. The figures tended to be smaller, and could be grouped in medallions to represent incidents, but individual pieces of glass, white or coloured, again formed the separate parts of each picture. This treatment gave a less vigorous result than that obtained by the artists of the Norman period.

The lines of the lead still enhanced the design. Lettering was again white on black, produced as before. Formal foliage designs formed borders and filled the spaces between medallions.

Also, in this thirteenth century, began the use of white glass

FIG. 119.—One of our oldest stained-glass pictures. Adam digging in the Garden of Eden. The original not later than A.D. 1178 is now in the great west window of Canterbury Cathedral; but it was designed for the north-west clerestory window of the choir (in which a replica of the panel has been inserted). The diagram is of the "cut line" made from the original, and it represents the mosaic built up of pieces of glass, each piece of one colour only. Thus the mosaic is a design of colours. This design is emphasized by the drawing in black only (see Fig. 120). The letters indicate the colours: PY, pale yellow; W, white; B, blue; F, flesh; Y, yellow; G, green; P, pink; R, ruby; PB, pale blue. The ruby glass is white with a thin red layer applied to it when the glass was molten, otherwise the glass would be too dense. All the other glass is one colour throughout. 56" × 29".

A COMPLEX PICTURE 207

figured in black pigment. This glass, generally called by its French name, *grisaille*, was arranged in patterns into which small pieces of coloured glass were sometimes introduced and

FIG. 120.—Is this the oldest stained glass picture in the world? The drawing of Adam: all this is done in black pigment which forms enamel lines on the surface of the glass. In modern glass these lines are on the inner surface, but Norman glass-makers did sometimes put the lines on the outside, where they might be damaged by weathering.

in which the lead strips played an effective part in strengthening and emphasizing the design. The ornament was frequently based upon the leaves of plants, particularly *Acanthus*. Behind the foliage, the groundwork was often cross-hatched with fine black lines.

In the fourteenth century (the Decorated period) *grisaille* glass was much used, but the cross-hatching behind the foliage disappeared. In other windows pictorial representation continued. Lettering in black began to be used from the fourteenth century, Where, in the fourteenth century, architectural features were introduced they naturally exhibited the Decorated style, but there was no over-elaboration of architectural design. A considerable amount of line-drawing was carried out in black pigment. Also in the fourteenth century we have the introduction of a new technique. It was found that if white glass were coated with silver sulphide and then fired, a layer of translucent yellow glass was formed on the surface. Also, the need to place leads around every feature of the design gradually became unnecessary because, about the same time, artists hit upon the expedient of grinding away the thin layer of red, which was fused upon white in the case of ruby glass, to leave patches of white surrounded by red. This naturally suggested flashing with other colours, especially blue, green and purple, to obtain similar effects with those colours. The use of this method made panels of glass much less of a mosaic than before and more like a painting.

Great use was made of this in the fifteenth century and, combined with methods already in use in the previous century, resulted in the production of glass which admitted much more light than before. The line-drawing included much delicate work.

As far as fifteenth-century design is concerned statue-like figures in niches are frequent, and canopies over them, sometimes very elaborate, often occur. The work is largely in white glass, with the fine lines enhanced by yellow pigment. Such a treatment gives a characteristic and readily recognizable appearance to many windows of the period. Coats-of-arms become more frequent and draperies tend to become very realistic. In some cases the glass is a patchwork of many colours, but, unlike the mosaics of two hundred years earlier (which, you will remember, were built up of small pieces of glass each of a different colour, held together by the lead), the differences are now due, in part, to the application of the principles of abraded flashings, already explained, and painting yellow in, with no necessity for lead separating colour from colour.

Sixteenth-century work includes some elegant and delicate designs, such as heraldic badges drawn rather faintly in black pigment on white glass, often on the inside of small diamond-shaped panes (quarries) and then coloured or enhanced in yellow on the other (outer) side of the glass. Rather clumsy human figures with the features less delicately drawn than in the previous century occur, and there is also a good deal of heavily coloured heraldic glass.

This phase was followed by the introduction of a new method of drawing lines on the stained or white glass. Previously it had been done by the application of black pigment only, and this was virtually an enamel. It was incorporated with the surface of the glass by firing. Now, powdered ruby, blue and green glasses were also used as enamels in which designs could be drawn or painted. By subsequent firing, the new pigments were fused with the surface and the design became much more like the work of the oil painter.

Swiss and Dutch glass of this kind, made in the fifteenth, sixteenth and seventeenth centuries, is to be found in England today.

With this phase, the production of stained glass came to an end until the Gothic revival of the nineteenth century.

At first the glass artists of the nineteenth century had to pass through an experimental stage and, though there were some very pleasing results, especially with bold lines on white glass and some in mosaic designs imitative of the thirteenth-century craftsmanship, a great deal of the glass of this period is poor when contrasted either with early work or with some of the best executed today.

Later designs and improved standards, less imitative and more original than those of the first years of the new period, have produced some stained glass which is generally regarded very favourably by contemporary critics. The best work seems to be that which avoids the mistake of the seventeenth century in the production of designs which could be better executed with oil on canvas.

Perhaps the greatest contributions that the twentieth-century glass artist can make to his craft concern the proper use of colours, their disposition in the design and their judicious combination to produce a pattern pleasing to the observer at a little distance. Freedom of drawing is also very desirable, and the use of lead to enhance the design already boldly executed in glass is as effective today as it was 750 years ago. The ample use of white glass as background also seems to be very desirable. Some of it may well be boldly figured in black, some of it with varied (not mechanical) cross-hatched backgrounds; coloured jewel-like pieces will enliven such a treatment. Most modern artists have already learnt the lesson that figures in stained glass must be figures in action not statues in niches. They may well go back to the beginning of things in England, and bear in mind the beauty and vigour of that glass at Canterbury, by which the artist of Norman days represented Adam digging.

Sometimes when ancient glass has suffered injury it has been necessary to repair cracks by inserting lead slips. This additional metal, not being part of the original pattern, detracts a little from the design. In some modern windows the artist has introduced similar slips of lead unnecessarily. They cut across the design and are an affectation; they are therefore to be deplored.

Weaving a Pattern

All that has been said so far in this book can be woven into one fabric, but *you* must do it. Take all the things that have been mentioned and some others too which you will find out entirely for yourself as you teach yourself archæology and merge one thing with another until you make the past live. In this way you will have some idea of the life and ways, the feelings and aspirations of the generations that preceded us. Remember the times we often think far distant are not really so remote either in years or in feeling: a hundred years is only the lifetime of a very old man, ten such lifetimes would take us back into Anglo-Saxon times and about a hundred years before the Norman Conquest.

None of us can expect to be expert in all the branches of knowledge into which we make some enquiry when we teach ourselves archæology, but all of us can take an intelligent interest in every phase of the complicated subject and find the greatest delight in doing it. In addition to learning much about different branches of the subject, we shall strive to become acquainted with the literature of archæology to know what books to consult when we are faced with a problem. Articles in most good encyclopædias give a number of references to an important subject at the end of the article which deals with it. It is good to be able to answer a question about the past ourselves, but it is almost as satisfactory to know *where to find the answer*.

Enquiries we wish to make are either general, when, for example, we want to know the period to which a piece of pottery belongs or wish to identify a coin we have found; or they are concerned with special localities, when, for instance, we want information about a particular castle or church or family.

For general enquiries we have many helpful works written by great authorities on their respective subjects, and additions to this class of literature are frequently made.

Public libraries possess a good many books of this kind, and if we personally do not know the titles of books we need nor the names of authors, an enquiry, I think preferably in writing, will generally elicit a very helpful answer, though we shall not give a busy public servant unnecessary work by making a careless or inexplicit enquiry.

In our study we shall naturally seek information from *up-to-date* books, because modern research has sometimes shown earlier ideas to be incorrect; nevertheless, some older books, some going back to the eighteenth century, are quite frequently of use and importance, and they often contain illustrations of objects found many years ago. Advice about the reliability of any particular work can be obtained at your nearest public library.

The pursuit of local information cannot, of course, be dealt with so easily in a book that is designed for use all over the country. Many counties have monumental histories, often written more than a hundred years ago and still used as standard works. Their archæological information is often of the highest importance. County archæological, historical and record societies in many cases publish very valuable volumes of papers covering a wide range of subjects, and the Victoria County Histories are valuable authoritative works up to the point reached in publication. Individual parish histories and guide books naturally differ very much in value, because sometimes the zeal of a local author exceeds his scholarship, and so care has to be exercised in accepting as authoritative any work about which we have no well-informed opinion. Avoid the common misapprehension that if you see something in print it *must* be true. A well-known author published a book in which he stated that a prehistoric burial-mound, which is actually two miles away in the next parish, is to be found in the place where I live. That mistake has been repeatedly copied in print by other writers; but that does not make it true.

Another thing to remember about books is that they are available for immediate consultation by all who own or are able to borrow them; an expert may not be available just when he is wanted, but his written word is a permanent record.

To most of our questions, but not of course to every one, there is an answer in print; knowing where to find it is the important thing, and learning how to get at the right books is a most important part of teaching yourself archæology.

Intelligent Interest

It is not to be expected that the industrious young man or woman engaged in the work of business or profession will ordinarily have time (or inclination for that matter) to become an expert excavator of Roman remains in Britain or a specialist in deciphering mediæval documents, but it should be possible for all of us who wish to have a wide outlook and an intelligent interest in the world around us to be able to teach ourselves enough to be able to appreciate the relics of past ages. We ought to be able, too, to people the past in our imagination from the patient examination of the antiquities that belong to town and country, when we come across them. By experience knowledge grows, and by comparison of one thing with another there is built up a wealth of interest. We use this not only on holiday in remote spots but for the daily observation of buildings as we pass down familiar streets or take an occasional look at a utilitarian excavation for building or for road repairs close to our home or near our place of business.

It is quite ordinary things that give us opportunities to teach ourselves archæology. In an ancient parish today we look at the church, an old barn, several ancient farmhouses, we note the arrangement of the pattern of arable, pasture and woodland. There is a stream passing by, and there are roads and field paths. How much, we ask ourselves, has the scene changed during the past fifty years? Those of us who can go back in memory that far may say, "*Very little.*" How much farther into the past can we carry this sort of enquiry? Church records, estate maps and knowledge of the road-system may convince us that here, at least, very little alteration has taken place during the last two hundred years or so. If that be true, then we are taken back nearly a quarter of the time that separates us from the Norman Conquest. It all makes me think that if we could travel back in time and could see the ancient scene, say at the Norman Conquest, we should say to one another, "Why there's old Whats-his-name's farm and the stackyard where we played hide and seek when you and I were boys together." And the reply would come back "Yes, and there's the fish pool in the river where I've spun for pike many a time. Just look at the woods and the arable and the meadow; why they are much the same as we find them in the twentieth century." "Look!" we would say again; "there is something very familiar about the roads and lanes."

In fact, I think that if we could go back 2000 years, instead of being content with a look at the local scene in 1066, we should often be surprised to see familiar things in familiar places and a little astonished, perhaps, to find that that ancient world was our world, in spite of the passing of the centuries.

Human Progress

All the subjects we have considered together in this book are part of the story of human progress which began on the day when an early ancestor of ours first found that a stick or a stone made his task a little easier in winning wild fruit from a tree or helped him in digging in the ground with his fingers for a fleshy root to eat or a succulent grub to tickle his palate.

In every age there were men who raised themselves to pinnacles of skill. The Solutrean tool-maker could flake flint better than any modern imitator. The Bronze Age workers who turned out halberds and lurs were masters of their craft. The Anglo-Saxon scribes set modern lawyers an admirable example of handwriting when they drew up their charters. Mediæval architects and builders provided a standard of excellence which remains an inspiration in the twentieth century. No later poet or playwright has equalled the genius of Shakespeare. The exquisite workmanship of the Black Prince's tomb at Canterbury and the virility of his funeral achievements fill us with amazement and appreciation today. The men who accomplished all these and many other superb triumphs of human invention and workmanship were exceptional people. Practice and the improvement of traditional methods had made every one of them supreme in his own speciality; their works stand out as landmarks in the vista of human progress down the centuries from the days of Adam to this present hour. And though each giant arose with such brilliance of execution in the crafts of his own generation that no one has since surpassed the masterpieces of that particular phase of human progress, new needs, new materials and new methods superseded the old, and there was no further need for the particular skill that had previously risen to such heights of excellence. The wonders of electrical science upon which we rely today for many of the marks of our civilization will one day grow old and perish because atomic power, or stranger marvels still to come, will make old fashioned and virtually useless many of the devices now in everyday use for transport, domestic equipment and popular entertainment. And yet human progress will sweep on.

Each age in human advance has left behind it objects that were fashionable and of great importance to the men and women who used them. But when that stage had passed, those things were completely superseded and were never employed again. The shapes and sizes, the forms and minor features of the tools or domestic pottery used at any given time are recognizable by those who know them well; they are types that characterize the period in which they made them. These types are like lines upon a scale of measurement, for we use them to give us our time-readings. They do not, especially in the earliest ages, give us absolute dates, but they indicate for us, clearly enough, the succession of events and give us the relative ages of the periods to which they belong.

So as you teach yourself archæology you will gain an ever-increasing perception of the unity of the subject. Each piece in the jig-saw puzzle helps to complete the picture. One piece is a fragment of thirteenth-century stained glass, another is a flint arrow-head of the Bronze Age. Here is an Anglo-Saxon charter, while close beside it lies a Roman coin. It is going to be a big panorama of mankind, and so the number of pieces is almost infinite. They each contribute something to the fascinating picture which begins to take shape as many of them fall into their proper places. But our jig-saw will never be quite complete, for some of the bits are lost for ever. Nevertheless, many of the pieces now unknown will eventually be found, and they will be fitted in to give a still better idea of the whole.

The subject abounds with delightful possibilities. You who teach yourself archæology are one of the people looking for missing pieces or trying to fit in some that have already turned up. You need perseverance, and you must cultivate a cautious, careful method of enquiry. Then you will have more than one exciting moment when some unpromising-looking, awkward shape suddenly falls into place and gives precision and finality to one little corner of the picture. You are in for a good time (as a friend of mine once said, when he was lecturing in a prison), and we wish you every success.

But, above all, do not think of the objects you handle as being merely specimens. They were in their own day part of the equipment of living men and women, and so archæology will never be complete until we are able to picture the families and individuals of the past using not only these tools and weapons and ornaments but other things, too, so perishable that they are lost for ever. Only when we have formed a clear impression of what happened in the lives of such people shall we be in the fullest sense archæologists. Our archæology will be a real thing when we can, at least to some extent, enter into the difficulties and hopes of their lives and into some of their anxieties and joys.

EXERCISE

You will find a note-book useful. In it you can jot down the things of archæological interest you see or hear about day by day. Some points you may find useful to enter in your book have already been mentioned; others will frequently occur to you.

Try out methods suggested for copying brasses and incised slabs.

If you wish to study stained glass, I think that the way in which the subject has been handled in the present chapter will put you on the right lines. Make a table showing the different periods.

By the time you have worked through a number of the exercises suggested in this book, you will be able to undertake new ones of your own invention.

But I promise one thing: however many exercises you complete, there will always be another one round the corner, and it may contain some questions that none of the experts can answer.

LITERATURE

In addition to the works referred to at the ends of Chapters Two and Twenty-two, attention may be drawn to the fact that there are many works on Brasses, one of which is *English Church Brasses*, by E. R. Suffling (London: Gill, 1910); this work contains a chapter on the literature of the subject. The subject of stained glass is discussed in encyclopædia articles, and attention is directed to *The Ancient Glass of Canterbury Cathedral*, by B. Rackham (London: Lund Humphries, 1949 (£12 12s.)), which might well be consulted by those interested.

INDEX AND GLOSSARY

(*Most of the words in the index are, in fact, explained in the text*)

ABBEVILLIAN, 42–43
Acanthus (Several species are ornamental plants. *Acanthus* leaves are used in the design of early stained glass in Canterbury Cathedral and the Norman builders adorned capitals of pillars in the choir there with representations of the *Acanthus* leaf, in the classical manner. In the nearby Precincts, in July 1953, a friend showed me a flourishing example of the living plant), 118–119, 207
Acheulian, 42–43
Achievements (in heraldry), 184, 186
Agriculture, 73–74, 88, 103, 110–111
Agrimensor (surveyor), *frontispiece*
Alfred the Great, 24
Alphabets, 111, 174, 181–182
  see also Futhorc, Ogham.
Altamira, 46
Amber (a fossil gum), 83
Amphora, 105
Anglo-Saxon architecture, 135, 140, 153–155
Anglo-Saxon Chronicle, 130
Anglo-Saxon pagan religion, 131
Anglo-Saxons, 121–134, 140, 171, 190
Annual rings of wood, 26
Anthropoid apes, 32
Apes, 32
Archæology, v, 13, 18, 133, 194–195, 212–214
Architecture, 107, 135–167
  Anglo-Saxon, 133, 135, 137, 140, 153–155
  contemporary, 148
  debased, 147

Architecture (*contd.*)
  Decorated, 135, 136, 138, 143–145
  domestic, 151–167
  Early English, 135, 142–143
  Georgian, 147–148
  Gothic (style arising in the late twelfth century by the introduction of the pointed instead of the segmental arch), 135, 148
  Norman, 135, 137, 140–142
  Perpendicular, 135, 136, 138, 145–147
  Renaissance, 135, 147, 162–163
  Roman, 153
  Romanesque (that is derived from Roman sources: the Romans introduced the segmental or semicircular arch, and this is the mark of the Romanesque style in England. The Romanesque styles are Anglo-Saxon and Norman), 135, 137–138, 140–142
  Tudor, 135, 136
Arms, *see* Heraldry.
Arretine ware, *see* "Samian" ware.
Arris (in architecture), 137
Art, Anglo-Saxon, 128, 129, 130
  early, 39, 40, 46, 68, 128–130
Aurignacian, 40 (Fig. 12, *a–g*), 42, 45 (Fig. 15)
Axe, 43, 83

Banker-marks, 148–149
Barbotine, 113
Bas-reliefs, 201–204
Beaker-folk, 77
Bede, 124, 172
Belgæ, *frontispiece*, 91, 98, 171
Beowulf, 131–132, 134, 154
Bewcastle cross, 175

Bible, the Holy, 31, 73-74
Blazoning (in heraldry), 184-186
Books, 171
see also Literature.
Bowtell (in architecture), 138
Brachycephalic, 81
Brasses, 187, 199-201, 204
Bricks and brickwork, 106, 140, 165-166
Bronze, 76
Bronze Age, 22, 76-89
Bronze Age clothing, 22, 83, 84, 85, 86
Bronze Age implements, 76, 77, 79, 80, 82, 83, 86, 87, 88, 89
Bronze Age pottery, 77, 78
Brooches, 125, 128-129, 131
Bucket (cista), 97
Building, see Architecture.
Bulb of percussion, 36
Burial, 16, 17, 18, 19, 20, 22, 54, 78, 83, 84, 85, 86, 91, 98, 103, 104, 107, 124, 125, 126, 131

Canoe, Bronze Age, 78
Canterbury, 103 (Fig. 68), 111 (Fig. 74), 153, 189, 198, 205, 213
see also Durovernum.
Carbon, radioactive, 26, 27
Carving, 199
Caschrom (foot-plough), 58
Castles, 155-159
Castor ware, 118
Celts (implements), 69, 79, 82
Celts or Kelts (race), 69, 90-92
Cemeteries, see Burial.
Cephalic index, 81
Chamfer (in architecture), chamfer-plane, 137-138, 141-144, 147
Changing fashions, see Fashions, Typology.
Charters, 180
Châtelperron, 45
Chaucer, Geoffrey, 24
Chert (compact siliceous rock), 39
Chimpanzee, an ape, 32

Chip-carving, 129
Christianity, 103, 115, 121, 172-173
Chronology of Roman pottery in Britain, 117-118
Church architecture, see Architecture.
Cinerary urns, 125
Cista (bucket), 97
Clactonian, 43
Classical orders of architecture, 119
Claudius, 24, 114
Coats-of-arms, see Heraldry.
Coins, 103, 112, 121, 129, 171
College of Arms, 188
Combs, 93, 131
Composite order, 119
Conchoidal fracture, 35, 46
Copper, 76-77
Copying inscriptions, brasses and bas-reliefs, 201-204
Corinthian order, 119
Cornice (the horizontal band of masonry supporting the pediment of a classical building), 163
Cottages, 163-165
Court of the Lord Lyon, 188
Crambeck ware, 118
Creswellian, 46
Cro-Magnon, 45
Cromlech, 71
Cultivation of the soil, 57, 58, 59, 65, 99, 102
Cultures, 42
Cunobelin (Cymbeline), 171

Dark Ages, the, 24, 121, 172
Dates in archæology, 23-29, 69, 79, 87, 95, 101, 102, 114, 115, 117, 135, 166
Dates in geology, 61, 62
Dead, remembrance of, 16, 17, 18, 103, 130
Dendrochronology, 25, 26
Denmark, 22, 70, 82, 83, 84, 85, 86, 87, 174
Dolichocephalic, 80
Dolmen, 71
Domesday Book, 133, 170-171
Doric order, 118-119

INDEX AND GLOSSARY

Dragendorff, Hans (born at Dorpat, 15th October, 1870, died 29th January, 1941. He held various posts; chiefly Director of the römisch-germanisch Kommission of the Institute at Frankfurt-am-Main; and General Secretary of the archäologisches Institut in Berlin (till 1922) and Dean and Rektor of the A. Ludwiges Universität at Freiburg i. B.), 117
Druids, 73
Durovernum (Canterbury), *frontispiece*, 116 (Fig. 75)

Early Iron Age, 24, 90–99
Early Iron Age burials, 91
Early Iron Age pottery, 91, 93, 97, 98
Earthworks, 47
Embroidery (Bronze Age), 84
Emperors, Roman, 114–115
English, the, 121–134
Engraving, 199
Eoliths, 37–38
Evidence, weighing, 21, 22, 23
Evil spirits, 17
Excavation, 19, 20, 53, 102, 103

Fabricator, 35
Family names, 192–193
Fashions, changing (typology), 15, 74, 88, 94
Figurines (small figures sometimes in pipeclay or pottery, sometimes in metal—some were objects of devotion in the Roman period), 103 (Fig. 68)
Fillets (in architecture), 138, 144
Flaking flints, 34, 35, 36
Flint, 34, 35, 36, 37
Flint-mines, 74
Fossils (remains of living things —including Man—preserved in rocks), 32–33, 61
Franks casket, 175, 181
Futhorc, 175–176

Gaul, coinage of, 171
pottery from, 117
Geology, 57, 59, 60, 61, 62, 63, 64, 65, 119
Georgian architecture, 147–148
Georgian era, 24
Gibbon, an ape, 32
Gildas, 124
Glaciation, 27, 53, 64, 65
Glassware, 103 (Roman); 122 (Anglo-Saxon)
Gley, 54
Gold, 76–77, 83
Gorilla, an ape, 32
Gothic architecture, 135–136, 142–147, 148
Graffiti (scribblings), 111 (Fig. 74), 112, 172
Grave-furniture (the various objects placed in a grave with a corpse or ashes), 103, 121, 125–128
Gravettian, 45
Greek architecture, 118–119

Halberd, 77
Hall-house, 160–162
Halstatt, 93, 95–99
Harpoons, 67, 69
Hatchments, 186
Hengest (less correctly, *Hengist*) and Horsa, 122, 124
Heraldry, 183–189
Heralds College, 188
Homes, 102, 151–167
Homo neanderthalensis, 33
Homo sapiens, 32–33
Hypocaust, 106

Immigration, 92–93, 123–124
Implements, stone, 35, 37, 38, 41, 42, 43, 44, 45, 88
see also Microliths, Neolithic implements, Palæolithic Age.
"Incense-cup", 78
Incised slabs, 201, 202
Industries, 42
Inscriptions, 104, 106, 121, 127, 133, 172, 174, 176, 181, 187, 199, 200, 202, 207
Ionic order, 119
Irish Genealogical Office, 188

INDEX AND GLOSSARY

Iron, 77, 90, 98, 99
 see also Early Iron Age.
Iron Age, see Early Iron Age.

Jones, Inigo, 147, 163
Jupon, 184

Kelts, see Celts.
Kilns (pottery), 103, 113, 116
Knightly equipment, 184

Lamps, 74
Land tenure and land use, 132–133
La Tène, 93, 95
Lead (metal), 106
Levalloisian, 42–44
Literature, 29–30, 46, 66, 75, 89, 99, 119–120, 134, 150, 167, 173, 182, 189, 198, 210–211, 214
Lombardic alphabet, 181, 205
Long-headed race, 80
Loom-weight, 92
Lost century, the, 24, 121
Lozenge, 186
Lurs (musical instruments), 87
Lynchets, 57

Magdalenian, 40 (Fig. 12 h–k), 42, 45
Man (*Homo sapiens*), 32–33
Man, origin of, 31, 32, 33
Manuscripts, 130, 168, 170
Masonry, 105, 141
Masons' marks, see Banker-marks.
Megalithic (large stone) monuments, 71, 77
 see also Stonehenge.
Menhir, 71
Mesaticephalic, 81
Mesolithic Age, 39, 67, 68, 69
Metals, 76, 77, 106; (in heraldry) 185
Microliths (Mesolithic implements), 67–69
Mirror, 94
Mosaic work, 102, 106
Mouldings (in architecture), 137–139, 141–145, 147
Mousterian culture, 42

Mousterian Man = Neanderthal Man (*q.v.*)
Musical instruments, 87

Names, 91–92, 190–193
Neanderthal Man, 33
Nennius, 124
Neolithic Age, 69, 70, 73, 74, 152–153
Neolithic implements, 16, 69, 70
Neolithic pottery, 16, 73, 74
New Forest wares, 118
New Stone Age, see Neolithic Age.
Norman architecture, see Architecture.
Norman stained glass, 204–207

Ogee (in architecture), 138
Ogham, 176–181
Old Stone Age, see Palæolithic Age.
Orang utan, an ape, 32
Orders (in architecture) a succession of arches within arches, 138
Orders of architecture, see Classical orders of architecture.
Ordinaries (in heraldry), 186

Pail (situla), 97
Palæolithic Age, 39–44, 151–152
Palæontologists (those who study fossils), 33
Palladian principles, 163
Palladio, Andrea, 147, 163
Palstave, 79
Peat, pollen in, 27
Pediment (the uppermost triangular part of the façade of a building erected in a classical style), 163
Place-names, 190–193
Ploughing, 57–59
Pollen, 27, 28
Post-holes (these are often visible because they are filled up with material different from the surrounding rock), 127
Potters' marks, 103, 105, 117

INDEX AND GLOSSARY

Pottery, 16, 73, 74, 77, 78, 91, 93, 97, 98, 103, 105, 112–113, 116–118, 125, 133
  coarse, 117
Pottery kilns, Roman, 113, 116
Preselau (preferred to the spelling *Prescelly*) Hills, stones, 72, 77
Provenance in archæology, 27

Quartzite (a metamorphic, compact, hard rock composed of silica), 39
Quern, 73
Quirk (in architecture), 138

Radioactive carbon, 26, 27
Rapier, 79
Religion, 103, 109, 131–132
  see also Christianity.
Remembrance of the dead, 16, 17, 18, 130
Renaissance architecture, 147
Ring, 127
Ritual floors, 54
River terraces, 63–65
Rivers, work of, 62, 63, 64
Roads, 197–198
  see also Roman roads.
Rocks, 60, 61
Roll (in architecture) or round, 138
Roman altar, 104
Roman antiquities, 53, 102, 153
Roman architecture, 118–119
Roman city, *frontispiece*
Roman coins, 103, 112
Roman Emperors, 114–115
Roman masonry, 105
Roman period, 100–120, 153
Roman pottery, 103, 105, 112–113, 116–118
Roman roads, 102, 109–110
Roman theatre, *frontispiece*
Roman tombstone, 104
Roman walls, *frontispiece*
Romanesque architecture, 135, 137–138, 140–142
Roofs, 165
Runes, 127, 174–175
Rusticated ware, 113, 118
Ruthwell cross, 175

"Samian" ware, 113, 117
Sarcophagus (stone coffin), 107
Saxons (Anglo-Saxons), 121–134
Scramasax (sword-knife), 113, 175
Scroll-moulding (in architecture), 138, 144–145
Sculpture, 199
Segmental arch, 137–138
Ship burial (Sutton Hoo), 17, 126, 132, 134
Shoes, 86, 103
Short-headed race, 81
Sickle, 73
Situla (pail), 95, 97
Slip-ware, 113
Sloden, 113
Soffit (in architecture), soffit plane, 137, 142, 143, 144
Soil, 47, 48, 49, 50, 51, 52, 53, 54, 55, 60
Soil-profile, 49, 50, 51, 52
Soil-texture, 54, 55, 56
Solutrean, 42, 45
Spandrel (the triangular space between an arch and the rectangular frame enclosing it), 145, 163
Spear, 43, 76
Stained glass, 204–210
Stonehenge, 14, 70, 72, 73
Stratification, 59–61, 65
Stuart period, 24
Sub-ordinaries (in heraldry), 186
Surnames, 91–92, 192–193
Survival after death, 17
Swanscombe, 43
Sword-knife, 133
Swords, 79, 83, 95, 96, 97

Terra Rossa, 53
Terra sigillata, see "Samian" ware.
Tesseræ, 106, 165
Thames pick, 68
Theatre, Roman, *frontispiece*
Tiles, 106, 107, 165
Timber-framed houses, 161, 163–165
Tin, 76
Tooling of masonry, 141
Tools, *see* Implements.

Tranchet, 68
Tricking (in heraldry), 184–186
Tudor period, 24, 136
Tuscan order, 119
Typology (changing fashions), 15, 74, 88, 94

Upchurch ware, 113
Urn field, 91

Varves, 27
Victorian times, 24
Vikings, 130

Volute (Latin, volutus, *rolled*), (the spiral ornament typical of the Ionic capital), 118

Wall, city, *frontispiece*
Wall, Hadrian's, 109, 114, 120
Wall-plane (in architecture), 137, 142, 143, 144
Weaving, 92, 93
Wood, sections, 26
Wren, Sir Christopher, 147, 163
Writing, 111, 133, 168–182

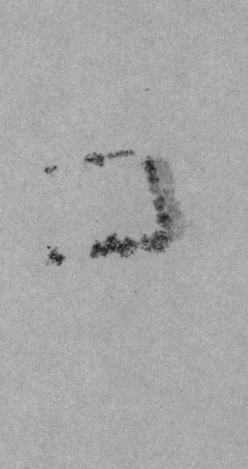